UNSUNG PIONEERS: Willie Keil's father (the founder of Aurora, Oregon) had promised he would lead the wagon train across the plains, but he died before the journey began. Willie led the train, though, in his hearse, preserved in Golden Rule Whiskey, and the Sioux were awed by the corpse-led, hymn-singing procession, and protected it, while savagely attacking other trains through the summer of '55.

REMITTANCE MEN of British Columbia, some of whom turned to the early wilderness and the life-style of the drop-outs of the 20th century.

TALL TALES AND MYTHS: The Rawhide Railroad, and the often hilarious origin of names that have become a part of the culture.

THE LONGEST BAR IN THE WORLD: An honor worth fighting for in the Old West, but undeniably won by Erikson's in Portland.

THE BIRTH AND GROWTH OF GREAT CITIES, Seattle, Portland, Spokane, Tacoma and others, and the

CITIES OF ILLUSION founded on idealistic principles of 'development' or 'communal living,' and today have merged with the land.

FAR CORNER

A PERSONAL VIEW OF
THE PACIFIC NORTHWEST

Stewart H. Holbrook

A COMSTOCK EDITION

For Sibyl
A Native Daughter

Copyright, 1952 by Stewart H. Holbrook
Renewal 1986 by Sibyl Holbrook Strahl

ISBN 0-89174-043-0

First Printing: April 1973
Second Printing: October 1986

Additional copies of this book may be obtained by sending a check or money order for the price of the book plus a dollar for the first copy and 75¢ for each additional copy ordered. A free catalog of books published by Comstock is also available.

COMSTOCK EDITIONS, INC.
3030 Bridgeway, Sausalito, CA 94965

Contents

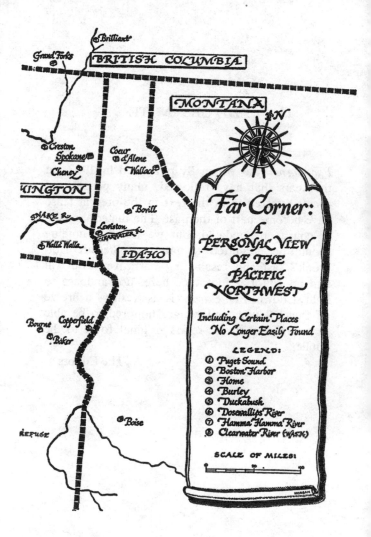

EDITORS' NOTE

Far Corner was originally published in 1952. In the years that have followed, many people and events referred to in the text in the present tense have become part of the past. The material could, of course, be updated, but we felt that nothing should be permitted to interrupt Stewart Holbrook's fast and fascinating narrative. You will find no editorial footnotes here, no sandbags to hold it down. *Far Corner* is as fresh as a breeze off Puget Sound, and we are honored to be able to return this classic in its original form to the public.

The Editors

PART ONE

TRANSITION

1. The Frontier Lingered

WHEN I CROSSED THE ROCKIES FOR THE FIRST TIME, AND came down the West Slope to Vancouver, I was wearing the only derby hat in British Columbia. I had bought it in the Jordan Marsh emporium in Boston on the day I purchased a ticket that promised to take me to the Coast and also return me, within a period of six months, to the Hub of the Universe. It was a thoroughly durable hat. Three years later I nailed it to a big stump deep in the British Columbia timber, then took off for Oregon.

Buying in Boston a ticket to so distant a place had naturally called for a decision of some sort. Buying a derby hat in that time and place was as casual a thing as stocking up with sufficient Sweet Caporal cigarettes for the seven-day ride. Young men in Boston and all other parts of New England wore derbies. So did older men. I had grown up seeing captains of industry, and plumbers, farmers, drummers, and pick-and-shovel men, wearing derbies. I had worked with river drivers, chasing logs down the Connecticut and Androscoggin, who wore derbies. A stiff black headpiece was the thing a newly arrived French-Canadian bought with his first wages. A derby hat, in short, stood for maturity, sophistication, and general competence. Incidentally, in British Columbia I was made to feel the uniqueness of my hat only by the stares and occasional remarks of city people. In the camps, where genuine sophistication is always greater than in urban circles, the derby did not create a ripple, though it might have, had I not been a seasoned logger and able to prove as much.

I belabor this hat business chiefly because it tells me now, more than thirty years later, that my attitude toward the Far West could not have been greatly influenced by the Diamond Dick and Buffalo Bill literature I had read in my

3

teens. This was fortunate. It meant that I had no pre-
conceived notions that must be rubbed out and wholly obliterated before I could begin to look at the Far West with
objective eyes. In more recent years I have known young
men from the East to arrive in Oregon wearing gallon-size
white Stetsons and packing genuine Colt revolvers. Perhaps
the writers of Westerns are getting better; or perhaps it's the
impact of the movies.

By the time I moved from British Columbia to Oregon,
I had long since sold the return portion of my railroad
ticket to Boston. I have never been quite certain what inspired me in the first place to come to the Northwest, unless
it was to find out if those picture postcards of vast trees
were fakes. Nor am I sure I ever made up my mind to stay
permanently in the Northwest. I think this decision came so
gradually that it could not be considered any decision at all.
The effect of the region reminds me of the antinicotine
tracts read in my youth which warned of the subtle and
sinister spell of tobacco. This, so it was made to appear, crept
upon the innocent one softly, and presently enveloped him,
the Victim, with pretty wreaths of blue smoke that turned
out to be, in caps and italics, the *Iron Bands of Vice*. I
dutifully read the tracts, then joyfully welcomed the hideous
habit; much as later I read the booster pamphlets which
somehow left the impression that one could have a decent
living in Oregon and Washington simply by eating the gorgeous scenery; and in spite of them settled down to earn a
living in God's own country in the Northwest corner of the
United States.

This Northwest is the one where men have their faces to
the sea, and can go no farther. It's time Minnesotans gave up
calling their state the Northwest. For over a century they have
been one thousand and more miles short of the goal. Once
upon a time Ohio was the Northwest. Manifest destiny changed
all that. Both Ohio and Minnesota became merely a part of
the Midwest as long ago as August 13, 1848, when Congress
passed an Act creating Oregon Territory, an immense piece
of geography. It was a triumph no less for American state-
manship than it was for American poetry. The new Territory's name had become familiar to Americans largely because William Cullen Bryant had applied it to a river that
rolled as majestically as did the strophes of his sonorous verse.
Neither Bryant nor anyone else knew where the word came
from, nor does anybody today. It is likely a corruption of

"Wisconsin" as set down on a map by some French explorer. The French, a peculiar people, have no *w* in their alphabet; and, after sufficient copyings of "Ouisconsin," the word, or the name, of a river that was thought to flow from the Great Lakes to the Pacific Ocean, became Oregon. But this is only one of many suggestions as to parenthood.

Most of us who live here think of the Northwest as being the states of Oregon, Washington, and Idaho, with perhaps a piece of western Montana thrown in for good measure. It extends roughly five hundred miles north and south, and some seven hundred miles east and west. In it is almost everything from stark desolation to lush green jungles of almost tropical growth. I have been in all of its 127 counties. Two of these counties each contain more than half a million people. Many of the others can scarcely muster crowd enough for a decent picnic.

Northwest people are generally given to thinking of their region as remote. If remote it is, then few of them know how fortunate they are; they do not realize what it is they are remote from. They have never seen the industrial wonders of Illinois, Michigan, Ohio, Pennsylvania, and New Jersey; nor the grotesque sight of eight million human beings swarming on and around a small island between the Hudson and the East rivers. They do not know that Manhattan is on the verge of learning exactly how many people can stand upright on its acres if stacked properly. This is called Progress. Once upon a time the people of Grays Harbor on the coast of Washington liked to measure Progress by the number of stumps in the neighborhood. They do not do so any more.

Being remote is, of course, a relative condition. Within the past decade a plane nonstop from Russia dropped casually, and without previous notice, into one of the Northwest airports. A Jap plane out of a Jap submarine let go an incendiary bomb on Oregon's Curry County, and started a forest fire. It was the first time continental United States had been bombed from the air. A little later, at a Sunday-school picnic, five youngsters were blown to bits when one of them, boy-like, picked up a strange gadget he found on the picnic grounds near Bly, Oregon. It was one of those little balloons the clever Japanese sent sailing across the Pacific, each complete with an infernal machine.

In the other direction, the Atlantic seaboard is less than a day's travel from the Northwest. The Northwest's feeling of

remoteness probably stems from the days of the covered
wagons. There is always a lag between public awareness and
history. History is as up to date, always, as today's newspaper. The public's awareness limps along anywhere from
five to fifty and more years in the rear.

In any case, one of the Northwest's charms is this feeling
of being tucked away in a forgotten far corner of the United
States. Isolation from the bedlam of teeming populations is
anything but unpleasant. The sense of isolation also contrib-
utes to the restless pioneering spirit, the opening-up-of-the-
country idea. I became conscious of this characteristic thirty
years ago, when I started to range all over the Northwest.
Everywhere I went something new was going on. It was
wonderful. The people around Coos Bay were enthralled because a jetty was being built to deepen their harbor entrance.
The Milwaukee Railroad, completely maddened by its first
salty whiff of the ocean, at Tacoma, on Puget Sound, had
just pushed its tracks still farther west, on through the wilderness to Willapa Bay, on the Pacific shore. In spite of the
warning fumes of gasoline, the Great Northern was building
into California from Central Oregon. The Union Pacific was
laying tracks to Burns in eastern Oregon. The Southern
Pacific was building a line over the mountains at Oakridge.
Some four hundred logging railroads were operating or under
construction.

The papers in many sections of the Northwest were running exciting stories of irrigation projects planned, just being
finished, or under way. It struck a stranger that hardly a
month passed that did not witness some celebration of letting
the first water from this or that new dam into the ditches.
In North Idaho lumbermen trooping in from the Lake
States were erecting white-pine mills, and villages to go with
them, so close to each other that one might go almost anywhere in the Panhandle and be within sound of the whine
and thump of the head rigs.

It was all new and wonderful, at least to one from a long-
settled community whose industry and commerce had case-
hardened into patterns which seemed to be as incapable of
change as the tides of Maine and the granite of New Hampshire.

At the junction of the Columbia and the Cowlitz, I found
a whole army of men clearing land and burning brush,
building dikes and bridges, laying tracks for the new Longview, Portland & Northern; putting up a city hall, schools,

churches, a library and a hotel; digging a lake and a scenic
waterway that would remind me of the Fens around Boston
—all to the end that Longview, Washington, should be the
biggest and finest lumber city on earth. It is, too. On my
first night in Longview, as a reporter, I slept in a bunk in a
shack. It was the best the place afforded. A year or so
later, when I came to see the million-foot sawmill cut its
first log, I was quartered in a fine new hotel, of metropolitan
aspect, where Joe Knowles, the artist and once-celebrated
Original Nature Man, was putting the finishing touches to
his murals in the lobby. The paintings depicted "Pioneer
Scenes in the Northwest." Neither the artist nor any of the
other ten thousand men engaged in building a new city reflected that they were engaged, if anybody ever was, in
pioneering.

Pioneers never know they are pioneers until time passes
and one day along comes somebody who wasn't there,
notices that the varnish is dry, or that the shingles have
accumulated moss, and says, "Lo, the pioneers." Then they
form a Society of Pioneers.

There were still many living who had come to the Northwest as children of the covered-wagon trains. A few men
were left who had fought Modocs and Nez Percés in the
Northwest. In Seattle and vicinity were perhaps half a dozen
of the Mercer Girls, the generic term for a crew of New
England spinsters who had shipped around the Horn to Puget
Sound with the tacit intentions of holy matrimony. That had
been in the sixties, and now the survivors were aged, re-
calling the wild seas of their long voyage, and their first discouraging sight of helter-skelter, jerry-built Seattle, where they
were made welcome by young men who had plastered their
hair with bear's grease. When a Mercer Girl died in the
1920's, she was good for almost a column in the papers.

The aged men who had fought Indians were by all
odds the most cantankerous military relics of the nineteenth
century—especially the enlisted ones. They seemed to feel that
veterans of all our wars, except those against the redskins,
had been given all the honors. True, the Indian fighters got
pensions, and they had a medal with a bright red ribbon;
but they felt they had been cheated of the glory rightly
theirs. Was the Civil War more dangerous than fighting Indians? Didn't Custer and Canby survive the former? And
had they not been killed by redskins? No two veterans of the
Indian wars could agree on a single battle, much less on a

single campaign. Newspapermen of my era quickly learned it
was unsafe to quote them on anything except the fact that
General Oliver Otis Howard had only one arm. And I have
heard two veterans argue as to which arm.

The old veterans, of course, had no influence on the
Northwest in my time, but another cantankerous crew did.
These were the Industrial Workers of the World, the I.W.W.,
the so-called Wobblies, by all odds the least inhibited labor
union the United States has known. The bloody and melancholy riots known as the Everett Massacre and the Centralia
Conspiracy, both titles composed by Wobbly propagandists,
were still fresh in mind; the penitentiary at Walla Walla still
held half a dozen Wobbly participants in the latter affair.
All of the larger cities and many of the smaller towns each
had a Wobbly hall. It was a part of the scenery. Its windows
commonly displayed eye-shaking posters in red and black,
calling on the stiffs to arise and shake off their chains. Hor-
ribly grinning cats sitting in wooden shoes (sabots) stressed
the workers' duty to commit sabotage. Pictures of clocks
showed sabots hanging from the hands, slowing the works.
Inside the hall, the standard piece of *décor* was a primitive
painting of Joe Hill, Wobbly poet and martyr. On November
19th, this icon was often draped with crepe, while a hand-
lettered card noted that this was the anniversary of Hill's
"murder by the constituted authorities of the state of Utah,
1915."

From the Wobbly halls emanated the traveling delegates
and other agitators who did their best—and it was pretty
good—to keep the wage slaves in an uproar. No employer
officially recognized them, nor did any conventional union.
Their weapon was the wildcat strike, always sudden, usually
developing violence on both sides. The I.W.W. operated in
other parts of the country sporadically, but the Northwest
was their favorite campaigning ground.

In the course of a Wobbly strike I attended on Grays
Harbor, two men were shot and killed. Another was stabbed
to death in a Wobbly affair I covered at Raymond. At the
latter place I saw Big Jim Thompson, Wobbly soapboxer,
run out of town by a mob. The Wobs never turned the
other cheek. They were courageous enough, and often as
witless as they were bold.

One day I got off the train at Marshfield, and started for a
big sawmill the Wobblies were picketing, though I did not
know this and saw no sign of pickets. But as I walked

along a road through dense timber toward the mill, rocks began sailing not too far over my head, to go *plunk* in the tidewater below the road. I mended my pace. So too must have the Wobblies—either that or there were many of them in the woods above me, for the bombardment continued the half-mile or so to the plant. They could not have known that I was merely a reporter, and it wouldn't have made the least difference anyway. Unless I was a reporter for an I.W.W. paper, then I was naturally a tool of the capitalist class, fit to be driven into salt water by their neolithic artillery.

Wobblies added much to life in the Northwest of the twenties. Their lumber union had zip and bang, a wild-eyed and completely chaotic viewpoint that predicated everything on a world revolution. This revolution might as well start, say, in the logging camps of the Mutual Lumber Company, Bucoda, Washington, as anywhere else. Wobblies recognized only two kinds of people—working stiffs and capitalists and their tools. In their ranks were many idealists, no few downright thugs and criminals, and a large number of young footloose men who merely wanted action and excitement. They got both with the Wobs; and the Wobs did put fear of the Red Dawn in many backward employers who thought a workday of twelve hours just right; and who believed working stiffs *liked* to carry their beds on their backs. It was asking too much of these hardshell employers to accept the cooperative industrial group called the Loyal Legion of Loggers and Lumbermen, the 4L, which was founded on the principle that industrial wars are as needless as they are costly to all concerned. In another fifty years, perhaps, industry may be ready to operate on the 4L plan, which was born far in advance of its time.

Another outfit, the Knights of the Ku-Klux Klan, was at the height of its power when I came to the Northwest. On the plains of Issaquah, one night, I ran head-on into what Seattle papers next day said were thirty thousand Klansmen engaged in holding a Konklovation and initiating a class of three thousand new members. I can believe it. An immense field was swarming with white-robed figures, while over them played floodlights. Loudspeakers gave forth commands and requests. Highway traffic was being directed by robed Klansmen. I was more than two hours getting through the jam.

For another couple of years the Klan in the Northwest

was something to contend with. It was still fairly strong when the people of Oregon elected a Jew to the governor's office. This inconsistency seemed as welcome as it was unexplainable.

Back in New York and Baltimore, Henry L. Mencken was saying that people joined the Klan because they were bored. Perhaps they did and were. What I could not understand was how anybody living in the Northwest could be bored. The whole place was filled with so much vitality, and there was so much going on and so many places and things to see, that I could not get up early enough nor stay up late enough to take it all in. Looking back now, the only boredom I recall was when I sat as a reporter through six endless evenings of the Reverend Billy Sunday's revival orgies in Portland. My only satisfaction was that the big and especially built tabernacle was not once filled to capacity. Being by choice a resident of Portland, this gave me pride in my town. Any place where Billy Sunday could not draw a full house must be more civilized than most.

It seemed to matter not at all which way I went in the Northwest; there was always something or somebody worth seeing. As an instance let me cite the short run of sixty miles on the Northern Pacific from Chehalis to Willapa Harbor: At Chehalis I saw a good mystery in the form of the trunk of a small tree through which was sticking, about head-high, a single-shot rifle that had been made at Springfield, Massachusetts, in 1839. Once upon a time, some men sighted that rifle over a crotch of this tree; but what had happened then? The gun was held so firmly in the wood, which had grown all around it, that it could not be moved. Had the unknown man taken bead on some foe, red or white, and been shot himself before he could pull trigger? The man who had discovered the relic near the hamlet of Rochester, Washington, and had sawed off the tree and brought it to Chehalis, held to that theory. Later I heard a story that had the gun placed in the tree as a peace offering by some pioneer who was much feared by the Indians. In any case, here was a dandy mystery of frontier days, and the imagination was free to work upon it.

At Chehalis, too, was the monstrous fir stump, some ten feet in diameter, which had been brought to town and set up by the railroad station for the express purpose of being a platform from which President William McKinley—and may God rest his kindly soul—should address the assembled citizens of Chehalis and vicinity on his Western tour. But a psychopath at Buffalo, New York, had changed all that; and it was Teddy Roosevelt who at last appeared and spoke from the noble stump.

Pe Ell, where the tree of the stump was felled, got its odd name in one or another of twoscore ways, none of which matters much. I might feel differently about Pe Ell had it not been for the worst restaurant meal I ever encountered. I recall that meal, after more than thirty years, distinctly and with shudders. Its main course was composed of two great pork chops which had barely been warmed through, then served in grease of room temperature. The dessert was a pudding of an appearance to turn the stomach. I have no knowledge of what was in it or of what it tasted like.

More interesting than Pe Ell was a curiosity in the neighboring sawmill village of Walville. There, occupying much of the front end of the big mill, was a truly gigantic black cat made of painted wood, its fierce whiskers fashioned from haywire. For thirty years this cat had bared its clamshell teeth and held its tail above its head. The Japanese who worked on the green-chain of the mill seemed to think the cat was some sort of white man's magic, a totem or good-luck symbol; and as such they honored it. The cat was really a symbol of Hoo Hoo, a lumbermen's fun organization, and it had been made and erected by one of their number as a pastime.

The big black cat of Walville told me the reason why so many people were bored, if bored they were. Hundreds passed the cat every day, for the railroad ran close to it. People couldn't help seeing it. Yet I talked to many persons, perhaps more than a hundred, before I found one to explain the presence and meaning of the cat. I wonder if no good epigram has been made on the connection between boredom and a lack of healthy curiosity.

There was Pluvius, too, just beyond Walville. Pluvius was a spot near the summit of the Coast range. It comprised two weatherbeaten log cabins and a small shack of a depot. I wanted to know who had named Pluvius. Nobody knew, not even the train crews who passed it every day. Months later I found a man who had been there when the railroad was built. He said there had been but a single resident then, a testy old man who had taken a homestead years before and had continued to stay on after he had proved-up. Why he remained was a mystery, for he cursed the spot with malignant eloquence. Said he never sat down to breakfast until he had consigned it anew to all the devils in hell. He told my informant that right there, in Pluvius, he had seen it rain for 362 consecutive days, and recalled that the other three days "was goddam cloudy." So he named it, and Pluvius it was and is.

Then, at McCormick, some homemade scientist had built an enormous sundial which covered the entire upper half of the south end of the planing mill. It worked well, too, and its roman numerals and the shadow of the sun could be seen a quarter of a mile away. It was probably the only sundial of its kind and size in the Northwest. A few miles west of McCormick was Lebam, to prove that our latter-day hucksters invented nothing new by spelling words backward. Lebam, if turned end to end, was the name of a daughter of Lebam's founding father. Then, at Sutico, named for the Sunset Timber Company, was a logging camp with *steam-heated* bunkhouses, in 1923, and for many years more, surely the only steam-heated bunkhouses on earth.

All of these marvels were to be found in a sixty-mile stretch of the backwoods of Washington State. I knew, of course, that none of them had much, if any, influence on the life and times of the country, yet I find, after three decades, that they stand out in my memory, although I probably have forgotten many important things concerning the district. I still wonder about the Springfield gun of 1839, and try to conjure up the shadowy figure who sighted it, or at least placed it, in the crotch of the tree. I honor the stump of Pe Ell, too, prepared by labors approaching the heroic; put aboard a flatcar, taken to Chehalis, then bound with stout hoops of iron and erected close by the depot where the President of the United States might speak, possibly about the tariff, but surely, too, about the pioneers. It is an artifact of patriotism, that great fine stump of a tree which had been a sapling when Columbus sailed West, a tall tree when George Washington was born, a real giant of a tree when Lincoln was splitting rails. And at last, in the early years of the twentieth century, Roosevelt the First had taken his stance on its broad surface to speak to people most of whom had never before seen a President.

The great black cat of Walville must have added something to life in the dreary clearing by the track, for one evening there I watched while five Japanese, parents and three youngsters, walked hand in hand to the end of the mill, looked up at the cat, then all bowed low and gravely, and returned to their hut beside the millpond. I like to think, too, though I have no evidence of it, that the big sundial at McCormick may have created an interest in the sun's daily course and its effect on the blowing of the mill's starting and stopping whistles. Perhaps the slowly creeping shadow may also have given substance, far more than a clock, to the adage that time never stops, that it is indeed fleeting; and to the I.W.W. slogan that time was made for slaves. As for Pluvius, it was the only place of that name in the *United States Official Postal Guide,* which is reason enough to mark it.

Where the branch railroad that served these places came to tidewater at Raymond was a city of five thousand, all of it built either on pilings or on dredged-in land. Its business district contained several new concrete buildings, but also block on block of structures straight out of Western or Yukon fiction: false-front establishments, many with fearsome architectural embellishments, called poolrooms, cardrooms, tobacco stores, clothing stores, hotels, rooming houses, sports centers, restaurants, and what not. A big business on Front Street was the retailing of moonshine and homemade beers and wines, all illegal in the days of Prohibition. The upstairs of many of these places were made into rooms for transients, and there was generally believed to be a chambermaid for every room.

The juke box had not penetrated Pacific County, but the electric player piano was well settled, and the insistent beat of a dozen of these hurdy-gurdies made an evening on Front Street memorable, while the tides washed and gurgled underneath the shacks and brought rich aromas to the guests and the customers. The Raymond sea gulls never slept. Busy all day, they held convention in the evening, wheeling and darting, screaming high and eerily above the pounding bass of *Dardanella,* fighting for scraps of food, lighting on window sills to glare at the people inside.

The sidewalks and some of the streets were planks set on stringers supported by piling. At low tide they were about ten feet above water; and during the June and December tides they either sank out of sight, or floated off. They rattled and thumped much of the night as lumber carriers moved over them. The town was none too well lighted, but it was never really dark; the hot red eyes of the sawdust burners at the mills blinked, then flared and smoked, twenty-four hours a day. Great seagoing ships steamed in to dock and await cargo. Two railroads shunted cars the night long in order that siding and flooring and shingles might be loaded next morning.

The whole place was throbbing, fairly bursting with the energy and the urgency I came quickly to associate with pioneering—with pioneering even sixty years after the covered wagons had ceased to roll. Raymond, and many another Northwest town, did not remind me of anything I had known in New England. I found the rawness and the spirit new and wonderful.

Pioneer smells yet lingered. Any stranger in the West Side sections of the Northwest, thirty years ago, noted at once the pleasant aroma of wood that permeated most homes. This came from the fir slabs that were brought in four-foot lengths and piled between sidewalk and street to dry until fall, when an army of itinerant power saw men appeared as suddenly and as mysteriously as so many locusts, to cut the slabs into fuel for stove and furnace. Its mild pungency struck me as a sort of aromatic hospitality. Nor was the aroma lost when sawdust burners came into use. But it disappeared with the newer oil burners. As with almost all improvements, something was lost as well as gained. In this case it was the perfume of Douglas fir, one of the most comforting smells I know of.

In the country districts I was at first disagreeably surprised at the poorly built barns and the houses that were little better. I came in time to comprehend that this casual construction was due in part to the mild climate. So far as the West Side of the region was concerned, one did not have to build thick and tight and strong. I thought the farmers unusually chary of paint. If they painted a house or barn as soon as it was built, they apparently considered that protection sufficient to the end of time. Even today the rural Northwest is probably the most unpainted of any farming region between the Aroostook country of Maine (much paint there) and the Pacific shore.

For all its comparative youth, I discovered the Northwest to have developed its own peculiarities of pronunciation, and to hold as fast to them as people in New England and the South hold to theirs. They insert an extra syllable in Snoqualmie, the name of a pass through the mountains, and of a river with a beautiful waterfall, to make it Sno-qual-a-mie. The Mackenzie River becomes the Mackinzie. The name of a big dam on the Columbia becomes Bonn-e-ville, which would have chagrined the somewhat pompous character who pronounced his name in two syllables. The place names that entranced me, however, were those along the arm of Puget Sound called Hood Canal. Here were places to match anything in Maine, Michigan, or Minnesota: Lilliwaup, Hamma Hamma, Dosewallips, Duckabush, and Quilcene, of which more later. They are infinitely more suited to the region than are the names of British brass hats such as Hood Rainier, Saint Helens, or the warmed-over Albany, Portland, Aberdeen, and Mount Vernon.

One other thing I noticed about speech in the Northwest was the use, even by persons who had been exposed to college, of "like" as a conjunction. I had never heard it used thus except by illiterates, yet here it appears even in editorials in the larger papers. Incidentally, one way to tell the stranger in the region is the manner in which he pronounces "Oregon." Most newcomers give it a careful accent on the last syllable, whereas the native and old-time accent the first.

The newcomer soon learns there are two general regions in the Northwest, known as East and West of the Cascade Mountains, which divide Oregon and Washington into vastly different climates. The East part also includes Idaho and western Montana. Paradoxically, the East-of-the-mountains country is far more "Western" than the West Side. Cattle, sheep, wheat, and mines are on the East, as well as much pine forest. Here are the great open spaces of the cowboy songs, and it is true that antelope yet roam in a few counties. The cowboys, however, are not all six feet tall, and lithe. Some of them run to an inch or so over five feet, and could be described as tubby. The East Side people are a shade darker of skin, because of sun and wind. Their speech is somewhat different from that of the West Side. I think there's more of a drawl in it, though there is no fast rule. One of Bend's most prominent citizens of long residence speaks State-of-Maine with Harvard undertones. Idaho's most celebrated killer, still in the prison at Boise, talked to me in pure Ontario. He had not been in Canada, or anywhere else but in prison, for forty-five years.

The worst habitations I saw in the Northwest thirty years ago were not in the city slums but on many ranches in eastern Oregon and in Idaho. Many of those ranchers were well to do, but they patently did not take much stock in the American dream of good living. Their houses were little more than sheds, bare of most conveniences, and bare too of any decoration save a pair of antlers and a calendar. I was told that many of the ranchers who lived in these sheds of houses could afford to, and did, shut up shop in winter and go to California. There seemed to be a time lag in respect to improved living conditions on the rural East Side. It is less now than it was. But the East Side folk impressed me as being even more hospitable than the West Siders, which is saying a good deal. Bend, Boise, Spokane, Lewiston, Wenatchee, Baker, La Grande and Butte all seemed incredibly filled with warmhearted, generous people. Hospitality on the ranches, of course, was taken for granted.

Although they were spotty, many evidences of the old frontier remained. I discovered that glorious Butte had come to tolerate a few chromium fronts and streamlined buildings, yet I could find little other of so-called modern elegance about it. It conducted its illegal and quite open gambling in resorts of pioneer simplicity. Its bars were obviously for men who stood while drinking, with one foot on a solid brass rail. "This is hilly country," a miner friend there told me, "and we've got used to sort of bracing ourselves when we're going to down a jolt." Butte's redlight district, lining blocklong Venus Alley off Wyoming Street, in the center of town, was starkly utilitarian. I doubt it had changed perceptibly since the eighties. Along both sides were small cubicles called cribs; on the north side were the famous double-deckers. Here the alley-level cribs were topped by a raised plank walk which in turn was lined with more cribs. Over the door of each crib, above and below, was a single blazing light, naked and white. At the doors or windows were the girls of The Line, mostly in the brightest of gowns, short and saucy.

It was my good fortune to be in tow of him who was perhaps Butte's best-known newspaperman, M. G. O'Malley, a veteran who dated back to the times of Daly, Clark, and Heinze. O'Malley was a local celebrity. He conducted me to the door of every crib whose inmate was not presently busy, and said I was making a survey of reading preferences in Butte, which naturally included Venus Alley. Whereupon I asked the girl to name her favorite magazine. Several said

they didn't "read nothing." Of the others, *True Story* led all
by a good margin, with *Liberty* second and *Cosmopolitan*
third.

Not many years after my visit, Butte saw fit to do away
with Venus Alley, and I am told that nothing remotely resembling it is now to be seen there, or for that matter in
any other Western town. Both Butte and Reno are claimed by
their partisans to have been the last city to permit a crib
street to operate with official recognizance.

Most of Butte, like any other city, is made up of honest
and hard-working citizens who possess a deep love for this
"richest copper camp on earth," and take a fierce pride
in their town. Their devotion blinds them to the basic ugliness
of Butte, and they spend untold hours trying to get grass
and a few flowers to grow in their yards. Viewed at night-
fall from the high pass where the Northern Pacific's Limited
emerges from the Rockies, Butte presents a dramatic sight,
twinkling all over its mile-high hill with astonishing brilliance
in the thin clear air of almost six thousand feet above sea
level. Below the hill is a brief rolling plain, then the mountains. It is a perfect setting for Butte, our biggest mining
camp, where men work hard and three hundred saloons are
required, I was told, to slake their consuming thirst.

The frontier lingered elsewhere. Near the headwaters of
the Clearwater River, on the Olympic Peninsula of Washington, I spent a pleasant day and night at the home of an
old lady, a log house that could be reached only by foot
trail or, at high-water, by boat. She and her husband had
come there early in this century to make a homestead amid
gigantic spruces. Years later he died, was buried on the
place, and the widow and a son carried on. Twice in nearly
forty years, she told me, she had made a trip out to the city,
meaning Hoquiam, to buy clothing. On one of these trips
she saw a motion picture, the only one she had ever seen. She
had not seen an automobile since 1917, or in twenty-five
years. She was standing up remarkably well, too, under these
blighting omissions. She served us fried elk steak for breakfast, meat she had put down the previous fall. The animal she
had shot herself, in the dooryard. She subscribed to a daily
newspaper, which arrived usually several in a bundle, whenever some friend or her son brought them from the distant
post office. She remarked, perhaps in explanation, that what

she read in her paper of the changing times had not been such as to make her wish for the outside. I had never met a more self-sufficient, nor happier person, in my life.

Much of North Idaho was still pungent with pioneer flavor. Coeur d'Alene had begun to suffer the lashings of Progress, and was tearing down many of its fine old false fronts and gingerbread houses, but the mining towns of Wallace, Wardner, and Burke carried on much as in the past, grim, like most mine towns, yet lusty, hearty, friendly, free-and-easy. There was no municipal hypocrisy here, no civic evasion or camouflage. These were mine towns. They made no pretense of being anything else. One respected them for it.

Near another mining town in this region, Orofino, lived Theodore Fohl, one of the old Nestors, and surely one of the greatest woodsmen here or elsewhere. Fohl had been born in Württemberg, Germany. After cruising and prospecting on Michigan's Upper Peninsula, he came to Idaho, in 1894, to file on a homestead where the town of Bovill now stands. For the next forty years he surveyed and cruised timberlands. By the time I met him, in his latter years, he knew that vast and rugged country as other men know their back yards. He was unique in that he never carried a firearm, though he was often alone in the woods for months on end—woods, incidentally, that for at least a decade contained many claim jumpers who settled all questions of argument with a gun. Fohl said he was in real danger only once, and that was when a bull moose charged him. A lucky blow of his ax felled the huge animal, and Fohl finished him. It was Fohl who guided Frederick Weyerhaeuser when that genius of the Wisconsin pines came West to see the pines of Idaho. Fohl went on to locate most of the Weyerhaeuser lands in the Idaho Panhandle.

I came in time to realize how swift had been the movement of events in the Northwest when, at Olympia, I talked with Mrs. Kate Stevens Bates, daughter of the first Territorial governor of Washington. The latter portion of her voyage from New England to Olympia had been made in canoes, with Indians who could not speak English doing the paddling. The speed of events must have struck Ezra Meeker, too. I watched him, aged ninety-four, crawl into a plane at Seattle, in 1924, to fly to Ohio, covering in a little more than two

days the course he had followed for many months when he
first came West in a covered wagon.

Ezra Meeker could recall the times before the Columbia
River was lined, in its lower reaches, with fish wheels. When
I first saw it, the Columbia's lower portion was still marked
with these great wooden wheels, set over the channels used
by the salmon, to scoop them as they swam, lift them up,
and toss them into receptacles, and so to the canneries. All
day and all night they turned slowly and steadily, creaking,
splashing, making fortunes for a few outfits, but progressively
depleting the prodigious runs of seagoing salmon. The
wheels have long since been banished by law, but only after a
bitter war in the courts and the legislatures of Oregon and
Washington. One sees their remains here and there along
the banks, antiquities of an era seemingly as ancient as
the ruins of Tyre.

Looking fully as ancient when I first saw it was the immense pile of concrete and stone called Maryhill Castle, set
high in the vast nothingness of a stark hill overlooking the
Columbia's gorge. The improbable pile was erected on this
spot by the eccentric Samuel Hill, son-in-law of James Jerome
Hill, the railroadman. There are only too many stories as to
why he built it, but not one to explain why he chose such an
inaccessible spot. Long after it was completed, it became a
museum; and it was dedicated as such, in ceremonies of
Second Coming size, by Queen Marie, who came all the way
from Romania to perform. Doubtless she got a thumping big
fee for her dedicatory efforts, for she was an astute woman
who could assess to the last dime the value of royal favor
as applied to the promotion of perfumes, deodorants, and
liver pads; and was probably just as shrewd in the business
of an honorarium proper for the royal launching of a museum in the far wastes of the State of Washington.

I have often wondered what went through the queen's
mind as she stood by the pile of stone and Portland cement,
through which were wafting the hell-hot zephyrs of the
parched region, and looked in four directions; though her
eyes were keen and she could see for many miles, she saw
naught but rock and sagebrush. Her logical mind must have
asked: Why this isolated monstrosity well beyond the limits
of where even God apparently had ceased to care?

When I ferried the Columbia from the Oregon side, then
girded my loins and climbed the precipice to Sam Hill's

castle, it was doorless, windowless, and swarming with bats. Since then it has been renovated to receive and display the somewhat incongruous mementos of Mr. Hill's wide travels, plus the queenly garments and other relics of the faded kingdom of Romania which the queen herself donated to this palace of art. A thousand years hence I hope that archeologists will discover it in the silts of time, and be vexed to explain how a tiny kingdom in middle Europe should have expanded into the desolate grandeur of the Columbia River gorge.*

Artifacts and other imported relics of past and foreign civilizations were no more needed in the Northwest than was more rain at Forks, Washington, and Valsetz, Oregon, two of our wettest spots. We had our own remnants of extinct cities. They have fascinated me ever since I trailed half a mile of sewer pipe, never used, that lay fair on top of the ground at ghostly Boston Harbor on Puget Sound. The pipe lay in the shade of brush twenty feet tall. Boston Harbor never quite came into being. It was one of our several cities of illusion, which I shall come to later.

The sewer pipes at Boston Harbor and decaying relics of other towns that had enjoyed planned parenthood but were never quite born were monuments less to outright fakery than to mistaken optimism, symbols of the pioneering state of mind, the haste to clear and to build, to "open up the country." The primeval automobile stage lines that were just coming into existence in the twenties were typical of this haste. I never rode one if boat or railroad would take me where I wanted to go. But occasionally I had to. The stages were desperately trying to go everywhere. To this end they bumped and plowed over mere trails winding among the stumps and amid virgin timber. They often had to back-and-go two or three times to get around a short bend. Their tires went flat every few miles. Wheels rolled off and into the brush. The stage interiors smelled most damnably. The printed schedules were pure fiction. Yet the lines persevered. The states began to subsidize them, making roads into splendid thoroughfares, turning trails into good roads. Hardly before one knew it, the many short-line railroads in the Northwest began to disappear. They were soon followed into limbo by the branch lines of the major railroads.

*In recent years Sam Hill's castle, though still comparatively remote, is more accessible. Art shows occupy it during summer months.

The major railroads seemed to make no great effort to retain their fading business. I was amazed to find, as late as 1926, on its branch in Oregon called the Tillamook Line, that the Southern Pacific's passenger train was composed of ancient coaches, each heated, after a fashion, by a coal-burning stove, and lighted by kerosene lamps. The seats made no concession to the human spine. The cars were filthy. The so-called right of way was such that huge fir trees were often blown down across the tracks. The baggage car always carried sufficient saws, axes, peavies, and wedges to have equipped a small logging camp. Twice, on trips to Tillamook, I took off my coat and lent a hand to the train crew engaged in bucking up and rolling a big tree from the rails. By fast work we prevented what its customers called with fine irony the Tillamook Flyer from being more than four or five hours late—on a run of eighty-odd miles. Little wonder the people served by this antiquated branch welcomed any mode of transportation that would supplant the Flyer.

It was much the same elsewhere in the Northwest. I got quite a start, no later than 1940. In that year I talked to a youth twelve years old who, though he had traveled much all over the Northwest, had never been on a railroad train. Not until then did I fully understand that I, even as old Ezra Meeker, had come to the end of an era.

Neither the railroad nor the new stage lines amounted to much in the region along the Oregon coast called Coos Bay, which, in the twenties, was the most charming area in the Northwest. Emanating from the bay were many miles of sloughs, inlets, and rivers navigable by small craft for long distances. The mail came in a boat. Children went to school in boats. The doctor came in a boat. There was an undertaker's boat. An oil barge anchored at a strategic place on the bay served as a gasoline service station for boats. The waterways winding back into the hills provided a panorama like nothing I had ever seen. In small clearings in the tall timber that grew down to the water, one saw cabins built of split cedar shakes, Monday's wash hanging from trees, corn and potatoes growing up among the stumps that still smoked from fires set to remove them, and cows munching ferns and brush. In larger clearings were logging camps, their steam donkeys snorting, big sticks coming in to the spar tree, to be rolled into the slough to make a boom half a mile long. At other clearings one might see a small church and a small schoolhouse, the bell of which was a short length of railroad iron.

Then, unannounced by signs or lights, one might come upon a typical general store, even to false front, looming two stories under the towering firs and cedars, all of whose merchandise and customers came in boats. Near the head of navigation on at least one of these interminable sloughs was the cabin of a chittam bark (cascara) gatherer, one of scores in the area. Peeling this bark was, and still is, one of the minor industries of Coos County. The product used to play quite a part in the lives of many bay dwellers; and one of the most interesting murder cases I ever covered was set off by a killing, on a Coos slough, over a division of bark peeled by two partners. It was typical of the area that most of the detective work on the case was done by police in boats. It had to be done in boats. There were no roads. Yet this waterborne civilization had disappeared by the mid 1940's. Roads had come. I can imagine there are now children in the Coos Bay region who have never had a boat ride or a trip on a railroad train.

What impressed the stranger to Coos Bay fully as much as the life carried on by boat was the pungent smell of Port Orford cedar being sawed into battery separators and, later, into venetian blinds. This wood is impervious to acids and termites. It smells like no other wood I know of. It used to be bragged locally, and for all I know may have been true, that Sir Thomas Lipton's racing yachts were made of buoyant Port Orford cedar. In view of Sir Thomas's racing record, this struck me as anything but a recommendation.

I had not been long in the Northwest before I discovered it to have elegancies. It first astonished then mildly amused me to run across, among the stumps still standing on logged-off land, a hunt club, complete with red coats, masters of the hounds, and considerable view halloo. Inquiry brought out the fact that there were several of these anachronisms emerging from the new-money classes of Seattle, Portland, Tacoma, and even smaller places. This was in the 1920's. Although I had not then read Thorstein Veblen, a common sense of proportion told me this leisure-class pose was a little pathetic in a region of fierce pioneering energy. An acquaintance, a genuine pioneer of bull-team days, who happened also to be the father of one of these elegant young huntsmen and of two of these young huntswomen, summed up the matter for me. "Yesus!" he said, for he had trouble with words like that, "Yesus!" Then he went on, bitterly, to say that the only hunting *he* had ever done, was to get meat for the family table. "Those kids seen the day," said he, referring to his hunt-club offspring, "when they was glad to get elk soup for dinner." Despite the shocked protests of his children, he still wore red woolen underwear because it prevented pneumonia, and liked to cool his coffee in a saucer. He might, had he wished, written a perfectly good check for $500,000. I loved him. I knew that until he and all his kind were dead, I would still be living in a region where pretense of any kind had little standing and even less influence.

The Northwest was spotted here and there with elegancies other than hunt clubs. I suppose all new countries go through like labors. Kensington Manors were appearing suddenly where one might yet hear the melancholy cadences of the owl. Out of newly drained swamps, as one watched, sprang Mayfairs, Windermeres, Highland Moors. A small convivial party of newspaper reporters once devoted an entire evening to conjuring up the most preposterous name possible for one of these raw new subdivisions. We finally settled on Buckinghamshire Mews. The promoter of the place was enchanted with it, when we submitted the name for his newly drained hog wallow, and would have so christened it had not his wife wanted the layout named for a daughter.

A Sandy Road became Sandy Boulevard. A Sucker Pond became Lake Oswego. A Seventh Street was thought to have gained stature, perhaps even glamour, by naming it Broadway. Little Hollywoods blossomed like so many lethal toadstools. There was also a brief period when the "Spanish influence," of which I could never find very much, was responsible for incongruities like Alameda, Estrelle, Avalon, and the Esplanade. Towns with fine frontier-flavored names like Baker City, Boise City, and Spokane Falls were already dropping the second half of their names. Yet all was not lost. You simply could not modify Yakima or Walla Walla or Steilacoom, and they survived. So for the same reason did Wenatchee, Hoquiam, Enumclaw, along with Duwamish, Snohomish, Kooskia and Quinault. One of my favorite pioneers took a good look at the map of Oregon, then called his clearing in the woods Remote, post office and all. Other early settlers did nobly in naming Wagontire, Neverstill, and Sweet Home. Then there is Elsie, the indestructible hamlet of

Oregon. Completely surrounded on at least three occasions by great forest fires, Elsie survived them all, and never suffered so much as a parched roof.

However it happened I was never able to learn, but a majority of the Northwest's big lumbermen, once they had made their piles, lived in brick houses that as often as not had slate roofs. I used to hear them at trade meetings speak heatedly of the hideous dangers inherent in "substitutes for wood"; namely, brick, slate, and tile.

Although virtually all of the larger cities of the West Side, and many of the smaller ones, were supported mainly by lumber, every one of them except Tacoma sought frantically to be known for some other reason. Tacoma was honestly proud of her sawmills, pulp and paper plants, and plywood factories. She erected a huge sign declaring Tacoma to be the Lumber Capital of the World. The other towns claimed distinctions they obviously thought were more aesthetic. Royal Rosarians cavorted in Portland, Cherrians in Salem. Other places started the custom of annual festivals, reigned over by kings and queens of this and that, devoted to prunes, pears, walnuts, hops, tulips, even daffodils. The go-getters of Grants Pass, Oregon, simply dressed up in bearskins, got some big clubs, and said they were Cave Men. Pendleton outdid them all by holding fast to its early tradition and erecting on it a stupendous affair called the Roundup. Everybody dresses up in cowboy suits and has a wonderful time.

These local events were used to attract tourists even before the several states had done much to publicize the Northwest's scenery. Our scenery is magnificent enough, and to it has been devoted, during the past twenty-odd years, an enormous literature that mounts steadily from the hurried and breathless pamphlets of the professional boosters to some really excellent verse by our more reflective poets. I shall not attempt to add to this literature, even though I probably enjoy a dramatic or a soothing scene as well as the next man. Often I enjoy it more if I know it was once witness to some piece of history, large or small, and can thus relate the scene to the event. When I look at Tum Tum Mountain in the foothills near Yacolt, Washington, I see it not only as a strange and striking pile of forested rock; I also see it as an old settler once saw it when, roused from sleep by a new noise in the night, he looked from his bedroom window to see Tum Tum and the whole ridge of hills back of it light up in ten thousand, perhaps fifty thousand spots, one after the other, quickly, as forest fire shot up the lengths of un-numbered old snags, dry as tinder. "It was like," he told me, waving his arm toward Tum Tum, "it was like a feller pressing electric buttons, the way she lighted up."

From my workroom window I can see the immensity of Mount Hood. There it stands, alone, aloof, complete, majestic. It is a superb sight, yet I never look upon it without thinking of my friends of the Crag Rats of Hood River, who have many times crawled over the mountain's inhospitable flanks, braved its blizzards and its crevices, and otherwise risked their lives to rescue somebody described as a sports enthusiast, who obviously should have never been permitted to go above timberline on Hood. And at Santiam Pass in the Cascades, I marvel to look on the world spread out so far below, and meanwhile give a thought to the late T. Egenden Hogg, and his heartbreaking attempts to put a railroad through this spot, where signs of his rock-drilling crews are still to be seen. Hogg's ambitions soared easily through the pass, and on and on, over the Rockies and the Plains as far as Manhattan Island, yet his rails never quite crossed the Cascades.

Of late years the matter of scenery in the Northwest has become serious business, something to sell; and it just hap-pens to be worth buying. Possibly some of our many mer-chants of fried chicken and hot dogs may gouge the tourist on occasion, but he is never cheated on the scenery. My only objection is that too many of us in the region have grown not only most possessive of the scenery, but speak as if we had had something to do with the erection of Mount Rainier and the digging of Puget Sound, and of adding the pigments that make Crater Lake so unforgettably blue.

I suppose that every region develops its own notions and peculiarities. In the Northwest we have a harmless sort of Mayflower Society method of designation, or classification. It applies only to natives. It concerns not at all where he landed or where he drove his stakes, but in what year Grand-father arrived in a covered wagon train. In former times there was a distinction: Did Grandfather come by ship around the Horn, or across the Plains in a wagon? The former route seemed to carry more tone. But the distinction, if ever there was such, has broken down. The numerous pioneer and old-timer groups apparently predicate membership on the basis of forebears arriving in the Oregon country before or with the last of the wagon trains. Quite naturally, I suppose, the pioneers of, say, 1842, rank those of 1859. This seems to be a simple way to settle such grave matters.

In the Northwest of three decades ago, the older natives often told me that the region had sadly deteriorated in the matter both of honesty and of friendliness, that those sterling characteristics had gradually all but disappeared with the passing of the frontier, whenever that was. Doors with locks, they vowed, had been unknown in that golden time. Everybody's coat and pottage could be had for the asking, even without the asking, if need were apparent, back in pioneer days. I never believed these assertions for a moment. I had grown up on the same sort of mythology in New England. There, so it was made to appear, the honesty and neighborliness which had disappeared in the era of Grover Cleveland had been common enough when John Quincy Adams was President; and had been even more prevalent, and of much better quality, in ye times of Plymouth Plantation. No magic I know of is so wondrous as that worked by time on the memories of men.

Both common sense and experience tell me that honesty in the Northwest is no more nor less than it is elsewhere. As for friendliness, it is probably silly to generalize. Yet I have never ceased to be astonished at the apparently illimitable source of that quality in Northwest natives. Possibly it is an inheritance from the time, not long past, when the quite real isolation and loneliness of pioneers made it more valued than anything else. I like to hope that we immigrants from longer settled and far more populous regions, where both courtesy and friendliness are thought to have faded from mere crowding, may absorb something of those qualities in this Northwest which to me, after more than thirty years, is still friendly, still new, still dynamic, still wonderful.

2. North of Forty-Nine

MY APPROACH TO THE AMERICAN NORTHWEST, AS INDICATED, was by way of British Columbia, where I lived for almost three years. At that time the stranger discovered, before he got to his hotel, that Vancouver was no Yankee city. His taxi ran on the left. So did all other traffic, including the specially built streetcars. This was odd enough even in Canada, where otherwise, except for tiny Prince Edward Island off the East coast, traffic followed the right-hand custom common to the United States.

It was confusing at first, though one ceased to think of it; and it was fair notice to the outlander, either Canadian or American, that the Province of British Columbia proposed to live up to its name. This was a true *British* commonwealth. But there had been a mounting opposition to the left-hand rule. This presently congealed into a strong parliamentary clique and, after a good deal of impassioned oratory, the provincial legislators passed an Act changing the rule of the road to right-hand. The time set for change was January 1, 1921.

I was still a resident of the province, and recall the uproar as the day drew near. The letter columns of the Vancouver *Province, Sun,* and *World,* and of the Victoria *Colonist* and other papers, were seething with bitter protests and denunciations concerning this un-British, even traitorous adoption of "Yankee notions." Various societies, associations, and clubs were galvanized into action. They held meetings. They passed and drew up resolutions damning the whole business as the work of Satan in league with Uncle Sam. Communications signed John Bull and True Englishman, both gentlemen obviously close to apoplexy, were given prominence. What was good enough in the times of Gladstone, it appeared; what was good enough for the Pitts, both Elder and Younger, and doubtless, too, good enough for Beowulf, was good enough for British Columbia in the twentieth cen-

tury. It was freely prophesied that collisions and wrecks
would strew the streets and highways with carnage compared
with which the field at Balaclava was as nothing.

The awesome day came and passed. The local press
reported that not a single accident occurred that could have
been charged to the change. Disappointed John Bull and
True Englishman returned to their more usual subjects of
letters to the editors, things like the first crocus in Kerris-
dale, and the correct ingredients of a proper chutney.

There were reasons other than the right-hand rule why
British Columbians might well resent American influence.
Since the middle of World War I they had been exposed to
numerous Hollywood-made motion pictures based on the
theme of one or perhaps two noble American doughboys
holding at bay the entire Prussian Guard. No matter the
complete idiocy of these films, they did not endear us to a
people who thought of American soldiers as arriving at
the front a full two years late. Another reason for hearty dis-
like of things American was the generally held opinion in
British Columbia that the local or provincial prohibition
of liquor, continued for two years after the Armistice, was
due somehow to prohibition in the United States. It was a
striking paradox that on the same New Year's Day British
Columbia began turning to the right in traffic, the province
shook off the shackles of prohibition and put into effect the
government sale and control of liquor, the first political
unit in North America, I believe, to adopt such a sensible
law.

Vancouver was so new a city when I got there that almost no one, except children, was a native of the place. In
the back yards of many an imposing home was to be found
the eight-foot stump of some gigantic fir or cedar. Men
hardly of middle age could recall the arrival of the first train
of cars, which rolled in on Queen Victoria's birthday in
1887. Only a year before that the collection of log
cabins and board shacks clustered around a sawmill had incorporated itself. Meanwhile, it had been completely wiped
out by fire and partially rebuilt. The town could muster less
than two thousand persons to greet the first transcontinental
train of the Canadian Pacific Railway to reach the West
Coast.

The site had been chosen for the railroad's terminus by the
general manager of the line, and named for Captain George
Vancouver, the English explorer who had mapped much of

the Northwest coast, and who already had a city named for him on the Columbia River in the State of Washington.

The British Columbia city might have been named even better for the railroadman himself, who was born William Cornelius Van Horne, in Illinois. He chose the spot from several possibilities, and said, like Brigham Young on another occasion, "This is the place." The great Mormon leader chose no better than did the genius of the Canadian Pacific. I thought when I first saw it, there was no city anywhere with a more dramatic setting than that of Vancouver, British Columbia. I haven't had to change my mind.

When Van Horne left his superintendent's job with the Milwaukee Railroad, in 1881, to take charge of pushing the Canadian Pacific tracks across the plains and mountains, the road had long been harassed by politics and vacillating direction. It had been brought into being with the idea that it would bind together the immense territory that was called, on paper, the Dominion of Canada. The road must reach and cross the Rockies, too, for the Crown Colony of British Columbia had been wavering. A vote of its primitive parliament had indicated a strong, though not quite majority, desire to join the United States. Although this vote was probably more a resentment against the Dominion Government than it was a genuine wish to join the United States, it was effective. To make certain no such hideous thing came to pass, Sir John A. Macdonald, Canada's prime minister, promised British Columbia a railroad to connect it with the rest of the Dominion.

Sir William Van Horne (he was knighted by the Queen in 1894) was just the man to build such a railroad. In six years from the day he took charge near Winnipeg, the first transcontinental train reached the shacks of Vancouver. Many think that our own Union Pacific story, epic though it is, was no greater than the epic of the Canadian line.

Van Horne had been urged, and pressure brought to bear on him, to make the terminal Victoria, on Vancouver Island. It was pointed out that tracks could be laid across the narrow tidewater at Bute Inlet to reach the island, then south to Victoria, seat of provincial government and then the largest city. Instead, and to the horror of all islanders, Van Horne chose the site elsewhere, and named it Vancouver. Incidentally, Sir William was an amateur artist of considerable talent. He painted in oils, and painted well, in the academic tradition. I like to think that he saw Vancouver's gorgeous setting no less as an artist than as a peerless railroadman.

Vancouver when I got here was not quite thirty-three years old, yet it was already Canada's fourth city, and well on its way to the third place it holds in 1951. It occupies a promontory of the mainland almost surrounded by water. Across the harbor to the north are great white-capped mountains. Five minutes' ride from the city center are the thousand acres of Stanley Park, all virgin forest to this day. Many of these noble old firs and cedars were huge trees before Captain Vancouver was born in 1758. On the edge of this superb primitive area of darkest green, Vancouver rises and glitters in the northern sunlight with a sparkle all its own. Mist and, in season, downright fog hang mysteriously over it. Snow is rare.

It is the most cosmopolitan city in Canada. Its Chinatown, next to San Francisco's, is the largest on the West Coast. One sees many fine turbaned Sikhs on the streets, along with Westernized Japanese, and both mountain and tidewater Indians. There are Seaforth Highlanders in white jackets and tartans, their kilts swaying. A suprising number of dowagers with boned lace collars survive, though the victorias and broughams in which I saw them riding in past years have disappeared. Most of these survivors of the lavender age do their own shopping, whether for some bauble or other at Birk's, or for food at one of the several small and excellent shops known as British pork stores—and so home to a spacious shingled horror crawling over a lawn on Shaughnessy Heights, or to a stone mausoleum on Marine Drive.

At rare intervals, too, one may see a group of Dukhobors, the men mostly bearded, the many-petticoated women wearing babushkas.

Lumberjacks in town seldom invade the purlieus of Granville Street, which is the quality district. They find the Skidroad of Cordova, Powell, and a part of Hastings streets more relaxing and not so expensive. These lads fancy themselves able drinking men. They are good, too, but they cannot hold a candle, or rather a bottle, to a species peculiar no less to Vancouver than to British Columbia as a whole. These are the long-retired army colonels, men who have taken their gin and bitters at Jodhpur and retain an inordinate appetite for liquor, any sort of liquor, and especially free liquor. But they are not parasites, for their excellent conversation is usually well worth the expense involved. They live in clubs, rooming houses, and "in chambers" all over town, and in small cottages in the wilder suburbs. They carry canes, and like bloaters for breakfast.

The old custom of military ribbons survives in British Columbia. Not only doormen and bank guards, but policemen, firemen, postmen, and even porters often wear at work the campaign ribbons that tell of Mons, of Diamond Hill, and the Relief of Ladysmith. The venerable Hudson's Bay Company, operators of one of Vancouver's finest stores, has always been hospitable to men who have, as the saying used to be, served the Empire. Thirty years ago a roll call of their employees would have turned up veterans from all of the Empire's wars from the Crimean to the one ending in 1918.

Whether or not the tendency in Vancouver and the rest of British Columbia has been toward "Americanization" these past thirty years is debatable. It is still the most British of all the Canadian provinces, but nowhere except in the city of Victoria does there seem to be any conscious effort to keep it so. In Victoria is a tweedy and sensible-shoed older population that firmly, and to my mind most properly, resists any effort at change. Working with them to this end are commercial interests that self-consciously keep Britishness alive to attract American tourists who enjoy scones and quaintness with their tea and are enchanted with Yule logs and policemen dressed like the bobbies of Old England. But cricket, which was in a thriving condition when I first went to British Columbia, is now played virtually in private, even in Victoria.

In the coastal country of the mainland the Rockies come right down to the sea. There are no roads worth mentioning. Everything moves by ships which ply north to the Queen Charlotte Islands, and around Vancouver Island. No highway yet circles the island. Parts of it are still hardly explored, to say nothing of settled. As on the mainland, logging and making lumber is the chief industry.

The region in and east of the Rockies, a mountainous country devoted to mining, and in less degree to logging and the raising of fruit, is known as the Interior. Here also are some fifteen thousand members of the Christian Community of Universal Brotherhood, Limited. These are the Dukhobors.

The United States has had scores of strange sects, but nothing at all to compare to these fanatics. One day in 1921, when I was in Vancouver, there emerged simultaneously from the men's and the women's toilets in the Canadian Pacific railway depot, one naked man and one naked woman. The cops promptly took them to jail. There they said their naked performance was a protest against the government, which demanded that their children attend school. They did not, they said, want their children to attend school, any school. This, so far as I am aware, was the first public notice that the Sons of Freedom had arrived in British Columbia along with the main group of orthodox Dukhobors. The Sons are an inner sect often at odds with the others.

At a logging camp where I worked, we once had six young Dukhobors briefly in the crew. All were under forty. All were bearded. They could neither read nor write, in English or in Russian. They would not eat meat. They did not use tobacco. They said they never touched liquor. They were good workers, but they didn't stay long. In the middle of a morning, and for no reason apparent to the rest of the crew, they trooped into camp and asked for their time. No, nothing was the matter. Nothing at all. It was merely time for them to go, and away they went to buy railroad tickets back to their chief settlement at Brilliant in the mountains.

To most Canadians and virtually all Americans, Dukhobors are known only as a wild crew of "foreigners" whose favorite amusements are the staging of nude parades, and arson committed on public schoolhouses. They have been the delight of the Sunday-supplement writers. Typical of this literature was a recent article which in text and highly illuminating pictures described one of these orgies. The article alleged that "several hundred naked Dukhobor men and women," led by a "raven-haired and nude young woman on a white horse" had swept through the British Columbia interior, torches in hand, spreading fire and destruction in their wake. If you didn't believe the text, then you could gaze at a picture, a pen-and-ink drawing, of the "pretty Queen of the Dukhobors," her raven hair flowing like Lady Godiva's, astride the white steed, while in the rear came a riotous gang of men, women, and children, all stark naked, the men bearded, flaming torches in hand.

Although both text and picture were sheer fiction, the article was true in one respect: it presented to the public what has long since been the public's own conception of Dukhobors. The raven-haired beauty on the white horse was merely an extra added attraction in the best Sunday-supplement tradition. Had she been a blond-beauty, then her horse would have been "black as night," according to the strict rules of the Sunday-supplement feature writers' union.

For almost half a century the Dukhobors have literally asked for, and received, the worst press imaginable. For this their leaders have been largely responsible. A bad press has singularly failed to bring about any reform or change in the Dukhobors. They have become one of British Columbia's greatest problems. If it is to be solved, something besides jail sentences and weird stories in the papers will be needed. I have long taken more than a casual interest in this strange sect, and only in the past two years have I seen anything to encourage belief that its troubles may now be on the way toward settlement.

The sect originated in a seventeenth century schism in the Russian Orthodox Church. For the next two hundred years its adherents were shunted from one Russian province to another, beaten by Cossacks, robbed regularly by government agents, and imprisoned. Their great crime was that they refused to serve in the army. In time they came to be vegetarians, nondrinkers of vodka, nonusers of tobacco. In the nineties Count Leo Tolstoy became interested in the sect. So did Aylmer Maude, an Englishman, and the Quakers. These people aided the Dukhobors to migrate to Canada.

Ten thousand came in 1899 to settle on homesteads in what is now Saskatchewan. Later their leader, Peter Veregin, who had spent many years in Siberian exile, was permitted to join his people. They called him Peter the Lordly. I once saw him in the Manor Hotel in Winnipeg. He was huge, though not fat, and perhaps looked bigger than he was because of the fur coat and cap he wore. He was bearded, and the papers said he looked much like his mentor Tolstoy.

Peter the Lordly was an able and crafty leader. He publicly deplored the mass nudism and other didos of the select Sons of Freedom, but seems to have encouraged them privately in their antipathy to public schools. The fanatical Sons staged parades of protest whenever the spirit moved them. Sometimes they were clothed during these demonstrations. More often they were nude. One of such orgies took them a thousand miles across the prairies of Canada to Fort William, Ontario. Every now and then they set fire to their own homes and the homes of others. Purification, they called it. They destroyed agricultural implements. At one time they got an overdose of Tolstoy's ideas, as transmitted by Peter the

Lordly, and came to think of the gophers as their "little brothers." So, they sat patiently by the holes to snare the pests alive, and when they had several boxes filled with the squeaking animals, they rowed across the Swan River and released them on the fields of their neighbors the Mennonites.

It was the Sons of Freedom who prevented most of the entire sect form getting the homestead lands they had farmed so industriously. The Sons maintained that to sign for the land was to become liable for military duty. This was not true; they had an agreement with the Dominion Government by which Dukhobors were expressly exempted from military duty. It has never been violated. Yet, excepting for a few hundred so-called Independents, the Dukhobors refused to sign for their homestead deeds or to swear allegiance to the Crown. They were dispossessed, and Peter led the majority of them to British Columbia, where he purchased land in the name of a corporation, the Christian Community of Universal Brotherhood, Limited.

Here at Brilliant the hard-working sect started raising fruit. They put up a big jam factory. Their products were noted for quality, and for a time they prospered. They erected a large sawmill. They built a waterworks.

All of this was too much for the Sons of Freedom. It was departing from the primitive Dukhobor way of life. The Sons set up a village of their own, a grim place they called Krestova. The first public schoolhouse in the Dukhobor district was destroyed by fire of unknown origin in 1923. (Some fifty more have been burned since.) Then came the event beside which all others in Dukhobor history paled.

On the evening of October 28, 1924, Peter the Lordly boarded the Canadian Pacific's Kootenay Express at Brilliant. With him was a Dukhobor woman. Eighteen other persons, mostly non-Dukhobors, were in the same day coach. It is perhaps worth knowing, though it does nothing to clear up the mystery, that Peter presented the conductor with two tickets to Castlegar, only two miles from Brilliant. Neither he nor the woman got out of their seats at Castlegar. He bought from the conductor two new tickets, this time to Grand Forks, a hundred miles farther on.

The train never got to Grand Forks. Near the hamlet of Farron it was stopped by a mighty blast that tore the day coach into splinters and twisted steel. Peter was killed. So were the Dukhobor maid and seven other passengers. Officials held the blast to have come from an explosive within the car. The mystery was never solved, although years later a Son of Freedom told me Peter had been "murdered by the government."

Peter's death marked the beginning of a slow disintegration of the sect. His son, who became leader, was much given to the bottle, and seemingly worked to undermine the spirit and economy of his people.* The Dukhobor jam factory and sawmill were mortgaged, then lost. The finances of the group at last became so involved that the provincial government stepped in to "lift the burden from the backs of the loan company and place it quietly on the shoulders of the taxpayers." For several years the province has been aiding ex-community Dukhobors to set up as independent farmers. Schism split the sect again in 1947, when Michael the Archangel led a group of eighty in a migration to Vancouver Island. I visited this colony recently. It was a collection of log cabins straight out of Chekov, but showing one bit of British influence—an empty Lipton's Tea can on a stump. I asked to see the Archangel himself, who turned out to be a hulking bearlike man, surly one moment, loquacious the next. He told me that his group comprised the "only true Dukhobors." "Here," said he, indicating the cluster of log huts, "here we are all one. We own nothing. We own everything. All of us belong to the community."

Whether or not the domestic arrangements of these island Dukhobors are, or were, in violation of Canadian law was something pending with Mike the Archangel's appeal from a conviction on charges of "conspiracy to promote adultery" among his followers.† Then, in 1949, all hell broke loose, not on the island, but in the older Dukhobor villages in the Interior. From the Sons' settlement at Krestova assaults with dynamite were made on Peter the Lordly's tomb at Brilliant. Another blast ripped up Canadian Pacific tracks. Another damaged a power house. Meanwhile, Sons set fire to, and burned several of, their own homes at Krestova. Four schoolhouses in the district were destroyed by night fires. An army of constables moved in and made several hundred arrests. At the trials most of the Sons readily admitted the charges,

---

*This is the opinion of J. F. C. Wright, Canadian journalist and scholarly writer on Dukhobors, whose study of them, *Slava Bohu* (1940), is a sound and fascinating book.

†The case doubtless was settled on July 28, 1951, when the Archangel died in a Vancouver hospital.

which ran from mere nudism to arson and assaults with dynamite. Three hundred and ten were sent to prison, bringing the total number jailed to more than four hundred.

For well over a year, as this is written, there has been a tentative peace along the Dukhobor front. If it is permanent peace, then its establishment is due in no small part to Emmett Gulley, a Quaker from Oregon, who went to British Columbia at the height of the Dukhobor violence and has remained there, working quietly and most effectively among the warring Dukhobor factions and with the government.

Quaker Gulley is an immense figure. He stands six feet four inches and weighs about 250 pounds. He is in his mid-fifties. He speaks quietly, as befits a lifelong member of the Society of Friends, but there is nothing wishy-washy in his speech or manner. His rugged face indicates the strong character which one is prepared to believe necessary to keep the faith when working in such unpopular and "hopeless" causes as that of the Dukhobors.

From the work of Gulley and others came a Dukhobor consultative committee on which are University of British Columbia people, provincial officials, pastors, a board of trade man, and several Dukhobors. The committee prevailed on the government to release from prison all Dukhobors who would sign a statement to work for peace among the factions, and abjure the Sons' favorite tactics of nudism and arson. Most of them signed. Since then, Gulley's committee has apparently made progress. No act of violence has occurred. It is too soon to predict complete and lasting peace. Yet it looks as if more progress has been made in one year than in the previous half-century.

I have talked to a number of British Columbians who seem to think the province's most harassing problem of the past two decades is really well on its way to solution. Others are still skeptical, and at least one was cynically hopeless about the whole business. "It is too bloody bad," he said, "that the whole pack of Duks didn't set up their bloody colony at Frank, Alberta, any old time before April 29, 1903." (I'll get to that presently.) He thought that the Dukhobors had been "coddled," and that coddling simply made them act worse than ever. "Lock all of them up and keep them there," was his considered opinion.

To such attitudes, Quaker Gulley replies that education and not incarceration is the answer.

Until the reference was made in relation to Dukhobors, I hadn't thought of Frank, Alberta, for many years. This was the little mining town in the Rockies, almost on the British Columbia border, which was suddenly buried deeper than Pompeii, so deep that, unlike the old Roman ctiy, it has never been excavated.

My friend, I found on checking, had the date right. The disaster occurred in early morning. Most of the town was asleep. There was no warning. With the suddenness of thunder from a cloudless sky came a deep rumble that probably roused some of the sleepers. The rumble grew into a roar. The earth trembled, and then a good part of Turtle mountain split off and came crashing down to bury the village and almost two miles of Canadian Pacific track.

Homes, stores, and other buildings were covered, some to a depth of well over two hundred feet. The inmates of the houses probably never knew what happened. Many of them rest to this day where disaster found them. Their number was more than fifty.

Survivors knew only that some terrible thing had happened. They came out into a night of chaos, and set about in the dark to do what they could. They worked dangerously among the huge boulders that continued to roll long after the main slide. When morning made the task easier, the people saw that the sheer wall of Mount Turtle, which had dominated the settlement, had wholly disappeared, along with most of the village.

Thoughts turned to the night shift which had been at work in the mine of the Canadian-American Coal & Coke Company. These men were given up for lost, yet by the night of April 29th eighteen had somehow managed to work themselves up and out.

From the débris the bodies of nineteen villagers were recovered. A check of the survivors showed that at least fifty-one others were still buried. Thus the total casualties were seventy.

What caused the great slide was never clearly established. I found one government report which said the mountain "had been of doubtful stability"; it was "filled with faults."

By the time I came to British Columbia, seventeen years had passed since the disaster. That is just about the right length of time for myths to congeal; and I heard all of the myths in bunkhouses, in saloons, in private homes, in smoking cars. The best and most formidable of them all concerned

a female infant found in the wreckage of a house that was
buried in rocks. A rescue party—so went the story, with
minor variations—a rescue party heard wails coming from
somewhere beneath them. They dug furiously, and lo, there
was the little girl, alive and well, crying lustily.

That was no place for a good story to stop, nor did this
one stop there. It went on to relate how the child's parents,
whose name was not known, had been buried far beneath
the slide, beyond recovery. So the child was "adopted by a
family in Pendiction, British Columbia," by the name of
Smith.

At least two tellers of the tale called her Frankie Jones.
Better than that, better than all else, was the storyteller
who vowed, in the modest though authoritative manner of
really great liars, that the child had not been named Frankie
Smith or Frankie Jones.

"It wasn't Frankie This or Frankie That," he said, becoming more indignant as he reflected on such deviations from
fact. "She was named—and christened, too, by God—Alberta Frank."

This name, neatly joining both the province and the town,
surely was close to genius. The man immediately became my
favorite authority on the subject, and I often bought him a
couple of drinks to have him repeat the tale. He had more
to say about it, too, for he was no fellow to leave anything
hanging.

"Alberta Frank," said he, "growed into a fine woman, and
she was wooed and won by some millionaire back East.
I forget his name, but he was a rich son of a bitch. Lots of
dough." The couple presumably lived happily ever after.

It all makes for the perfect mythical story, believed to
this day, so I have discovered, by many Canadians. Ron
Moxness, a newspaperman who has written of the disaster,
told me he has run across Alberta Frank again and again.
Often he has attempted to disillusion the narrator, or at least
correct him, and he is never thanked for his pains. You just
can't do that to little Alberta Frank. Men in bars still weep
over the tragedy of Alberta, and smile through malty tears
at her presumably happy end. The eyes of women, sitting
and sewing together for St. Mark's Guild or the Ladies' Improvement Club, grow misty at the tender story.

Meanwhile, however, these makers and supporters of
myths seem to shed no tears for the seventy actual victims.

Such is the manner in which the improbable, the incredible,

and the preposterous thrive in folklore and at last become immutable facts, refined and documented by talented liars. We might just as well gather round, all of us, and drink a toast to Alberta Frank and her many-times-a-millionaire husband. She is as safely enshrined in her special Valhalla as Lady Godiva and Barbara Frietchie are in theirs.

Remittance men were often superb tellers of tales. In my day there must have been several hundred authentic remittance men in British Columbia. One ran across them living in some shack along the beach, working in logging camps, holed-up in chambers in Victoria or Vancouver. Others lived on small stump ranches. Most of them were probably actual younger sons of blooded houses of England, or at least of the gentry. And most of those I happened to meet were fine company. Their characters varied, of course, and ranged in my acquaintance from worthless, in the case of two, to admirable in half a dozen of the others. I knew only one who was not British, and he was a native of New York City.

Ed Fellows was the name he went by. That was the name on the letter that came to him once a month, addressed in care of Phil Wilson, logging operator of Loughborough Inlet. Loughborough was as remote and lonely a place as I was ever in, an arm of the sea hemmed on both sides by virgin fir and cedar that grew down to tidewater. At some time prior to 1912, Ed Fellows made his way to the far end of this long seaway, and there built himself a cabin of split cedar shakes. His only neighbor was the Wilson logging camp, some ten miles distant. Once a week the Union Steamship Company's *Cheakamus* from Vancouver steamed into the inlet to deliver supplies and the mail at the Wilson camp. Once a month, and never oftener, Ed Fellows rowed to the camp to buy groceries from the outfit, and to get his letter. The letter was never late. It was postmarked at New York City, usually on the first day of the month. In the envelope was a check for $15. Ed always endorsed it over to the logging company, then drew groceries to the amount, and went back to his lonely shack on the shore.

He was a soft-spoken man, and his talk was patently that of a well educated person of no common learning. Not that he wore his learning on his sleeve. He never showed it off. You came to appreciate his knowledge only after considerable acquaintance. Phil Wilson, himself a graduate of Cornell, managed to draw Ed out, and learned he had spent four years at Princeton, though he said he had never graduated. Phil Wilson told us younger men that Ed Fellows showed an easy familiarity with the classics of literature such as he could not recall of the Cornell faculty. When he made his monthly trip for his mail, Ed usually stopped for dinner at the logging camp, for he obviously enjoyed talking with Wilson.

Ed Fellows did not pretend to do any remunerative labor. He hunted a little, fished a little, and read a great deal in his books, of which his small cabin harbored perhaps a thousand. Perhaps he read too much, if that is possible. In any case, he was much alone.

What happened to the mind of Ed Fellows is not to be known. He was moody, certainly, and given to brooding by the shore when the tide was running and the gulls circling and making their wild cries. The gulls of Loughborough Inlet, it seemed to me, gave forth the wildest cries I ever heard. I came to wonder if the birds themselves were not conscious of the immense loneliness of the inlet and were protesting. Anyway, Ed Fellows used to sit on a rock by the shore with the gulls wheeling and screaming around him. The sun would go down suddenly, the way it does when you live in the midst of timber two hundred and more feet tall; and Ed would sit there on the shore, brooding still, as the moon came up, the gulls retired, and owls began to call from the woods.

A friend of mine, Boone Kerlin, saw Ed sitting like that a couple of times. So had Phil Wilson. But they were not there on the night when Ed Fellows came to the end of his brooding. Something in his fine mind snapped. He killed his faithful dog with a rifle shot, then turned the rifle on himself.

Two weeks or so passed before anybody knew about it. There was the man, there was the dog—both dead. The two loggers who discovered the tragedy went into the cabin, which they found in good order and filled with Ed's good books. These two barbarians piled a new tragedy on the other; they took the books out, made them into a pile, and set it afire. Then they buried Ed near his cabin, and buried his dog nearby.

The two loggers brought back word of the affair at the far end of the inlet. On the next Sunday Boone Kerlin, a highly literate saw filer, and myself, got into Boone's small motorboat and ran down to Ed Fellows' place. We hoped to retrieve a book or two from the holocaust set off by the two illiterates. The best we could do was to assemble two or three handfuls of odd pages from several volumes, charred but still readable words of Plato, Shakespeare, Fielding, Herbert Spencer, Schopenhauer, and Ralph Waldo Emerson.

Among the remains was one page from the Yankee philosopher's *Essays*. Marked in pencil was a passage: ". . . but in the solitude to which every man is always turning, he has a sanity and revelations which in his passage into new worlds he will carry with him."

What was the sanity and what were the revelations that came to Ed Fellows before he pulled the trigger? Doubtless he believed he had discovered an answer, perhaps the answer, to the Great Riddle. And possibly he had, or did.

A month later, when Ed Fellows' letter came to the camp, Phil Wilson marked it "Deceased," and returned it whence it came, which was some office building in New York City. Nothing further, not even an inquiry, came from that address or from anywhere else.

I became well acquainted with an English remittance man who lived in a world wholly different from that of Ed Fellows'. I will call him Cyril Robinson, which was not his name. His base of operations, and I use this term correctly, was a small cottage in North Vancouver, where he lived in happy sin with a woman he described as having more than a little bow-and-arrow in her lineage. Cyril was in his fifties, a public-school boy from the English Midlands, and the youngest, so he said, of six sons of a lord. The survival in fact, if not by law, of primogeniture had sent Cyril to Canada at manhood, and scattered four other brothers in the British dominions of India and Australia.

The estate of the late lord, Cyril's father, had apparently held up well for many years, or until World War I, and Cyril had been in receipt of remittances that kept him from all except casual work for a full twenty years. But around 1919 the remittances became less frequent. They were also smaller. Cyril was inclined to charge this condition less to actual circumstances concerning the estate than to an increasing niggardliness of his eldest brother—or rather to his brother's own manner of living.

"The bounder's bought himself a Rolls," Cyril complained, "and he's damned well keeping his horses, too." This appeared to Cyril as excessively Tory. "There is only one way to deal with Tories," he said. "They won't be driven. One must use guile."

Guile in this case soon took form in a beautiful letterhead which Cyril talked a North Vancouver printer into doing, on spec, as he termed it. Cyril was proud of the job. In conservative script the letterhead announced: "The British Ophir & Grubstake Mines, Limited, North Vancouver, B.C., Dominion of Canada." In smaller, extremely modest type, lower down, was the legend: "Cyril Allen Henty Robinson, Managing Director."

"That's an odd name for a mine," I remarked.

"It is a carefully calculated name," Cyril replied. "My brother knows all of the implications of Ophir. The Grubstake part of it will appeal to him as the fine vulgar essence of frontier country—a real mining region. Romantic and rich. I fancy he will respond like any wealthy and voracious coney—or what we call a sucker."

The plan was clear enough, but I wondered aloud to Cyril what he would do about ore samples. "People who invest in mines," I told him, "like to see samples of ore. It is often the only ore they ever see."

"I know all about that. I've already sent him samples, though the first lot I sent was a mistake. I just wrapped up some iron pyrites I washed out of the creek here and put them in a packet. They looked superb, but too late I learned they were not heavy enough. Lord save us, if he had taken the trouble to show them to an assayman, all might now be lost. He was too stupid to do so."

Cyril went on to say that the next sample he sent was a hunk of rock that did contain gold, not much, but enough to look well and to stand up to any assaying business.

I asked him if he were selling stock in British Ophir & Grubstake to his brother.

"Not exactly. The printing of stock certificates is too expensive for a poor chap with a niggardly elder brother. What I have done, though, is just as—just as effective. I have promised him fifty per centum of the profits."

The profits, Cyril went on, were of course something for the future. Now and then he wrote his brother a long letter relating "developments" of the mine, always pointing out that the modern mining of gold was a long and costly process. It wasn't the way it had been in early days on the Rand, or in the Yukon, where free gold was to be found. This was hard-rock mining. Lesser ores had to be separated from the precious metal. To keep his letters convincingly authentic, Cyril devoted considerable time to reading technical works on mining in the Vancouver Public Library. And no letter failed to imply the certain fortune that lay in the depths of the British Ophir & Grubstake.

In his letters Cyril usually suggested his brother send a draft, sometimes for as little as £5, again for as much as £100. The brother always sent some money, commonly about half what had been asked for.

To keep things warm, Cyril clipped every item he could find about the fabulous success of the mines at Flin Flon, Manitoba, some two thousand miles distant from the alleged Ophir & Grubstake. "No Englishman at home knows anything of the geography of Canada," he remarked, "and no Englishman will trouble himself to look at a map of Canada. So far as my stupid brother is concerned, Flin Flon is merely up the creek a way from the gigantic operations of British Ophir."

The last I knew at firsthand of British Ophir was about 1926. The vein was petering out. Cyril was discouraged, virtually beaten. He had, in fact, taken a position as bookkeeper in Vancouver, but something had gone wrong with the job, or with the books, and he had been discharged. He was still living in the shabby little cottage in North Vancouver, though his dark-skinned partner had disappeared. "She just went away," was all he said. Two years later Cyril himself had gone away. I could not learn where he had gone. Wherever he is, if still living, there is good company, as good company as ever I knew, a cheerful, thoughtful, philosophical, witty, and humorous man. And imaginative, too. Clods do not become managing directors of things like British Ophir & Grubstake Mines, Limited.

But there would no longer be much chance for "improvement funds" from an England where lords and ladies have come to the pass of showing their estates, at a small fee, to the masses. Cyril Allen Henty Robinson's mine would not be able to raise an assessment of tuppence-ha'penny.

In the days of Cyril Robinson's mythical Golconda, the exploitation of British Columbia's mineral lands had hardly begun. It is only now, almost thirty years later, that major activity is under way. It is much the same with the province's other natural resources, save for timber. (And of timber there are yet millions of acres which have known no ax.)

A good portion of the province is yet to hear the whistle of a locomotive or the pounding of a motor, except in the sky. The visitor to British Columbia seldom appreciates the vastness of the region. Let no Texan go there to brag of the size of his state. It would be wholly swallowed in British Columbia, which contains 359,279 square miles, and leave no trace.

Exploitation of its resources, as I said, is just now beginning on a grand scale. It is not my story. I know nothing of it at firsthand, nor does it interest me overmuch. My three years in the province were rather circumscribed. Most of my time was spent in logging camps, one of which was as isolated as could be imagined. My visits since have taken me into little new territory. Because of this, my personal knowledge of the country is too narrow, or special, to permit me to describe or to attempt to "interpret" it. I would refrain from doing so if for no other reason than that British Columbia, and for that matter all of Canada, has already suffered from too many once-over-lightly treatments by itinerant American and English journalists, no few of whom have displayed remarkable ignorance of what they were writing about. No, I respect British Columbia and its friendly people too much to saddle them with "impressions" and "interpretations." There have been too many of these in the wake of fast-moving journalists.

I feel competent, however, to speak up on a subject which earlier in this book I said was debatable. I mean the tendency toward Americanization. It *is* a debatable subject, too, though it is so no longer so far as I am concerned.

Thirty years ago I found British Columbia to have an individuality as striking as it was refreshing. It was no mere copy of Ontario, or of England, or of anything in the United States. It had a distinct flavor as quickly felt as it was difficult to define. Of recent years this distinctiveness is less marked. I could wish it were otherwise. Yet of late Vancouver has come to seem like any other city on the make, filled with the same bigger and better boosterism that infests so much of the Western United States. The town has been growing rapidly in population. It has been getting large doses of American capital.

Victoria, as I have intimated, is a handsome town whose dominant commercial interests are now self-consciously "British" for a purpose. It used to be a delightfully and honestly stuffy place.

What I have seen of late of the country towns and cities indicates that they have become almost indistinguishable from country towns and cities across the line in Washington. Neon has them in thrall. Glass block and chromium have captured them. These and packing-box architecture are transforming them into replicas of dismally "modern" towns in the United States. Their newsstands are dominated by a clutter of American periodicals, including movie-fan magazines and comic books. I was hard put on a recent visit to Victoria to discover a copy of *Punch,* and failed to find a copy of that century-old classic of scandal *The News of the Day*. Every city and town, of course, has a gaudy temple for displaying the art of Hollywood. I believe, too, that a survey (which I have not made) would show fewer hotels named Queens and Wellington and Connaught than of yore. In this respect I have often wondered why so few hotels in Canada have been named for General Brock, a native Canadian whose brief military career indicated him to be a commander of great ability, possibly of genius.

Now and then, as I happen to know, some old-fashioned Canadian or Scot or Englishman raises his voice to protest the copy-cat Americanization he sees on every hand. I am stoutly on his side. Were I living there, I would be as vocal as he, and doubtless as bitter. And of course just as futile.

The British Columbia I used to know was as delightful a country as man ever lived in. It had, and still has, gorgeous scenery. Life was not too hard. The people lived calmly. The pace everywhere, town or country, was leisurely. The people had their own ways and customs and heroes and symbols. They held fast to these. I do not think this is true any longer. People and province have been caught in the heady current called Progress. Anything new is wonderful. Anything old is to be deplored.

The province is now beginning to know Progress in full measure. Backed by natural resources as great as any in North America, and possibly greater, I can see nothing to prevent British Columbia from becoming the hive of population and of industry and commerce that a majority of its citizens seem to want. I wish them well, and remain happy in my memories of a British Columbia that wore its own clothes, including its own collar; and when, in all its immensity, there were only half a million people—only a few more than are now living in greater Vancouver alone.

Why, then, did I leave this Eden? Well, I was determined

to be a writer. I had begun to write during the long evenings and even longer Sundays in logging camps. I soon discovered that Canadians who made a living by writing wrote either for American or for English periodicals, but mostly for the former. Canadian markets were few, and Canadian editors patently believed that writers needed neither food nor clothing. A little tobacco, perhaps, but nothing more. English editors were not much different. American magazines, I learned, were not greatly interested in Canadian subjects. If I were to earn my living by writing, and planned to remain in the field of nonfiction, then the United States was the place to be.

But I had come to love British Columbia. I did not leave it without many regrets and a few misgivings. It was my wonderfully good fortune that the pressure of economics should have taken me from the most charming part of the Dominion into what proved to be the most charming part of the Republic.

PART TWO

SYMBOLS

1. The Pioneer

THERE IS NO RECORD OF HOW MANY PEOPLE FROM ELSE-where came to live in Oregon during 1923. That was the time I arrived from British Columbia, and I had to wait another seven years to find that I was one of 170,387 new residents of the state in the decade ending 1930.

That was small distinction, surely, yet it was some gratification to know I was among the first million, a figure Oregon did not attain until about 1940. It is always comforting to be among the first hundred, or thousand, or million, and I like to think of myself as among the first 800,000 Oregonians living at one and the same time within the state's borders. (Incidentally, Washington passed its first million by 1910. Idaho reached its first half-million in 1940.)

Immigrants in the Northwest like to distinguish their era of arrival as, say, the time before Portland had built even one bridge across the Willamette, or before Reedsport had either a name or a post office, or before the Flood in Heppner, or the Big Fire in Seattle or Astoria. All of these milestones of time are considered of local importance. They carry the authority of long residence. And long residence, by what seems a rather comical *non sequitur,* means good solid citizens.

The business was often carried to the extremes of unconscious burlesque. One of the earlist residents of Longview, Washington, Leith Abbott, used to recall that in Longview's pioneer days, which is to say 1923–1924, the barber there was disdainful of anyone who hadn't been in town long enough for two haircuts. Those who had undergone his ministrations twice or more he greeted deferentially as old-timers.

It is a natural tendency, I suppose, to want to belong in a select company of some sort. The great trouble with being in the select company of long-established citizens is that by the time you have achieved the status you begin to notice the number of funerals you are obligated to attend. You go along for years thinking of your place as being in one of the rear seats; and then some day or other, it suddenly occurs to you that you are right down there in the front row. Noises you hear in the night are no longer, as they were in childhood, the walking of a ghost, nor yet, as in middle years, the intrusion of a burglar. They sound more as if someone, in a field not far off, were applying whetstone to a scythe. . . .

The process of becoming what passes for a long-established citizen varies. There is no general rule. Roughly, it takes from ten years or so in Seattle or Spokane, to twenty-five years in Oregon City, Walla Walla, Boise, or Portland. This rather speedy conversion of raw immigrants into old citizens may have no actual effect on a man's arteries, though I think it ages him psychologically, especially if he were born and reared, as I was, in a country where long-established citizens are made not by the passing of years, but of generations.

The Northwest was the last corner of the United States to be settled. The Northeast corner began permanent settlement in 1620. By then the Southeast corner was a long-established colony of Spain. The Southwest corner dates its settlement from long before the American Revolution. But the Northwest had nothing comparable to these until the 1840's, though it had a lone trading post as early as 1811.

History moved swiftly in these parts. Our blockhouse era lasted only two years. It had passed by 1856. That was the end of the only genuine pioneer-Indian war fought in the Northwest; later Indian troubles were local uprisings, and were put down by professional soldiers. Nowhere else in the United States did a blockhouse era pass so quickly as here. Nowhere else, too, did the railroads arrive so late and begin to disappear so soon. The history that elsewhere required from two hundred to three hundred years for its unfolding was in the Northwest compressed into much less than a century. In a period of thirty years, 1859–1890, Oregon, Washington, and Idaho were admitted as sovereign states to the Union. In my own thirty-odd years in the Northwest, I have known men and women who came here in sailing vessels around the Horn, in the covered-wagon trains, by railroad, by automobile, and by airplane—plus one hardy character who walked here from Illinois pulling a little boy's express wagon containing his effects along with a sign that said here was John the Messenger.

The Covered Wagon is our great tradition. The people who came in those wagons are our Pilgrims. We have, however, no Plymouth Rock. The Willamette Valley takes its place. This was the New Canaan of our first settlers. Our Bradfords and Brewsters and Standishes are named Lee and Nesmith and Applegate, and sometime McLoughlin. We have not yet discovered a Priscilla, but give us time. Priscilla Mullens Alden had been in her grave for a century and a half before Longfellow got around to her.

We have no *Mayflower*. The many vessels that brought settlers to the Oregon country had names, but none of the names have survived as symbols. Our symbol comparable to the *Mayflower* is the Covered wagon. It does not matter that those wagons were not all covered or that they were numbered by the many hundreds, or that they rolled westward continuously from 1843 until well after the railroad had arrived on the West shore. They have long since separately dissolved to merge into the classic symbol of the Northwest, that of the Covered Wagon and the Pioneer.

It is true that no few of our pioneers arrived in ships; and it is easily proved that many of these became leaders in the new settlements. Yet our *Mayflower* symbol has four wheels, and its canvas is a top, not a sail. A cult naturally grew from the symbol, and took form in pioneer associations. Membership in these groups was predicated on the time of arrival, that is, in or before a stated year. Immigrants by ship were of course eligible, but the cult symbol was the Covered Wagon. Then, as time passed and the actual pioneers were removed from the scene, the cult was continued in the form of the Sons and Daughters of Pioneers. By mid-twentieth century the actual sons and daughters of actual pioneers were, in turn, beginning to grow scarce; and it would seem that the cult must soon either ignore the patent falsity of the title, as do the Sons and the Daughters of the American Revolution, or change it to Descendants of Pioneers.

Occasionally, as in all cults, the cultism becomes fatuous. In 1890 one pioneer, his nostrils filled with sage and the smoke from remembered campfires in his eyes, stood up at the annual meeting of the Oregon Pioneer Association. "I say to you," he declared, "that there was no honor in having come to a country already opened up."

Many a latter-day immigrant has resented the pioneer cult. I rather enjoy it. Its mild snobbism is harmless. It has its foundations in one of the greatest American experiences. What if it does make for parochialism? Most of the descendants of pioneers I happen to know do not allow the fact of their antecedents to affect their own decency as human beings. And besides, the cult tends to maintain a vicarious pride in one of the great classic events in American history. That alone, to my mind, weighs the scales in the cult's favor, just as it weighs the scales in favor of the several cults in my native region. Anything that makes for proper pride as an American is good, whether it be a forebear in the *Mayflower,* or one in Bunker's pasture, or one who walked two thousand miles beside a covered wagon. It is the fact of participation in the event that counts. It is a heritage infinitely finer than "blood" or "gentle birth."

It was here in the Northwest that the men and women of the wagon trains, grown old and conscious of their parts as Pioneers of the Oregon Trail, remembered their youth in the circle of campfires blinking like small red eyes in the endless dark. This was not the dark of the woods, which they had known in Maine and Tennessee and Illinois and Missouri, and had understood. This was the dark of the great American void, that vague and mysterious region which the very maps they carried in their wagons designated in so many sinister words as the Great American Desert, or worse, as simply the Unknown.

Because where knowledge ends, the imigination takes over, this was an uneasy dark. Here, too, were the biggest sun and the biggest moon in the biggest sky any of them had ever seen. It was the hottest sun, and the coldest moon; and the sky—or something—played cruel tricks. Mirages danced ahead of the wagons, or flickered in their wake; and the kids cried with joy, then wept bitterly as a handsome blue lake suddenly appeared, shimmering cold and inviting for a few moments, then sank out of sight into the horizon.

It came to seem, in their increasing agonies of travel, as though both the horizon and their goal beyond it kept moving in unison; that the horizon always kept ten miles away, moving steadily westward with the wagons, and that Oregon itself moved with the horizon, keeping a safe distance of a thousand miles beyond it.

The wind never ceased. For weeks on end it blew straight from the hottest corridors of Hell, then shifted to blow from the top of the world and to pile up purple murk that split in thunderous crashes. Out of the murk came salvos of cast-iron hailstones to stun the imagination, and to stun man and beast. The poor oxen groaned and staggered and stopped, and their drivers were glad to hide under the wagons until the fury had passed.

The wind never ceased. It coated throats and lungs with dust. It carried corrosive alkali into the eyes, where it became as emery powder, and ground the lids raw. It ground tempers raw, too, and men cursed one another for no other reason than that there was little satisfaction in cursing the wind.

Some said the sun was worse than the wind. In their native homes these people had welcomed the sun, for there had always been a place where they could hide from it when need be. Here in the great American void there was no hiding place, nothing to break the endless glare and heat of that immense and hated thing. These people devoutly believed that God was everywhere, and they came to believe, too, that here on the Plains not even God could hide from the great blazing sun He had made, possibly in a moment of aberration. Was it any wonder that once they had got there, few of them ever wanted to move from the Willamette Valley, where skies were often gray and the sun was a passing occurrence rather than an immutable and continuous experience?

Here on the Plains, too, the everlasting glare played hob with one's eyesight and sanity. In its confusing brightness a gopher was seen plainly to be a coyote, a clump of sagebrush became a mounted Indian, a wrecked wagon grew and grew until it loomed up as a monstrous barn of many mows and stables, topped by grotesque weather vanes that waved and glinted, then fused into nothingness. Men argued as to what that object in the near distance was. One vowed it was a buffalo, another swore it was nothing but a gigantic lone rock. Sometimes they came to blows before it was seen by them both to be a chair or a chest that had been tossed out to lighten some wagon ahead of them.

These discarded chairs and chests, these old claw-footed tables and massive bureaus of carved oak had been cherished through generations of decline from ancestral prosperity in colonial days on the Atlantic seaboard. They had been battered once when they crossed the Alleghenies, battered again when they were moved along the Wilderness Road, and stained and scuffed as their owners took land in Missouri. Parkman the historian saw them along the trail he helped to name. He recognized, as did lesser men, that these things were not the mere trumpery of households, but were the last physical evidence of family importance, or at least of family continuity. They were not discarded lightly. Next to food and powder, they were the last things to be left beside the trail. The family who jettisoned them was a family close to desperation.

Desperation might come from several causes, but it almost never failed to appear. It could stem from a dead ox, or a paper-thin sheet of ice at the water hole. In either case, something had to be done to lighten the burden of the wagon. Time might not have meant a great deal in Kentucky or Tennessee, but here on the Plains one could not allow Time to pass him. The Rockies were still ahead, and beyond the Rockies stood the Cascades. You could not let Time reach the mountains ahead of your wagon, no matter what you threw out to keep pace with the hours. From the day when the wagon trains passed the one hundredth meridian of west longitude, men began to think of winter, and the thought remained a nagging worry until they reached the comparative safety of the dripping mist-hung forest on the west slope of the Cascades.

Though they had never been in the mountains before, they knew well enough that they should not winter in the high places of the continent. The knowledge was in their bones, for these people who took the trail to Oregon were the final development of generations of pioneers. They were professionals engaged in following the calling of their fathers and grandfathers and great-grandfathers, which was generally known as opening up the country. In a manner, they were greater pioneers than their forebears had been, for they had set out on the longest wagon road in American history.

This road through the hell-wrought desert and the threatening mountains beat all manner of things out of human beings. Men and women displayed prodigies of courage and self-sacrifice one day, and on the next showed petty traits and meanness beyond understanding. A man might live fifty years back in the States yet reveal fewer points of character than he would display here on the long road within a week. It was much the same with the women. She who quietly got into a wagon at Independence, Missouri, might emerge at Fort Laramie a virago.

In later years, in their old age, when they had long since attained the status of hallowed Pioneers, the men and women of the covered wagons were sure that the trail had done something to their characters to set them apart from all others in the Oregon country. Their attitude seemed to be that they had endured the most, hence their needs and opinions should be given first consideration in all regional matters. I think their attitude was natural, and perhaps it was morally right, too. The Northwest, and especially that portion of it that became Oregon, was to them more than a Territory, more than a state. It was something like hallowed ground. They had cut its first logs. They had cleared and plowed its first fields. They had fought its only war. And they had done all this and much more *after* they had already covered the longest wagon trail in history. You do not perform feats like those and remain without a cult, or some special form of aura.

Cried one of their number: "Patient toilers of pioneer days! What shall I say of your lonely, isolated lives. . . ." She recalled the pathetic funerals along the trail, and the shuddering apprehension with which the perils of maternity were awaited in dismal cabins. During an Indian uprising she saw "the slow caravan of returning comrades who bore their mutilated dead." She never forgot the blinding tears that accompanied the sudden disasters of pioneer times. She never forgot "the haunting specter of homesickness that moved about the house and the clearing. . . ."* No, you did not emerge unscarred and unchanged from such scenes. Man or woman, willing or not, the experience made you over, turned you into the classic character of the Pioneer. It was a sort of reincarnation, typical of America, that had begun when Plymouth Plantation grew too populous and an exodus resulted. It recurred every few generations for the next two hundred years, and each time it happened out of it came the Pioneers. The poet Whitman identified them: They were the

---

*She was Catharine Amanda Scott Coburn, and she wrote from personal experience, including her trek with the covered wagons at the age of thirteen.

ones who must bear the brunt of danger. It was they upon whom the rest of us depended.

As our Pioneers in the Northwest passed from the flesh, they were immortalized in the arts. The most favored medium was sculpture, and over the years statues in marble, granite, and bronze have gone up in memory of the men and women of the covered wagons. Here and there, among our parks, is a cast-iron general or statesman, but they are rare. So are the wreaths laid on them, though these are lavished at the bases of the bronze or stone Pioneers.

We could do with at least one more statue of a Pioneer. I began to learn about him many years ago, when I first visited the ghostly hamlet of Willapa in southwest Washington. Near there I noticed a tiny graveyard among a clump of fine cedars. In it, along with a few more graves, was the last resting place of young Willie Keil, doubtless the strangest of all immigrants to Washington in the times when it was a part of Oregon. There was and is nothing at the little graveyard to indicate the part Willie Keil played with the covered wagons. I had to put his story together over the years. I had to tap many sources to get it. There is nothing else like it in the story of American migrations. Where are our poets, that they have not sung of Pioneer Willie Keil?

His trek with the covered wagons was unique. He was dead before the teams were harnessed. The train in which he crossed the bloody plains and mountains came in complete safety. No arrows, no bullet, nor any sort of Indian harassment was directed against this caravan of German Christian communists, who took off from Bethel, Missouri, on May 23, 1855, and arrived almost six months later on the shore of the Pacific, unscathed and with nothing but good to say of the redskins, who had been particularly savage that season with other wagon trains.

The immunity of the Christian communists was no miracle of Providence. It was achieved by Willie's father, bewhiskered William Keil, Sr., the communist leader, a man who in no circumstances needed a Marx or a Fourier to tell him what to do. At the head of his train of thirty-four great wagons, Keil in a stroke of genius placed a homemade hearse in which, carefully preserved in Golden Rule whisky, was the body of his son. No flanking riflemen ever awed the enemies of a column of pioneers half so well as Willie and his hearse.

These first communists to cross the plains were not followers of Karl Marx, nor did their philosophy stem from Charles Fourier, whose Phalanx scheme of communal life had already been tried at Brook Farm, Massachusetts, and in New Jersey, Ohio, and Wisconsin. They were mostly disgruntled Rappists whom Keil had persuaded to follow the special brand of Christian communism which he himself had invented.

Keil was admirably equipped to weld his fellow Germans into a tight group able to brave the many dangers of the American West and to found a colony which persevered until time had removed all need for it. He was a Prussian, born in 1812, who came to the United States in 1831, well ahead of the high tide of German immigration. Six feet tall, of rugged build and great strength, he had deep-set blue eyes that took in any situation immediately and seemed either as cool as ice or burning with heat, according to circumstances. He wore a fringe type of beard, though it was more luxuriant than the one grown and made famous, a bit later, by Horace Greeley.

Keil's early years seem to have been restless. He had been reared in the Lutheran faith, but became enmeshed in the occult practices of necromancy and mesmerism. After arrival in the United States, he worked as a journeyman tailor, and later established his own shop in New York City. In 1838 he turned up in Pittsburgh, operating a small drugstore. Here he compounded drugs and experimented with formulas supposed to ensure life everlasting. He also practiced medicine, though he had no formal training for it.

Then, one day, a great hot light beat upon William Keil, and he joined a church of German Methodists. He gave up his devilish brews, and in a formal ceremony "burned a secret book of mystic symbols and formula written in human blood." He vowed to devote his life to evangelical Methodism. This, however, did not turn out to be what he wanted. He began to study the methods and beliefs of the Rappists, followers of George Rapp, also a German, who had founded colonies of religious immigrants at Harmony, Indiana, and Economy, Pennsylvania. The Rappists, like so many other sects, had undergone schisms. A part of the Economy branch of Rappists was ready for a new prophet when William Keil turned up with the idea of establishing a Christian community somewhere in the new West.

The forties were an era of experiment in the United

States. Communal living was a part of the yeasting, and many groups, both religious and secular, were trying it. The Perfectionists were beginning to bubble in Vermont. The various Shaker villages had been successful for many years. Swedish communities were about to be settled in Illinois. The Zoar Separatists, all Germans, had but recently received five hundred new immigrants from the Old Country to their colony in Ohio. A group of advanced thinkers was playing farmer in Massachusetts.

William Keil was an uneducated man but a dynamic speaker and person. He spoke to the schismatic Rappists, lost and looking for a Moses. More than two hundred joined him. Dr. Keil, as he had come to be known, acted swiftly. He made a small payment on 6,300 acres of land in Shelby and Adair counties, in Missouri, and led the group there in 1844. He named the settlement Bethel, and laid down rules for community government. All the land was communally owned, though the title was in Keil's name. Marriage was permitted. (It was later discouraged, though apparently not often forbidden. Each worked according to his abilities, and everybody had to work. The children were trained in several crafts. Keil was the only leader, though he often asked for counsel, and sometimes even acted upon it.

The Bethel community was a hive of industry. Up went the houses, gristmills, sawmills, and a distillery. What they could not use they sold, and all of their products gained a reputation for unusual excellence. They seem to have been wine, not whisky, drinkers, and the large surplus of their Golden Rule Whisky was considered notably good in whisky-drinking Missouri. They set up their own schools, blacksmith shops, and a store where colonists got what they needed without question. No cash exchanged hands, no charges were made.

There were other industries. The Bethelites made fine boots and shoes to meet a steadily increasing demand from outside the group. They wove woolen cloth. A few dissidents left the colony at various times, but this seems to have been done without hard feelings. Bethel, and their later home in the Oregon country, Aurora, were never troubled by the lawsuits which shook more than one colony to pieces.

The Bethel colonists kept much to themselves, except for actual commerce. Unlike the Mormons, they attempted no proselyting. For more than a decade they lived among Missourians, and seem to have had no trouble with their neighbors; but they were being exposed constantly to the greatest migration of Americans in history. Missouri of the forties was the jumping-off place, the point of departure of the wagon trains to Oregon and, later, of those to California. The building of wagons and equipping of the trains had become a big local industry. The Bethel artisans went enthusiastically into the business of making the big wagons. Like all of their merchandise, these were honest goods. They were sold as fast as they could be made.

Some of the current Oregon fever obviously got into the souls of the Christian communists at Bethel; at least it attacked Dr. Keil. He observed to his flock that Missouri was fast filling up. Bethel Colony itself had grown to have more than a thousand persons. Buying more land in booming Missouri, said Dr. Keil, would be very costly. In 1853 he felt the time had come to move a part of the flock to a New Canaan, and New Canaan, he said, might well be somewhere in the wondrous Oregon country. Dr. Keil, however, was no man to trust everything to Providence. He forthwith dispatched a party of nine scouts to look at the far country.

A year later two of Dr. Keil's land seekers returned to Bethel. They had, they said, found a likely location on the Willapa River in what is now southwest Washington. The other seven men had remained there to make a clearing and build houses for reception of the colonists. Dr. Keil prepared for the move. It was to be no wild, hurried departure. Months passed while every colonist turned in a grand effort to prepare everything for the exodus. Some 250 elected to go; the others were to remain at Bethel and carry on as in the past. Then, in May of 1855, the thirty-four great covered wagons, packed to the guards, were ready. Young Willie Keil was to have driven the leading team. Four days before the date set for departure Willie died.

This was, to be sure, a grievous occurrence. But the Lord ordereth all, and even the sons of prophets are subject to His orders. Dr. Keil had promised the lad that he should go with the wagons. Dr. Keil was a man of his word, always. Willie's body was put into a home-made and lead-lined coffin and covered with the one preservative close at hand, which was Golden Rule Whisky, and the box sealed. The coffin was placed in a long light wagon, open at the sides, and given the place at the head of the column.

On the appointed day, on schedule to the minute, the long

train moved out of Bethel with the immigrants singing to the accompaniment of guitar, flute, zithers, and drums. At Saint Joseph, the last outpost of civilization, the wagons were ferried across the Missouri. Ahead of them lay two thousand miles of desert and mountain. Eighteen fifty-five was one of the most dangerous seasons to cross the plains in the entire history of the Oregon Trail.

The Germans had little more than passed the Big Muddy when they met a wagon train moving eastward, returning to the States. Members of it told the Bethelites that the Sioux and other Plains tribes were out in force, determined to stop for good the invasion of their hunting grounds. Whether or not the colonists were given pause by these omens, they had no discernible effect on Dr. Keil. "The Lord will guide and preserve us," he said, and the column moved on, singing a none too happy song, "Das Grab ist tief und stille," which the doctor had composed for the occasion of Willie's funeral, to be held on arrival in the Oregon country.

The column reached Fort Kearney on June 18, stopped briefly, and were advised by the military personnel to go no farther. Dr. Keil thanked them politely, and the train proceeded. A few days later they were halted by a small party of Sioux. They had not come to raid, however. By signs and grunts they indicated a desire to inspect the strange wagon at the head of the column. Somehow or other they had heard that the box contained a dead man who had been miraculously preserved. They were permitted to look closely at the coffin. They looked in awe, too, and then the colonists broke full-voiced into Luther's hymn, "Ein' feste Burg ist unser Gott." The Sioux were entranced at the melancholy music, like nothing they had ever heard, rising and swelling in the thin high prairie air to a mighty crescendo, then dying away on a long harmonious note. Silence was upon the redmen when the hymn was finished.

After a moment the Sioux asked for more. The colonists responded with a couple of old folksongs and closed with the rollicking "Ach, du lieber Augustin." Dr. Keil indicated that the concert was over. The leader of the Sioux party made a gesture of thanks, and by a few words and many more gestures told the colonists that their singing and the strange dead-wagon at the head of the column were very strong medicine indeed. Aye, the Lord would guide and preserve. . . . The train moved on.

When they reached Fort Laramie, the commandant there

strongly opposed the emigrants' going farther. He related stories of horrible massacres of whole wagon trains in recent months. He told Dr. Keil that the party should start back for Bethel at once, or should go into winter camp near the fort and remain until the Indian uprising had passed. The be-whiskered prophet heard him out. "The Lord," he replied with all the force of an Old Testament character, "will watch over His own." The train moved on, singing.

Along the Laramie River, encamped for the night, the train was visited again by Sioux, this time a huge band of hunters. They seemed to know all about the magic of the preserved dead man and the music of the big medicine. They lined up to ride one by one past the hearse, then gathered to sit their horses silently while the colonists sang. The chief gave thanks, made gestures of friendship, and the band rode off. At least two more Indian bands visited the column, one of them estimated to contain more than a thousand warriors, all armed. They looked, they listened, gave thanks, and de-parted.

In the Green River country, where the trail grew dim for many miles, two Sioux left their own party and spent several days guiding the Germans over the difficult terrain. It was all quite wonderful, but it was also, as Dr. Keil took pains to point out, quite in keeping with the Lord's wishes.

At one dismal spot along the way, the colonists saw what could happen to wagon trains that did not move in the sight of the Lord: there were the ashes and the twisted iron, as well as more sinister remains, of a column of Missourians that had been set upon and massacred to a man. Dr. Keil offered prayers for the departed souls, and on went the colonists. As they approached the Oregon region, more tales of depredations and massacres were heard, this time in con-nection with the Cayuse and Yakima tribes, who were bent on clearing the country of immigrants. At this point it began to look as if even the chosen of God might be in for serious trouble, especially after one night when several of their cows disappeared. But riders sent out next day soon came upon a band of Indians who were driving the missing cattle, not away but patiently toward the Keil encampment. The ani-mals had strayed, and the friendly redmen were driving them back to the Germans.

In September the colonists were crossing Idaho. In Octo-ber they reached the Columbia. In November they arrived at their goal on the Willapa River, where they found that the advance guard had done wonders of labor in making a clearing and erecting cabins. The great trees here ran six and even eight feet in diameter, and stood so close together that one might stand and touch the trunks of two of them. Before anything further was done, Dr. Keil called the group together, and they sang praise and thanks to God. On the day after Christmas, 1855, funeral services for Willie Keil were held, and the body was interred.

Dr. Keil was not too pleased with the new site. It rained a great deal. There were fogs. The place was an immense forest of big timber. It was isolated from Portland, the chief city of the region. The doctor sent out scouts to find a better location. He himself went to Portland to practice medicine during the winter. His scouts eventually reported an ideal location, twenty-eight miles south of Portland in the Willamette Valley. Dr. Keil went to see it. He called it good, naming it Aurora for one of his daughters. In the spring of 1856, colony workmen began construction of houses and shops and mills, and within a few months the entire group assembled in their new community.

Aurora was to be a happy and prosperous settlement. In addition to the sawmill, gristmill, and distillery, the colonists made beds, looms, and other furniture for sale, as well as candlesticks, spoons, gloves, and woolen braid for trimming dresses. They organized two bands, for which they made the instruments. They manufactured horns for sale; and a colonist named Henry G. Ehlen made clarinet reeds so well that demands for them were presently coming from professional musicians in California and many Eastern cities. The two Aurora bands were the talk of Oregon. Directed by Conrad Finck, a German of sound musical education, they were in demand for concerts up and down the Willamette Valley. When Ben Holladay, the pioneer railroad builder, wanted music for some spike-driving or first-train festivities, he engaged an Aurora band. (The director's son, Henry T. Finck, went to Harvard from Aurora, and later became the music critic of the New York *Evening Post*.)

Except for music, however, the colony had little time for cultural activities. Keil did not encourage them. The little school taught elementary subjects, all in German, and little else. But the colony cooking was wonderful. Travelers made it a point to stop overnight at the Aurora Hotel, which was open to all. Dr. Keil, of course, was an autocrat. Although he had fathered nine children, he now began to urge celibacy. He permitted most marriages, but forbade a few; and no marriage whatever was permitted with outsiders. Although his leadership was more intelligent than that of many other religious communities, it retarded intellectual progress, and also retarded Americanization. It doubtless hampered individual reliance. In the end the doctor found that his powers were limited by events wholly beyond his control. He could do nothing about the steadily increasing numbers of "gentiles" who were hemming Aurora on every side.

Worse things happened: Now and then an Aurora maiden disappeared from the colony, to turn up later as the bride of some youth from outside. Young men of the colony were running away to work elsewhere and to marry outsiders. The English language infiltrated the citadel; by the midseventies the younger colonists were using it in preference to German. The older people fretted, but there was not much they could do. And then, on December 30, 1877, the blackest day in their history, Dr. Keil proved that he had been unable to find a formula for life everlasting. He died quite suddenly, and for many weeks the colony was too numbed to work.

Andrew Geisy, who back in Bethel had acted as Dr. Keil's deputy, had no desire to take the doctor's place at Aurora. No one, apparently, had ever been trained or even considered by Keil as his successor. The Bethel-Aurora communities, two thousand miles apart, were liquidated in the Federal courts, and so far as any outsider ever knew, to the satisfaction of all concerned. At least, no lawsuits were brought; and the grateful colonists presented a handsome silver bowl, suitably inscribed, to Judge Matthew P. Deady, the pioneer Oregon jurist, for his wise counsel in the liquidation proceedings.

There are yet in Oregon a very few aging men and women who were born in Aurora while Dr. Keil was living. They speak well of the colony, although two of them have said that the place had become an anachronism long before it was discontinued. It had simply outlived its need. The young people wanted to be Americans, not members of an eccentric sect of foreign-speaking "Dutchmen." A few of the old colony houses survive, and so does the Aurora post office. German names cling to the neighborhood.

Willie Keil still rests near the faded hamlet of Willapa. No guidebook so much as mentions his grave.* There lies the remains of him who by God's great grace, said the Bethel immigrants, had been their savior in perilous times and places. And so far as the State of Washington is concerned, he lies forgotten. I think it silly of Washington's official and unofficial boosters to repeat endlessly, as they do, that Mount Rainier is 14,408 feet above sea level, yet pay no heed to poor Willie Keil. After all, California has a mountain higher than Rainier; but I should like to hear of any other place, California included, that has an immigrant to match the lad who came full two thousand miles in death, and served to protect the wagon train of his people. I know of no pioneer story to equal that of the Bethel immigrants, and hope that the State of Washington will erect a historical marker to Willie Keil on Route 12 in Menlo.

But giantism is one of the ills we of the West are prone to; we measure our wonders more for size than for quality. It is the tendency of Americans everywhere. It merely grows as it follows the sun and passes one meridian after another: big, bigger, biggest. At somewhere around 85 degrees longitude, big becomes bigger; and almost anywhere west of 100 degrees things are likely to become the biggest, widest, tallest, longest. These superlatives are adequate for all Western states except, of course, Texas and California, where they are considered weak, if not actually demeaning.

2. Salmon Creek and John Johnson

NAMES ARE SYMBOLS OF PEOPLE, PLACES, AND THINGS; AND no matter what the Bard said of the scent of a rose, names are often of no little influence. Yet the naming of geographic features and of towns in their new home did not weigh

*It is in the pasture of the old Giesey place, Menlo, Wash., on State 12, together with other graves of Bethel pioneers. They are well cared for by Mr. and Mrs. E. D. Buell. Before marriage Mrs. Buell was Huldahmay Giesey, whose forebears were among the most prominent of the Bethel group.

heavily upon the minds of a majority of pioneer settlers in the Northwest. For all their readiness to undertake the longest wagon trek in history, and their courage in the face of hostile natives and hostile nature, they seem not to have cared if at the end of two thousand miles they settled for the rest of their lives along any one of a thousand Salmon creeks, or beside any one of uncounted Elk lakes, or in the shadow of this or that Old Baldy, or Huckleberry Mountain.

If it wasn't Salmon Creek, then it was Fish, Dry, Beaver, or Alkali Creek. If it wasn't Elk Lake, then it was Clear, Deer, Bear, Trout, or Goose Lake. If it wasn't Huckleberry Mountain, it might be Black, Bear, Elk or Quartz Mountain.

Here and there, of course, was a musical and unsual Tonasket Creek, ready-made, or almost ready-made, waiting for them; and a Siltcoos Lake, and a Tum Tum Mountain. Here and there, too, settlers christened a Remote, a Lookingglass, and a Bluestem. Other settlers listened to the incoherent sounds issuing from natives and transformed the grunts into incomparable Walla Walla, Hamma Hamma, and Humptulips.

Before the settlers, explorers by land and sea, and traders, had left their marks, the Spanish chiefly along the coast headlands which they named Cape Sebastian, Heceta Head, and so forth; the English, on mountains like Hood, Saint Helens, and Rainier, on waterways like Hood Canal and Puget Sound, and on places like Vancouver and Colville; and the Americans on Grays Harbor, the Columbia River, Astoria, and much else.

Before the white men, the natives had applied names to such places as they felt needed identification. It is probable that a fourth of our place names have been derived from this source, but the names have undergone mutations. For example, our French-looking name Willamette, and the perverse way we pronounce it with accent on the second syllable, was once upon a time the Wallamt, or something similar. I have an old map on which it appears as Wahlmet. It has also at various periods been Walla Matte and Wallamut. That it is now the Willamette is obviously due to the many workings-over it has had during the past century. It is also much improved to the eye, though our pronunciation is plainly idiotic.

What Willamette "means," if anything, is best left to the large number of people who believe one or another of several alleged translations. I am able to believe in none of the alleged translations of the alleged meanings of alleged Indian place nemes. What I do believe is that romantic white men, feeling secret guilt for the manner in which white traders and settlers treated the natives, sought, perhaps subconsciously, to make up in some part for the crimes by crediting Indians with a sense of poetry for which little evidence has been discovered. These are the men who founded the Laughing Water School. A poet named Longfellow gave it high popularity and much prestige.

I believe that many, if not all, of our musical "Indian" names came into being something in this fashion: In Idaho a settler noticed a stream of water that flowed through a pass in the Bitterroot Range. He asked a native if it had a name. The Indian, wanting to please, grunted something that sounded like "Lolo." The settler asked what it meant. The native replied that it was the name of a white trapper who lived for a while in the pass.

Now, no white trapper of record was named Lolo; but a paleface trapper had lived in this pass and his name was known to have been Lawrence. The natives, apparently, could not pronounce Lawrence, so the man became Lolo, or something similar. The stream became Lolo, and so the pass. But you are not to think that that finished it. Another settler asked another native what the name of the pass meant, and suggestively wondered if it didn't have something to do with the packing of supplies through a mountain pass. The native cared nothing at all what the pass was named or what it meant, but the easiest thing was to agree that Lolo did indeed mean a place for packing supplies through the mountains.

The matter was not yet done. Still another man asked still another native about the muddy water in the steam through the pass. Did Lolo by chance mean a creek of muddy water? Yes, said the native, it did. He would have agreed if the white man had suggested Lolo meant clear water, or no water at all. There the Lolo business stands to this day. You merely take your choice. I hasten to add that I wouldn't for a moment change Lolo. It is as musical as it is meaningless.

Anyone who knows something of the labors of Henry R. Schoolcraft will be skeptical of allegedly pure-Indian names. Schoolcraft was an Indian Service agent, a right good one, and a scholar to boot. He married an Indian. He compiled several large volumes dealing with native lore, history, and customs. He also did much else, and nobody knows just how many of the quite wonderful "Indian" names in the Lake States are due to his fertile brain and acutely musical ear. For instance, from the two Latin words of *caput,* meaning "head," and *veritans,* meaning "true," he fashioned Itasca, the source of the Mississippi River, the true head of it. Not one in a hundred thousand Minnesotans knows the word is else than pure Chippewa. Schoolcraft also invented many other fine names that are generally believed to be native. He wanted to call what is now Lake Superior, Algoma, a compound of "Algonquin" and the Latin *mare,* or "sea." It was not adopted, but the name Algoma itself survives on our maps in places as widely separated as Wisconsin and Oregon, in both of which it is considered authentic Indian. Michigan is covered with Schoolcraft's handiwork, and no finer "Indian" names are to be found in the United States than his inventions, comprised of Latin, Arabic, French, and Algonquin, such as Alpena, Arenac, Alcona, Oscoda, Tuscola, Illigan, Allegan, Leelanau, and Colcaspi. They are magnificent.

Although the Northwest corner never had an inventive genius of Schoolcraft's stature, we must have had a number of musical-eared settlers who worked wonders with the native grunts and gutturals. Around Puget Sound no few of these names have *ish* endings, much like the *keag* in eastern Maine. They appear in Duwamish, Snohomish, Samish, and Skycomish. I think these names are no more Indian than they are settler-made. Consider the name of our largest city. It stems from a local chieftain who called himself something approaching "Sealth." But this was impossible. White settlers merely said the chief's name was Seattle, and so he and the city became.

I imagine that some such modification had a hand in producing Snoqualmie, Nooksack, Siuslaw, Tillamook, and the best of our Q-names, such as Queets, Quilcene, Quinault, and Quillayute. All but one of these is now applied to a stream, though there is good authority for belief that the natives were not in the habit of naming streams.* Even so, settlers applied Clatskanie to an Oregon river, though the word *tlats-kani* was an Indian term for a system, or route, of waterways and portages by which the natives traveled to a spot in the Nehalem Valley, and perhaps elsewhere as well.

*Lewis A. McArthur, *Oregon Geographic Names* (1944), one of the best state books on the subject.

It is strange that only a few of the scores of names given
by Lewis and Clark have survived in the Northwest. Clark
Fork remains, but the former Lewis River is now the Snake.
Many years after the great expedition, Oregon named one of
its smallest rivers for the two explorers; and there is a Lewis
River in Washington.

The symbols and names of any culture are bound to be
affected when they are transferred to another people. What,
for instance, *were* those Indians in northwestern Oregon?
Were they Tlahsops, or Tschlahsoptchs? Whatever they may
have called themselves, they were gradually transformed into
Chatsops, Chadsops, Caltsops, and finally Clatsops. What,
too, did the Tillamook tribe really call themselves? Lewis and
Clark heard it as Kilamox, sometimes as Killamuck. Patrick
Gass heard it Calamex, again as Callemeux. Our present
Klamath region was once the Clammitte country. Its people
were Clamites. In all parts of the Northwest, the names of
native tribes and of places may well have been similarly
modified.

When the settlers did not adopt, or modify, or invent an
"Indian" name for a place, or a geographic feature, they did
the best they could with such imaginations as God has been
pleased to give them. Among these settlers were all manner
of men and women. A few were erudite, many were illiter-
ate. The more learned leaned, for a time at least, toward
names like Olympia, Olympus, Toledo, Rome, and similar
classical derivations; or they applied synthesis and gave birth
to Montesano (mountain of health) and Valsetz, the latter a
combination of the native Siletz and "valley." Town promoters liked to see what they could do with their own sur-
names, hence Bucoda, representing the labors of the Messrs
Buckley, Coulter, and David; and Faloma, from juggling and
adding to the initials of the Messrs Force, Love, and Moore.

Many of the pioneers were direct and outspoken, hearty
and jovial fellows, who bequeathed us innumerable Squaw-
Teat mountains, and made our anatomical observations that
we lesser men have seen fit to modify, by reference to Squaw
Mountain, Rooster Rock, and such euphemisms. These are
weak substitutes.

Perhaps the purest pioneer flavor is to be found in the
place names Wagontire, Canyon City, Cougar, Forks, and
Tenmile. The same is true of Oregon City, which almost of

necessity has retained its hindmost part long after Baker City, Eugene City, and Boise City dropped theirs.

Surely one of the prettiest names we have is Coeur d'Alene, yet it is highly uncomplimentary, and in its native French means heart-of-an-awl, or hardhearted, and not the heart of a maiden named Alene. In the matter of women's names, however, we have the only Sappho in the United States and, for all I know, in the world. It was named, no matter the spelling, for the heroine of Daudet's novel *Sapho,* and not for the scandalous Greek poetess of the island of Lesbos. It was the Post Office Department that chose the Sappho spelling in place of that suggested by the novel-reading wife of an Olympic Peninsula logger.

The early Mormon settlers might have done us much good in respect to names had they but planted in the Northwest several of the excellent and unique names they took from their *Book* and planted in Utah, such as Moroni, Deseret, and Moab. These have a special flavor not found elsewhere. Mormon settlers in Idaho did, however, supply the name of Limhi, a character in the *Book of Mormon,* even though it appears on the map in the corrupted form of Lemhi.

The great majority of our settlers were, like settlers everywhere, conventional. They preferred to name new places for old places they had known in youth, hence the proliferation of town names common in the south and eastern United States. Thus we have one or more towns called Medford, Bellingham, Lexington, Arlington, Aberdeen, Ashford, Auburn, Kent, and Centralia; and Old Testament names like Lebanon, Goshen, and Eden.

Names are things only too often bestowed with little or no thought. Once a name is given, it is more likely than not to stick. About once every decade, the citizens of Portland, Oregon, irritated that when away from home they must explain over and over again that they are not State-of-Mainers, attempt to rise and change the name of their city to Multnomah, which some think is musical and almost everyone considers would be an improvement. Nothing comes of it, or likely ever will. Yet Portlanders have something to console them; it was only the chance turn of a coin that prevented them from living in Boston, Oregon.

The case was different with a rambunctious settlement in Oregon's Linn County. This was Buckhead, and took its name in true pioneer style from a saloon over the door of which was nailed a big set of antlers. But propriety set in, when a post office was about to be established, and syrup flowed untrammeled. Buckhead the riotous became Sweet Home, and so it is today, one of three such in the nation.

It was natural and proper for the early explorers and early settlers to apply the names of noted Americans to geographic features and political subdivisions, beginning with the State of Washington, and going on to peaks like Jefferson and Adams, to counties like Benton, Lincoln, Grant, and Sherman; and to honor less prominent Americans like Whitman, Mullan, Douglas, and Harney. Reverting again to native sounds, Oregon did especially well in naming Tillamook and Umatilla counties. Perhaps the most difficult to pronounce is Washington's Wahkiakum County. None is more musical than the Washington county and river called Okanogan. It fairly rolls.

Names of things and places are just as personal as the names of men. What is a good name, or a bad name, is of course a matter of opinion. To my fancy, the State of Washington is in the top class so far as its pseudonative or allegedly Indian names are concerned. Its only rivals, to my way of thinking, are Maine and Michigan, though Wisconsin and Minnesota have some beauties. The Puget Sound *ish* endings have no counterparts elsewhere that I know of. The Q-names that I have cited are unlike Q-names in other states. And I can think of nothing superior to the sounds of names along Hood Canal, where, in less than thirty miles of highway, one passes and, if one has music in one's soul, sings of Potlatch, of Hamma Hamma, Lilliwaup, Duckabush, Dosewallips, and Quilcene. Only a few miles beyond, and he may sing again, this time to scored notes on the staff which compose the glorious or unique sounds of Sequim, Pysht, Sekiu, Ozette; and of Soleduc, Elwha, and Bogachiel. By night, if he drives on, he may camp along the rippling white waters of the magnificent Humptulips, or on the banks of the superbly wild Wynooche. These are peerless names. Happily, too, the places are as easy on the eye as you could wish.

There is another, if wholly unrelated, matter of names in the Northwest. I think of it as being the era of the John Johnsons. The era has faded, but remnants of it are still to be found in the tidewater communities of Astoria, Oregon, and Aberdeen, Hoquiam, and Bellingham, Washington. In and around Astoria, at one time, were approximately four hun-

dred men, each of whom was called John Johnson. They were
not all born that way; their names were manufactured from
whole cloth. Among them were Swedes, Danes, Norwegians,
Finns, Russians, Poles, and even Chinese. John Johnsons,
every one.

Now, Johnson is a widespread name in the Scandinavian
countries, but the hosts of them, of many nationalities, con-
centrated in and near Astoria were not due to unusual
fecundity. As immigrants fresh from the Old Country, they
were named John Johnson by employers who could not spell
or pronounce many foreign names, or at least would not
attempt to. These callous persons asked an employee his
name. If it seemed at all complicated, as it often did, they
merely set down another John Johnson on the payroll.

Foreigners themselves were quick to assume names that
Americans could handle without difficulty. County clerks
added to the near monopoly by turning out John Johnsons
when immigrants applied for their first naturalization papers.
This was notoriously the case in Astoria and environs, which
had attracted a large number of Scandinavians and Finns.
Presently it was found that the numberless John Johnsons
presented a problem of identity. The post office, tax collectors, and the lads who delivered groceries and telegrams,
in fact almost anybody who had dealings with a John Johnson, had to know which John Johnson.

The problem was solved by the manufacture and use of
nicknames. Beginning in the eighties, and lasting well into the
present century, Astoria and the neighborhood perhaps had
more John Johnsons per capita with nicknames than any
other community in the Northwest. Arthur Danielson, veteran surveyor of Clatsop County, in which Astoria is situated, has been collecting these nicknames for years. Among
his John Johnsons who acquired qualifying names from their
occupations were Sawmill Johnson, Cigar Store Johnson, and
Saloon Johnson. Harold Johnson, a restaurant man, was Pea
Soup Johnson, or Johanson. There was a Tideland Johnson,
a Fernhill Johnson, a Slackwater Johnson, a Tucker Creek
Johnson, a Gum Boot Johnson. How Rocking Horse Johnson
got his name is now forgotten, and the same goes for Copper
Tack Johnson and Sugar Foot Johnson.

The many Danish Hansens also called for a little effort,
and in Astoria, as a result, there lived a Forenoon Hansen
and an Afternoon Hansen, along with a Policeman Hansen.
Among Astoria's many commercial fishermen were a Tom-

cod Erickson, a Tomcod Linquist, and a Steelhead Nelson. There was a Lighthouse Nelson, a Sailmaker Nelson, and a Carpet Layer Olsen.

More obscure are the reasons for Hung-Up Johnson, Doorway Johnson, and Spruce Limb Johnson. Personal characteristics surely had something to do with naming Crying Olsen, Whispering Peterson, and Hungry Larson. Of a latter vintage, probably, was Six-Cylinder Larson and Caterpillar Johnson. An unusual case was an Astoria longshoreman known as Just-a-Minute Johnson, from his favorite expression, even when intoxicated and asked to come along to the station by a cop.

Collector Danielson has remarked that the very convenience of these nicknames is obvious from their predominantly plain character. They were for use, not ridicule. Only a few of them were of an insinuating nature, such as Canned Heat Johnson, who perhaps would not have been so named had he not stolen and sold fishing gear in order to buy the substitute for whisky implied in the moniker. Fire Bug Johnson may have been a dangerous character. Only a few nicknames made reference to physical handicaps, such as Cork Leg Johnson and One Arm Johnson. There were, of course, as in all pioneer communities, a number of men who got their special names from places where they had previously lived and about which they were prone to talk. Among these in Astoria were a Bellingham Bill, a Liverpool Jack, and a Klondike Erickson.

Walter Mattila, American of Finnish descent, who used to work on an Astoria newspaper, told me that of nicknames applied to foreigners, none poked fun at the manner in which the man spoke English. "Making sport of the foreigner's English," Mr. Mattila said, "was not cricket among them. This sensitivity has toughened with the years. After becoming acquainted with, and accepted by, the community, the foreign-born like to hear dialect stories and enjoy the native American's mispronunciations of all but their own names."

How many of the pseudo John Johnsons permitted those names to stand is beyond knowing. It is known that many John Johnsons paid taxes under their real names. It is also known that not a few Olsons, Carlsons, and Swansons had these names changed by court action and carried on with names which they considered to be "more American." Whatever the name, no region or country has attracted better emigrants than those from Scandinavia and Finland.

3. The Longest Bar

IN THE DAYS WHEN DRINKING EMPORIUMS WERE KNOWN only as saloons, many, if not all, Western states liked to claim a saloon "with the longest bar in the world." Having one of these colossi within state or Territorial borders was something in which Western males took considerable pride. They showed it to impress visitors, and when they were away from home they bragged of its immensity. They even got into bloody fights about it, for a longest-bar-in-the-world was no trifling thing; it was a cause worth defending, a kind of symbol of local greatness and potency.

We had one of those bars in the Northwest, and you should know that once upon a time the City of 'Portland, Oregon, was famed less for its gorgeous roses than for an institution commonly called Erickson's, a saloon patently designed for the refreshment of giants. It occupied the best part of a city block on Portland's Skidroad, which was, and is, Burnside Street, and its noble bar presented a total length of exactly 684 lineal feet. Men of Gath might have lifted their schooners here in comfort.

It was founded in the early eighties by August Erickson, an immigrant from Finland. It grew in size and magnificence until loggers, hard-rock miners, and other hearty men from all over the West, and sailors from the Seven Seas and beyond, vowed they had rather see Erickson's with its gaslights in full blow than to view Niagara Falls tumbling into the Grand Canyon of the Colorado, with Lillian Russell, nude, riding the rapids in a glass barrel, to music by John Philip Sousa. Praise could reach no greater height. Footloose young men of the West grew up with the notion that they had hardly reached man's estate until they had lifted a few in Erickson's on the Skidroad of Portland. This aura survives somewhat to the present day, though the saloon appears in dreadfully attenuated form.

Perhaps a score of Western cities staked claims to drinking

places having "a mile-long bar." These turned out, I have discovered by no little research and occasionally by actual measurement, to have been bars of one hundred feet or less. Erickson's mighty total was no myth. It comprised five great bars that ran continuously around and across one gigantic room. Two of these ran from the Second Avenue side to Third Avenue. Two more connecting bars completed the vast quadrangle. And the other bar ran down the middle. Incidentally, the stretch of bar nearest the Second Avenue entrance was known, because Russians liked to congregate there, as the St. Petersburg.

Size alone probably would have brought fame to Erickson's, but the place offered much else. The bars, fixtures, and mirrors were the best money could buy. No tony twenty-five-cent place had better. There was a concert stage, on one side of which was "a $5,000 Grand Pipe Organ." Around the mezzanine were small booths where ladies were permitted, though no sirens of any sort were connected with the establishment. And no female was allowed on the hallowed main floor.

Art was not forgotten. Besides numerous elegant and allegedly classical nudes, there was a thumping great oil, "The Slave Market," which depicted an auction sale of Roman captives and was highly thought of by the connosseurs of art who infested Erickson's. The late Edward (Spider) Johnson, onetime chief bouncer for Erickson, said it was common for these art lovers to weep into their schooners at the plight of the poor slaves.

Yet this was no place for tears. It was vital and throbbing with the surge of life, the place where men of the outdoors came to meet and to ease their tensions, a true club of working stiffs. Indeed, in time Erickson added an outside sign which designated his establishment as the Workingman's Club. Itinerants in funds made a beeline for the place. Five minutes after the swift *Telephone* or the graceful *Harvest Queen* docked, anywhere from fifty to five hundred wage slaves converged on Erickson's like so many homing pigeons. Seven minutes after arrival of a Northern Pacific or a Southern Pacific train, in barged another crowd. It was said, and with some truth, that if you wanted to find a certain logger you went to Erickson's, and waited; he would be there soon or late. It was common, too, to address letters to footloose friends in care of Erickson's. The place often held hundreds of such missives waiting to be claimed.

Patrons of Erickson's discussed almost but not quite everything over their beverages. Jobs, wages, working conditions
were popular subjects. Stupendous feats of work were
bragged about; so, too, noble stints of love-making. The
characters of logging bosses and other foremen were praised
or assassinated; but hot discussions of religion, economics, or
politics were forbidden. The mildest form of discouragement
from Erickson's corps of competent bouncers was a sharp
word of admonition. This was followed, if not instantly
heeded, by the bum's rush, performed by the finest practi-
tioners procurable—of whom more later.

Men might forget the Erickson paintings, or even the
$5,000 Grand Pipe Organ, but no man ever forgot the Erick-
son Free Lunch. This was really prodigious. On his business
cards August Erickson described this feature of his place
modestly as "A Dainty Lunch." The word was not quite
exact. Erickson's free lunch centered around the roast quarter
of a shorthorn steer, done to the right pink turn that permitted juices to flow as it was sliced. Bread for sandwiches
was cut precisely one and one-half inches thick. The Swedish
hardtack bread, round and almost as large and hard as
grindstones, stood in towering stacks. The mustard pots each
held one quart. The mustard was homemade on the spot; it
would remove the fur from any tongue. Round logs of
sliced sausages filled platters. So did immense hunks of Scandinavian cheeses, including *gjetost* (of goats' milk) and *gam-
melost* (meaning "old"), the latter of monstrous strength; one
whiff of it caused the weak to pale. "Gude ripe," Gus Erickson said of it, and he did not lie. Pickled herrings swam in
big buckets of brine. At Christmas generous kettles of *lute-
fisk* were added to the dainty lunch.

Beer was five cents, and the local brew was served in
schooners of thick glass yet of honest capacity. I possess two
of these veritable glasses. They each hold sixteen fluid
ounces. Strong men used both hands to lift a filled schooner.
Genuine Dublin porter was a nickel a small glass. Imported
German brews cost a dime. All hard liquor was two for a
quarter. Lone drinkers were looked askance, but when one did
appear it was taken for granted he would require not one
but two glasses of whisky.

The regiment of bartenders needed to operate a saloon as
large as Erickson's was carefully selected; the men ran to
grenadier size. All wore beautifully roached hair. All had
carefully tended mustaches. Across the broad white vest of

each was a heavy watch chain. Below the vest was a spick-and-span apron. No coats were worn. There was no regulation in regard to neckties, but all bartenders' shirts were white. Arm elastics were an individual matter. Scandinavian bartenders liked pink; all others had a weakness for purple. Trousers were held in place by distinctly he-man galluses, the Hercules brand, fit to stand the strain of lifting a leg and the torsion incident to heaving a bung starter. The bartenders were known for their courtesy, and were able to converse learnedly about prizefighters, bike champions, and such; to give sound advice in matters of love or business; to prescribe suitable eye-openers, pick-me-ups, and for lost manhood.

All of the Erickson beverages were sound. A handsome likeness of August Erickson himself appeared on the label of the house whisky. He was a good-looking, even a studious-appearing man, blue-eyed, blond, and had a neatly curled mustache. He wore, oddly enough for one of his occupation, pince-nez with gold chain. His broadcloth suits were tailored for him. He was a man who liked order, and this applied to his saloon.

Order in Gus Erickson's was kept, with rare recourse to the city police, by his own staff. My friend, the aforementioned Spider Johnson, was for a period chief of these bouncers. Spider was a tall, genial, and most courteous man, and of many intellectual interests. He handled men well too. But when stern necessity called, he was lightning-quick, and carried a punch that was rightly feared. One of his staff was a delightful person known as Jumbo Reilly. He was big, well over three hundred pounds, and though he really wasn't much of a fighter his size and general aspect were so forbidding that he had no difficulty holding his job. "Jumbo," Spider recalled, "had the appearance of a gigantic and ill-natured orangutan. He also could emit a hideous laugh-snarl that cowed almost anyone except the most stouthearted. His fighting tactics were to fall bodily upon his opponent. While not fatal, this was very discouraging. Jumbo's special ability lay in his version of the bum's rush. It was swift and expert."

A favorite story around Erickson's, which had five entrances from three streets, concerned a character called Half-pint Halverson, a troublesome Swede logger who liked to argue about the comparative abilities of different nationalities. On one such occasion, when he disregarded Jumbo Reilly's warning, the bouncer plucked Halverson by the collar and pants and threw him out the Second Avenue entrance. Halverson presently wandered in through one of the three Burnside Street doors. Out he went again in a heap. This continued until he had been ejected through four different doors. Working his way around to the Third Avenue side, Halverson made his entry through the fifth door. Just inside stood the mountainous Jumbo. Halverson stopped short. "Yesus!" he said, "vas yu bouncer en every place dis town?"

Loggers loved places as big as that.

Gus Erickson was a man who took things as they came. His place was but two short blocks from the waterfront, and when what is still referred to as the Flood of Ninety-four made much of downtown Portland something like Venice, and his own and most other saloons were inundated, Gus promptly chartered a big houseboat, stocked it complete, including the Dainty Lunch, and moored the craft plumb in the center of Burnside Street. Men in rowboats, homemade rafts, and catamarans, and single loggers riding big fir logs, came paddling for succor to Erickson's floating saloon. Spider Johnson remembered that a score of customers never once left the place during the several days of flood.

The glory of Erickson's lasted for nearly forty years. Prohibition did not close it, nor did it become a bootlegging establishment. It simply carried on halfheartedly with near beer and added an out-and-out lunch counter, not free. The paintings of the pretty plump nudes, and even "The Slave Market," were sold. So was the $5,000 Grand Pipe Organ. The size of the place was cut in half. The bar when I first saw it ran to no more than two hundred feet, and this has been reduced again, to fit the new and dreary times. August Erickson himself died in 1925, in mid-Prohibition. Repeal did not bring a return to the great days; Oregon's liquor law permits the sale of beer over a bar, but not whisky.

Thus does Erickson's, still the Workingman's Club, survive as a shadow of its former immensity. The stuffed head of a deer, sad-eyed and disconsolate, is all that remains of the stupendous old wall *décor*.* Beer, tea, milk, and—God forbid—soda pop are the only beverages to pass over the mahogany. Yet the fame of Erickson's has not wholly evapo-

---

*The most typical relic of the saloon's heyday is a cherished fixture now in Tom Burns's Time Shop, just around the corner from the present single entrance to Erickson's. It is a cigar lighter, in the form of a bronze and charming female, from whose pretty mouth issued a steady bright flame of gas. It is well worth seeing.

rated. Every little while some old-timer, filled with nostalgia,
stops off in Portland for no other reason than that of seeing
if the longest bar in the world still retains its old-time polish.
It does, but there is less than sixty feet of it left. Perhaps this
is just as well, for within a block of the old saloon is now
a manicure parlor that caters to lumberjacks and other now
thoroughly tamed men. In such a civilization, there could be
no place for the lusty joint that was Erickson's.

4.   The Legend of Rawhide

IN MY OCCUPATION OF NEWSPAPERMAN AND WRITER OF
books, I have perhaps been exposed to as many liars as the
next man. Of the hundreds I have heard in action, and often
listened to, only half a dozen could be called masters. I am
not speaking of the tellers of tall tales in the Davy Crockett
or Baron Munchausen manner, or the related school dealing
with Paul Bunyan, Mike Fink, and other purely mythical
heroes. I mean the genuine master who can relate some
patently improbable story with such artistry as to daze and
charm his auditors into at least temporary belief in the marvels under consideration.

Such narrators are as rare now as they were in Virgil's day.
We have had only one native master of that caliber in the
Pacific Northwest. He was the late George Estes of Troutdale, Oregon. I regret that I never met him in the flesh, for
it was he who fashioned our one Northwest tale that appears
to have the indestructible qualities of a classic. He called it
The Rawhide Railroad. It first appeared in print in 1916,
and he had to publish it himself. Book publishers and the
editors of magazines and newspapers had rejected the manuscript in heartbreaking numbers.

George Estes earned a living as an attorney, and meanwhile wrote hundreds of thousands of words of what he, and
apparently no editor, believed was historical fiction. And
when he came to set down his extraordinary tale of the
rawhide railroad, he founded it on an actual line, the Walla

Walla & Columbia River. His chief character, as well as several minor ones, were actual persons. The locale was real, too, and the fact that the locale was Walla Walla, Washington, surely did the story no harm. There is but one Walla Walla on earth. Estes's introduction of rawhide, that favorite symbol of Western pioneer ingenuity, into the story, was touched with genius.

George Estes, as remarked, was forced to publish the story himself, and the little booklet has all the stigmata of the small-time printer. The text opens with a dedicatory paragraph that would disarm any doubter. It has the perfect flavor of the typical amateur home-town antiquarian sending his labor of love out into the world. It is romantic, bombastic, filled with capital letters, laboriously punctuated, and ungrammatical. It is, in short, perfect. Here is Historian Estes in full voice, hailing all hands:

DEDICATED To the Pioneer Railroad Builders of the Pacific Northwest, WHO, undaunted by dangers, builded their Hopes and Dreams into The Empire of the Columbia, This Book is affectionately dedicated by the author, whose parents toiled over the Old Oregon Trail by ox-team in eighteen hundred, fifty.

Historian Estes next goes into his Preface, and here he begins to get up a head of steam and give his readers an idea of the forgotten, though authentic and marvelous, material he has in store for them. "This," says he, "is the story of a remarkable steam railroad actually constructed and successfully operated in the beautiful Walla Walla Valley many years ago, on which rawhide, overlaying wooden beams, was used in place of iron or steel rails." He goes on to say that this pioneer railroad has long since become a part of the Union Pacific System, and that all records of the rawhide era have been, regrettably, destroyed. Most fortunately, however, said Mr. Estes, he had some twenty-five years previously met an aged character, a veteran section foreman who had been employed by the railroad in its formative, or rawhide, days; and from him the author got "the wealth of detail and circumstantial accuracy" that could leave no doubt whatever as "to the truth of the story as a whole." Only with these typical flourishes of the local historian out of the way does the author get on with his narrative.

He begins it, as almost any amateur historian of the West-

ern pioneers school would do, with a sober, even reverent
discussion of the early missionaries in the Walla Walla region.
He leads up to, then describes, the celebrated Whitman Massacre; and at last comes to the first farmer settlers. All this is
done with proper gravity. The farmers, he relates, found the
soil good for wheat; but the grasping operators of the overland freighting lines charged so much for transporting the
grain to the banks of the Columbia River, some thirty miles
distant, that no profit was left for the growers.

Into this bucolic scene of pioneer times now comes Dr.
Dorsey S. Baker—an actual person—who was among the
first settlers in the town of Walla Walla. He was a practicing
physician who had crossed the plains from Illinois, and was
easily the most energetic and purposeful figure in Walla
Walla. He was into everything. No local project could get
under way without tremendously bearded old Doc Baker being a party to it. Thus when on his rounds he heard grumbling against the high cost of freight to Wallula, nearest port
on the Columbia, he swore he would remedy the condition.
He would, he said, build a railroad forthwith.

Author Estes requires a couple of leisurely chapters to get
a small locomotive and several sets of car wheels from Pittsburgh, Pennsylvania, to Portland, Oregon, then up the Columbia by boat to Wallula; and another chapter to collect a
crew of cowboys and Indians, and set them to making the
right of way. Doc Baker had looked into the matter of iron
rails. They were too costly, he pronounced. His trains, said
he, should run on wooden rails. These were laid, and one
day soon the first train of the Walla Walla & Columbia River
Railroad made a successful round trip. Presently Walla Walla
wheat was going to port for a fourth of what the despicable
freighter operators had charged. It was wonderful to behold.
Doc Baker was more than ever a hero.

"But," says Historian Estes, "it was soon found that the
gnawing movements of the tread and flanges of the locomotive drivers quickly wore off the tops and edges of the
wood rails." But do you think for a moment that Doc Baker
would face them with strap iron? He would not. It cost too
much. Anyhow, he had figured out the remedy. The remedy
was rawhide, that renowned "metal" upon which all Western
pioneers, time out of mind, relied to surmount all difficulties
of a mechanical nature.

Rawhide was then to pioneers what haywire became later
—the universal material of protean uses. It patched wagons

and harnesses. It held shaky guns together. It was clothesline, hinge, and weatherstrip; it was gallus, belt, and garter. Well, then, the Walla Walla & Columbia River Railroad should roll on rawhide.

This triumph of pioneer resourcefulness worked well for a number of years, as Historian Estes told it; and lest uninformed readers have any doubt that rawhide filled the need, the author took time out from his narrative to explain the nature of rawhide. In wet weather, said he, rawhide became soft and loose. But the Walla Walla Valley, as everybody ought to know, was a region of sparse rainfall. Occasionally, because of rain or snow, the rawhide railroad had to suspend for a day or so; then the sun came out, the rawhide quickly became taut again, and as hard as mild steel. It was as simple as that—all glory to good Doc Baker, a man with stout belief in the fundamentals of pioneering America.

Yet, disaster lay just ahead. It came during a winter of unprecedented severity. Provisions grew scarce. Feed ran short. Cattle were turned out on the snowy ranges to get such fodder as they might. They fared ill. Most of them froze. Wolf packs now swept down from the Rockies, devouring the frozen cattle, and at last crowded to the very edge of Walla Walla Village. One terrible night, as still another blizzard rolled over the land, two of Doc Baker's faithful Indian friends came pounding at his door. They brought hideous news of the railroad. Half frozen, they yet managed to tell the pioneer magnate what had happened: "Railroad, him gonum hell. Damn wolves digum out—eat all up—Wallula to Walla Walla."

Well, sir, old Doc Baker was understandingly shaken at this catastrophe, yet he rallied manfully, and in the spring had strap iron fastened to the top of the wooden rails. The era of rawhide had passed. The refurbished road operated successfully for many years more, and was then purchased by the Union Pacific.

Such was the rawhide-railroad story as set down most soberly and with fine attention to detail by Historian Estes. The story made little noise at the time, though it did irritate Dr. Baker's family (he had died in 1888) and many other residents of Walla Walla who seemed to think that even though the story was fiction, it served to put their city and region in the class of backward communities.

Then, somehow or other, Emerson Hough came across a

copy of the booklet. I've been told that Author Estes himself sent the famous writer an autographed copy in care of the *Saturday Evening Post*, with which Hough was for many years identified. In any case Mr. Hough, author of *The Covered Wagon* and prolific chronicler of the Old West, was all but bowled over. "This story contains," he wrote of *The Rawhide Railroad* in the *Post* "as much homeric humor of the American West as anything between covers since the days of Mark Twain's *Roughing It.*"

Then, the deluge. Bookstores from Portland, Maine, to Portland, Oregon, and from the Lakes to the Gulf, hastened to order stocks of *The Rawhide Railroad* from author-publisher Estes in remote Troutdale, Oregon. With his own hands he wrapped and shipped the major portion of the original edition, which for six years had been gathering dust in the Estes home. The orders continued. Happy George Estes of Route 1 got out a second edition. Being a man who liked prefaces, he naturally wrote a new one. Apparently he felt the need to clear up a few matters, for he mentions that "the Baker family have taken exception to the story, calling it a burlesque"; he warns his public that "the amusing incidents and humor of the story are from the author's brain."

What Author Estes was obviously trying to do was to forefend a possible libel suit, yet seeking at the same time not to destroy the flavor of historical authenticity of *The Rawhide Railroad*. I think he accomplished both objects. I cannot learn that he was ever sued for libel, nor was the "authenticity" of his story in the least impaired. Subsequent events have proved as much.

Rawhide was an honored Western symbol. Symbols almost never fade. Legends die hard, if at all. What now happened to George Estes's rawhide-railroad story was that it escaped its proper bounds of fiction and went—almost—into history. I have been told the story of this railroad by possibly a hundred different people, often by natives of the Northwest, who actually believed the rails to have been covered with rawhide. Doubt offended them. There were some, too, who believed the wolf part of it.

Belief in the story must have strengthened and spread. By 1934 W. W. Baker, a son of the doctor, had been so much troubled by *The Rawhide Railroad* that he went to considerable effort and expense to put the Estes tale back where it belonged, in the corral of fiction. In that year Mr. Baker published *Forty Years a Pioneer: The Business Life of Dorsey Syng Baker,* a fat volume that, among other things in the life of Dr. Baker, deals with the Walla Walla & Columbia River Railroad—as it was, and not as described by George Estes. Here one learns that the line was operated on wooden rails, true enough, but that they were from the first topped with strap iron, a common practice with many early railroads, both East and West.

The Baker book relates the life of a remarkable man, by all odds one of the ablest pioneers in Washington. It also seeks to lay the rawhide business for all time. "Several historians," remarks Author Baker, "have absorbed many of the amusing episodes told by Mr. Estes, and presented them, slightly distorted, as historical facts. This is not commendable from any point of view." He goes on to say that he has met "many persons who firmly believe that a railroad constructed along the lines described [by Estes] is within the scope of successful building and operation."

So, in order that those whom Author Baker terms, with almost a visible shudder, "this class of readers" might discern the difference between fiction and fact, he prints most of the Estes story, then proceeds to demolish its fictions.

For all the effect it has had on *The Rawhide Railroad,* Mr. Baker might just as well have printed a chapter or two from *Black Beauty* or *Uncle Tom's Cabin.* His book is a good and valuable piece of local pioneer history. It belongs in all Oregon-county collections. But as an exterminator of rawhide rails it is as the wind in the cottonwood trees along the old line of the Walla Walla & Columbia River Railroad.

As recently as 1951, an article in a railroad magazine accepted the rawhide-topped rails of Doc Baker's railroad as fact, while dismissing as fiction that portion of the tale relating to the hungry wolf packs. Recently, too, a distinguished American historian seriously cited the use of rawhide "on a railroad in the Northwest" as "the most remarkable example of American ingenuity of record." Visitors to the Walla Walla Valley, both Northwest natives and tourists from other parts, invariably want to know about the rawhide railroad. Is it still running? Where can they see the tracks? The personnel of Walla Walla's Chamber of Commerce have been harassed by the story for so many years that they have long since become weary of denying its truth. They wince, or smile wanly, when the subject is broached. A resident of that city told me recently he thought the rawhide business was gaining strength every year. "I can't understand," he said, "why the Chamber doesn't do something with it. It's a natural."

Except for his railroad story, George Estes composed nothing that is read or talked about. A subsequent work, *The Stage Coach*, is a dreary thing, though so eccentric as to indicate the success of his rawhide tale may have gone to Author Estes's head. In this book actual brass filings, to simulate gold dust, had to be glued by hand to one page in every copy of this two-pound volume; attached to another page is a package of cow-parsnip seeds. Still another, a tipped-in page, is an *original* water color, not a reproduction, of a blond and undraped young woman labeled "Undine." I hasten to add that Author Estes paid a printer for making *The Stage Coach* available to the public. The book is now a collectors' item not alone because of its eccentricity, but because a kindly Providence destroyed most of the copies by fire before they had left the binders.

Yet George Estes's place in the literature of the Northwest is secure—or rather his major work is secure. Thousands of people who never heard of him know all about Doc Baker's railroad, and a good many of them, I am convinced, believe implicitly in the rawhide tracks. Had Estes lived in, and written about, Indiana, say, one feels sure there would be today formal markers at both ends of his rawhide railroad's old right of way, and possibly a plaque honoring the house in which he was born.

Two factors have made the Estes tale durable, perhaps indestructible. One, which I've mentioned, was the imposing reputation of rawhide in all Western communities, the symbol of pioneer strength and resourcefulness. The other factor is the author's delicate sense of balance in the matter of exaggeration.

When at its best, exaggeration is a fine, a frail, and a tender thing. One foot too high or too long, one pound too many, one gallon, or even one quart, too much—let any of these or comparable exaggerations occur, and the whole structure of a narrative collapses into juvenile silliness, a simple tall tale. Only a master knows the exact point where a load will be too great for the story to bear, and stops short of it. I still half believe the story of the famous jumping frog of Calaveras County, California. It seems possible, even probable to me that there *was* just such a frog as Mark Twain wrote about; that he surely was loaded to the gunnels with birdshot, and was thus basely prevented from winning a championship match. I also have to fight a powerful urge to accept as gospel half a dozen legends about Ethan Allen, tales I know were cooked up by talented if now forgotten liars.

George Estes's little story has been quoted all over the country for thirty years. It is widely believed, and is certainly the nearest thing to a classic that has appeared in the Northwest. It survives and grows with the years chiefly because Estes judged with fine accuracy the exact amount of exaggeration the tale would bear, and because of the fortuitous circumstance of rawhide's place in the history of pioneering America.

Thus I begin to wonder about the Chamber of Commerce of Walla Walla. They ignore the rawhide railroad to babble of the delights and opportunities offered by their incomparable city and region. Do they not know that the annual Jumping Frog Jubilee attracts thousands of visitors to tiny Angels Camp, Calaveras County, California? If Walla Walla really wants visitors, let them stage an annual Rawhide Railroad Ruckus. It might well crowd the nearby Pendleton Roundup for attention.

5. The Cattle King

OF THE SEVERAL NOTABLE FIGURES OF THE OLD WEST, THAT of the Cattle King was perhaps the most romantic, or at least has been made so by the tireless labors of thousands of writers. Maybe he *was* the most romantic. It is certain that uncounted tons of pulp paper are required annually for the imprint of Westerns; and tons more both of slick and of book papers are needed to tell the identical story; while the film footage devoted to the Cattle King and his minions, the cowboys, and his enemies, the rustlers, is probably greater than that used for all other kinds of movies combined.

Why this should be so is a matter for psychologists, or possibly psychiatrists. Perhaps it is based on the ancient appeal of the man on horseback, the old plumed-knight-and-charger combination. In any case the Cattle King survives as a glorified symbol long after his kind has disappeared, at least in the Northwest. The annual celebration at Pendleton, Oregon, called the Roundup, is devoted to perpetuating the symbol. This is quite proper, for eastern Oregon, rather than any other part of the Northwest, was our great cattle country.

One has no difficulty naming the Northwest's most eminent cattle king. He was Peter French of Harney County, Oregon, and he easily stands first in the legend as he did once in fact. When he died, in his boots, in 1897, the twilight of the Northwest cattle kings set in. For a quarter of a century he had successfully held at bay all of the natural enemies of the cattle kings, including the United States Government, rustlers, Indians, competing cattlemen and, worst of all, the homesteaders. When he died, there was none of his kind left with the strength and ruthlessness necessary to hold out against encroaching civilization.

Not too much is known of Peter French's early years. He was born on his father's modest ranch near Red Bluff, California, in 1849. He ran away from home while still a youth, and went to work for Dr. Hugh Glenn, a wheat-and-cattle rancher of Chico. He must have shown great abilities, for Dr. Glenn advanced him steadily, and soon he married the doctor's daughter.

In the early seventies California sought to curb its powerful cattle kings and other large owners of land by a succession of fence laws. Dr. Glenn, who by then was one of the largest landowners in the Sacramento Valley, and was quick to note a trend, had heard tales of a vast range country in eastern Oregon. He had also seen some prime beef cattle from that region. In 1873 he sent his son-in-law, Peter French, to scout the land, and to buy, if it looked good.

Young French, twenty-four years old, ranged on horseback into eastern Oregon, crossing deserts marked by shallow shimmering lakes, great marshes of tule, buttes, and sagebrush. He did not find what he sought until he came to the Donner and Blitzen River in what is now Harney County. The Blitzen Valley enchanted him. There the river tumbled down the rocky slopes of grim Steens Mountain to thread a valley that for seventy miles was a fine wild meadow. The nearest railroad was at Winnemucca, 250 miles by horseback. There, in an area approximately that of the State of Maine, a scattering few ranchers ran cattle undisturbed, and were as yet largely unknown to the rest of Oregon.

In the Blitzen Valley French found an old prospector who also raised a few cattle, and used a P-brand. French bought him out. The P-Ranch was to become headquarters for the most stupendous cattle outfit in the Oregon country, the French-Glenn empire. No matter its name, Peter French himself built it—built it first with Dr. Glenn's backing, and after the doctor was presently murdered by his bookkeeper, without it.

Peter French would scarcely have fitted the pulp-paper and Hollywood conception of a cattle king. He was a mere five feet six inches tall, or nigh a foot under the standard for fiction. He was wiry, dark-haired, and wore the usual big mustaches of the period. Although he was usually genial and even-tempered, he was no mixer. There was something aloof in his character. He took his own place in any company, but never slapped backs. There was little of heartiness in him. His hospitality was openhanded, but that was in the tradition of range country, and could not be said to be a personal characteristic.

It seems generally agreed that he drove his men pretty hard, and drove himself more. He came in time to be the most feaerd and respected man in eastern Oregon. Perhaps he was loved, too, though I cannot find evidence of it. All accounts of him are singularly free of anything indicating devotion to Peter French. Certainly he was ruthless, yet ruthlessness in that time and period was held to be less a sin than a virtue.

With the comparatively small P-Ranch underfoot, French lost no time in acquiring the rest of the Blitzen Valley, and went on from there by various means to add to his holdings until they embraced some 200,000 acres. Meanwhile, he made his headquarters ranch into an outstanding spot in south-eastern Oregon. First he built a great White House. Every stick of lumber for it came 150 miles overland by twelve-mule team from the Blue Mountains. He erected barns, cookhouses, bunkhouses, and established a store for his help. His corrals were the best in the region; they were founded on clusters of posts lashed together with rawhide. His fences were of juniper stakes bored to carry the unbarbed wire. He built everything to last. In time his fences came to enclose 120,000 acres.

Then, as now, there was a great deal of marsh land in

Harney County. French set his men to draining it. One of his canals, said Julian Boyd, who knew French, ran a good fifteen miles and cost one dollar a lineal yard. At times the number of men on French's payroll was as high as two hundred.

He kept adding land all the time. It is likely that no little of this acreage was acquired through the help of a character known as the Oregon Swamp Rat, who said he had been christened Henry Owen. Hen Owen made his living from a law entitled the Swamp and Overflow Act, which permitted the purchase of marsh land at $1.25 an acre. The purpose of the Act, of course, was to cause the buyer to drain and otherwise improve the land. Peter French actually did drain much land. He also bought considerable land, at swamp-law prices, that was far from swampy. Everybody did so. It was a custom of the time.

Hen Owen's specialty was in "locating" good sound lands which, because of their remoteness from the likelihood of inspection by government agents, could be bought as Swamp and Overflow without great danger of detection. Stories are told of how Hen Owen and other locators often rode over a tract in a rowboat hauled by a team of horses; then they could swear, on any stack of Bibles, that they had covered the area in a boat. This was thought to be pretty cute business, not admirable, perhaps, but quite in accord with business ethics of the latter nineteenth century. These inspired land grabbers were known by the generic term of swamp angels.

Only once did French have to defend his empire against those who morally owned it. In 1878 the Bannocks, Paiutes, and Snakes made a determined raid into Nevada, southern Idaho, and eastern Oregon. They killed a number of settlers, burned houses, and ran off cattle and horses. A large party of them came rather suddenly over Steens Mountain to catch French and sixteen of his men at work on the Diamond ranch of the French-Glenn holdings.

French saw them coming. He ordered his men to ride for home, the P-Ranch, while he covered their getaway. This he did in a manner that would have made a nice film. Taking position on the roof of a hog house, French used a rifle to good effect, slowing the Indian advance until his men got safely away, though one of them, the Chinese cook, fell from his horse and was taken and killed. French himself managed to get away unscathed, and rode to meet his men at P-Ranch. He led his entire crew to Fort Harney, where they joined with other volunteers, and a bit later accompanied regular Army troops of General O. O. Howard's command to defeat the Indians at the battle of Silver Creek.

The next and worst danger to threaten the French empire came from homesteaders, when a government land office was opened at Lakeview, and the lands of Harney, Malheur, and Lake counties were thrown open to settlement. Swamp angels and homestead locators, who followed land booms as other men followed gold strikes, were well in the van. Homesteaders arrived in force during 1880. Sheepmen were coming in too. Something would have to be done, so Peter French sent his employees, one after another, to file homestead claims, which they sold later at token prices to the cattle king of P-Ranch.

At about this period, Mrs. Peter French decided she had had enough of life on Oregon's greatest ranch. She went back to California, never to return. There seems to be no record, or even a scrap of folklore, as to why Mrs. French went away, or as to how Peter French took her departure. His whole life, indeed, is pretty much undocumented. Probably nobody in Harney County gave any thought to French as possibly a historic character. He was less a fabulous person to them than he was a hard and immediate fact, something you accepted, like Steens Mountain, or perhaps as you did rattlesnakes. He was just *there*. You didn't write anything about him.

A few of the new homesteaders, however, tried to do something about Peter French; they took potshots at him from well concealed positions. He was never hit. Two or three of his ranch employees were less fortunate; they died from shots fired by unknown hands.

Then there were the French dams. Some of these had been built purposely to flood land, thus making it swamp, so that it could readily, and more or less legally, be filed on under the Swamp and Overflow Act. Once the land had been acquired at the $1.25-per-acre price, the dam could be taken out, and the land would revert to its pristine soundness.

But now, with homesteaders around, the French dams began going out before their time. Sometimes dynamite was used; at others, portions of dams were dug out by hand, sufficient for water to flow out.

Wherever homesteaders had managed to settle on a quarter-section within the French empire, Peter French tried to buy them out, and off. He had to keep his bounds intact;

you couldn't run cattle where homesteads interfered. For the most part French managed to buy off the new settlers within the bounds of his domain, but one of them, Ed Oliver, did not care to sell. Said he liked the country. Good healthy place. He ran a few cattle. He was getting along all right. Thought he would stay. And stay he did.

Such was the condition of things on December 26, 1897, a day when Pete French chose to work with one of his crews at the division of his ranch called Sodhouse. Ed Oliver was presently seen in the neighborhood. What happened next has been so much in dispute for half a century that no writer in his right mind would think of citing his account as accurate. It is certain, of course, that there was bad blood between the ruthless French and the obstinate Oliver. Folklore has it, too, that French had warned Oliver to keep off French land. This seems likely.

Well, on this 26th day of December, French rode off a short distance from his crew to meet Oliver. The crew saw the two men parley a moment. One story has it that French struck Oliver with a whip, then turned to ride away, and was shot and killed by the homesteader. Whatever happened, Pete French died in his boots, and Ed Oliver admittedly killed him.

And now David Crow becomes something of the hero of the affair. Crow was one of French's employees. Promptly on the death of the cattle king, Crow mounted horse and started for Winnemucca, Nevada. It was one of the great rides in Oregon annals. Crow was in the saddle forty-eight hours, and changed mounts nine times. He tore into the Nevada town with the news, and from there the wires spread it all over the West.

Ed Oliver does not seem to have attempted to flee after the shooting. He stood trial on a charge of murder, and was acquitted by a jury that found him not guilty by reason of self-defense. Incidentally, folklore has it that French commonly did not carry firearms.

The one thing about the passing of Peter French with which all parties seem in agreement is that the era of the cattle king began passing with him. He was the last, as well as the greatest, in Oregon of the old school, the kind who felt and believed and acted like the crowned heads of old Europe, and who ruled by the right of God Almighty.

Yet the homesteaders who put an end to the cattle king did not remain. Harney County is more of a wilderness today than it was when Pete French died. Only six thousand persons inhabit its 10,123 square miles, and of these more than half live in the cattle-and-lumber city of Burns, in the northern part of the county. Harney County is larger than the states of Massachusetts and Rhode Island combined. Its density of population works out at something like one person for each one and one-half square miles. Nowhere else in the Northwest are the open spaces so wide, or so uncluttered with the works of man. But in the old domain of Peter French are more wildfowl than you would believe unless you had seen what is officially the Malheur National Wildlife Refuge.

The Malheur project was established by executive order of President Theodore Roosevelt in 1908, when the Government set aside 95,155 acres around Lakes Harney and Malheur. Pete French's favorite Blitzen River empties into the latter. In 1935, and again later, the Government added more of French's old range, until the whole now runs to 174,000 acres. The refuge is almost identical with the French empire. It runs from near what is now Frenchglen, a hamlet with a hotel on the old P-Ranch, along both sides of the Blitzen to the two lakes, and around them, with bulges here and there.

Here to the refuge come wild birds by the millions, to nest and rear their young, then to take off, either north or south, for their other haunts. It is reputed, at least in Oregon, to be the greatest migratory bird refuge in the United States. It harbors virtually all Western species of ducks, as well as egrets, pelicans, terns, ibis, bitterns, and the rare whooping cranes.

Peter French's old White House has been torn down, though some of his stout fences still stand; and his empire, on which he cut ten thousand tons of hay annually, and over which he ran twenty thousand head of cattle, has now reverted to a state as primitive as it was before the first cattleman, or even the first white man, saw it. There is perhaps no greater area of complete and savage solitude in the Northwest than the old P-Ranch of Peter French.

PART THREE

METROPOLIS

1. Under the Gaslights

AS AN OLD SETTLER IN THE NORTHWEST, IT OFTEN STRIKES me, only half humorously, that in my time here I have watched the municipality of Bourne, an incorporated city of Baker County, Oregon, drop from a population of thirty to that of one, and in the next decade leap from one to nineteen.

I like to contemplate that staunch fellow who, when the census men of 1930 came within its portals, was the sole resident of Bourne. Was he still an optimist, making Chamber of Commerce speeches to himself, freely predicting Bourne's great future? I fancy him, standing alert and undaunted, though alone, amid the rocks and sagebrush, talking to the winds that blow down the Sumpter Valley from the Blue Mountains: ". . . and furthermore, fellow citizens, all indications point to a tremendous increase of population in our city during the next decade." How right he was, too, right beyond the wildest dreams of even a California realtor. Not even Los Angeles saw its population increase, as did Bourne, almost twentyfold within a decade.

The highly volatile business of population was either ruin or success to a settlement in new country. An area of 250,000 square miles is not going to see all of its counties teeming with people overnight, or over a century. Most Americans accept as infallible dogma the proposition that a town of ten thousand people is exactly twice as desirable as one of five thousand people. Size is what counts. Citizens of the smaller place are apt to be apologetic and on the defensive because their town has failed to attract a multitude. It is as if the citizens of the larger place somehow took on added stature, individually, and greater sophistication simply because more of them were huddled together.

My own method of judging the comparative importance

of places was just as witless: Did or did not a town have streetcars? The ones that did I automatically thought of as cities. All the others were just villages. Though during my boyhood in Vermont, Saint Johnsbury held as many people as did Montpelier, it had no streetcars, hence was a village. Montpelier, with a population of some seven thousand, plus a clanging car line, seemed a vast, hectic, somewhat dangerous, and wholly exciting metropolis.

When I came to live in the Northwest, I found that my juvenile method of assessing towns was as active as ever. The towns of Raymond and Chehalis, Washington, for instance, impressed me as being real, if small cities, while Bend, Oregon, with twice the population and probably twice the commerce and industry, was only a fine-looking village.

And when, as recently as 1950, the city where I live did away with its last line of streetcar tracks, and went whole hog into gasoline buses and trackless trolleys, Portland seemed to me to shrink infinitely. The rattle of wheels on tracks and the great urgency of streetcar gongs were to me the authentic sounds of Metropolis. Although the census figures tell me that Portland has almost doubled its population since I came here, it no longer seems a city proper at all. Nor do Raymond or Chehalis, which are also trolleyless. The same holds for Seattle. One must cross the border and go to Vancouver, in 1951, to hear the sound of a veritable city; or south to San Francisco, where, by efforts approaching the heroic, the citizens have managed to retain a few of their beloved cablecars.

In the eighties and after, no hamlet in the Northwest that aspired to greater things was without a street railway, even if it were only projected. Gaslights first, then streetcars. That was the way to grow into a city. Putting up a gasworks and installing street lamps, and running gaspipes into homes and places of business were not huge or terribly expensive undertakings. But a streetcar line came high. Hence the great number of projected streetcar lines that never came into being. The adjective was one of the most overworked words in the lexicon of town boosters. Street railways, steam railroads, steam sawmills, even gaslights, city halls, opera houses, and hotels could all be referred to casually as "projected." It was thought to help matters. Perhaps it did. Maps of states and of towns fairly crawled with projects. Webster says of the word "project" that it is a scheme, a plan.

"Scheme" has come to have a faint flavor of something underhanded, so perhaps it was the proper word to describe many of the projects that never got off paper.

Yet it would be unfair to say of all the town projectors that they were dishonest. They were filled with an enthusiasm so great and untrammeled that they came actually to believe anything projected as already more than half accomplished. It was a sort of occupational disease, a self-hypnosis brought on by looking long at town plats.

Political and military matters are usually the first interest of historians. Perhaps this is as it should be. But surely it is also of some importance to know of the manner in which settlements were originally made, and how this settlement grew to importance and why that one faded. After all, the military history of the Oregon country is neither extensive nor bloody. Oregon became a part of the United States without a shot being fired. Volleys of impassioned oratory, it is true, were loosed in Congress and in Parliament; Fifty-four forty or fight was a stirring alliteration; but the first part was not achieved and the second part did not happen.

The wars among Northwest cities, however, began as early as 1850, and have continued to the present. They have been bitter, too. Only on occasion did they erupt in gunfire and other violence, yet they may well have resulted in more tragedies, more heartbreaks, than all of our Indian uprisings combined. That is, so far as the white settlers were concerned. All the Indians got was tragedy and heartbreak, anyway.

Wars of the settlements were fought with promotional ballyhoo, whispering smear campaigns, and political skulduggery in low and high places. Occasionally, an armed mob from one place raided the courthouse at another to steal the physical properties of the county seat and remove them to their own struggling metropolis. Indeed, these county-seat wars were so numerous as to make a standard Western legend not only in the Northwest, but elsewhere in the West.

Stagecoach outfits often had an influence in making a town. So did steamboat operators. Railroads had incomparable influence; they could snub a town into picking up and moving to a new site, or fading where it stood.

Things moved swiftly in the Northwest. Once settlement was begun, there was no possibility of a new town remaining static. It either went ahead steadily to gain importance in the neighborhood, or it shriveled even more quickly into insignificance. The bustling hamlet that suddenly grew up around a stagecoach stop was turned into a dreamy antique when the new steamboats docked, perhaps less than a mile away, on the riverbank, to attract a rush of stores and hotels. The steamboat-landing towns disappeared, in turn, if the line of the railroad passed them by a few years later.

For a long time the railroad towns seemed secure. Then, during the 1920's, they began to feel the era of the motor-car. The new highway might pass, say, half a mile east or west of the railroad. When it did, spiders often began weaving their webs undisturbed over the old depot's windows. The express truck rusted, then fell apart. The stove in the waiting room went cold. The depot roof started to moult shingles. The paint on the brave bold nameboards flecked away until you could barely read the dim letters that spelled Napavine or Vader or Castle Rock. The station ceased to be a regular stop. Often it ceased to be a whistle stop. If the village survived as a community, it did so by moving its business district, say, half a mile east or west, there to line the new highway and hope to retain a little of the trade that was going in larger amount to the bigger cities.

These things have, of course, happened elsewhere in the United States. My point is that nowhere else did they happen so soon after a town had come into being. In 1927 the fine new city of Longview, Washington, opened its spacious railroad depot, complete with marble waiting room, covered train shed, and all. Four years later it was ready to be boarded up; and would have been, had the city not converted it into the Longview General Hospital. The active life of many another railroad depot in Washington, Oregon, and Idaho spanned less than twenty-five years.

Men still living can recall the rise, decline, and disappearance of a whole civilization in a back corner of Oregon's Columbia County. There, in the eighties, came a group of emigrants from Scotland, familes named McKay and Reed, and such, bringing with them their women, their children, their oatmeal and bagpipes. They went into the deep forest of the misted hills to set up a colony. They made a great clearing, those hard-working Scots. They built substantial homes. They erected a steam-powered sawmill and shingle mill. Soon the primeval forest was scented with the heady tang of fresh sawdust, as the great firs and cedars were made into boards and shingles. Gardens and orchards grew among the stumps. Oats waved bright yellow beyond the mill.

But the bold venture had come too soon. Markets were far away over mountain trails called roads. The colony dissolved, and the Scots scattered elsewhere in Oregon. Then the forest started closing in again, marching across the big clearing, strangling the new orchards, crushing the houses, trying to obliterate every last trace of civilization, which Nature naturally considers a disgrace.

Go look at it now. I did, in 1950; and the place where the bold Scots had their colony is now in twilight from trees so tall and thick that a pulp company is thinning them, taking out thousands of cords of wood, leaving other trees to grow with accelerated speed as sunlight touches them. No longer should one stray far off the road there without compass; men have been lost in the great woods that have grown up on the site of the mills, the homes, and the oatfields of the Scottish settlers. Wilderness is there again. Columbia County has seen the rise and fall of a civilization. No country can record a greater event.

Apparently there was no sure-fire recipe for making a city, no combination of factors to which one might point and say with assurance that these things would result in a metropolis. The very first settlements, if trading posts be counted as such, were Astoria and Vancouver, both on the Columbia. As the fur trade disappeared, these places grew slowly, and without much trumpeting, into business centers. In time they came to have not only gaslights and streetcars, but each also achieved that triumph of culture called a radio station. But of all the trading posts thad dotted the Northwest, only those two survive as important communities a century later.

Many people who live here will tell you that Spokane grew up around a trading post. This is not so. The trading post called Spokane House, of the North West Company, was a good ten miles from the present city. Spokane Falls, as it was known for many years, was wholly independent of the old trading post. It took hold, as the phrase had it, chiefly because the falls of the Spokane River at that point offered excellent power for grist and sawmills. The mills went up, a store was opened, and local patriots awaited the coming of the Northern Pacific. They had to wait only eight years for the first train to arrive in 1881.

But the railroad favored nearby Cheney, and for the next few years the Cheney-Spokane fight was bitter. A contested election in regard to the county seat brought a Cheney mob to Spokane one night when almost everyone in town was at a dance. They broke into the courthouse, secured the county records, along with the auditor himself, who happened to be working late, and started back to Cheney. Spokane's lone watchman took a futile shot or two at the departing gang. Although Spokane grew rapidly and Cheney did not, another six years elapsed before the county seat was restored to the larger town.

Oregon City's early growth also centered around water power, this time on the Willamette. The town's founding, however, was unlike that of any other. The first cabins were erected by John McLoughlin, the Hudson's Bay Company's chief factor in the region, solely as an outpost of empire. The company's headquarters in the Northwest were at Vancouver, on the north side of the Columbia. As the dispute over sovereignty between the United States and Great Britain warmed up, the astute company informed Factor McLoughlin it was important "to acquire as ample an occupation . . . on the south as well as the north side of the Columbia." The factor forthwith erected a couple of log cabins near the falls of the Willamette, and planted a patch of potatoes. Indians burned the cabins. The doughty McLoughlin was not discouraged. He set men to digging a mill-race and to squaring timbers for a mill he planned to put up.

None too soon. In fact, hardly soon enough, for Americans had begun to infiltrate the region in increasing numbers. A group of them promptly settled on land near the falls, organized a company, and put up grist and sawmills on an island. These Americans, typical of their era, also formed a Temperance Society, a circulating library of three hundred books, and the Oregon Falls Lyceum and Debating Society. The *Oregon Spectator* started publication. Local Masons set up the first lodge West of the Missouri River. The place was growing at such a rate the town fathers felt need for additions. The new plat was surveyed not with compass and chain, but with compass and rope which, in the manner of rope, stretched, then shrank, according to moisture conditions, presenting the town with the irregular lots it has to this day.

By 1844 it began to appear as if nothing could stop Oregon City from becoming the metropolis indicated by its name. The provisional legislature met there. For the next eight years it was the Territorial capital. Local boosters had every reason to believe their town was headed for great things. By then, however, the newer settlement of Portland, twelve miles downriver, started to intervene. The importance of Oregon City faded as Portland grew.

The more one reflects upon it, the more does the rise of cities seem to depend often on some slight thing or event having little or nothing to do with the site selected. Sometimes, it would appear, the difference is made by one man, or one incident. The case of Portland comes to mind.

Even with the hindsight of a century, I think I should naturally have chosen Oregon City rather than Portland, in 1850. Those big tumbling falls, pouring over a ledge, dropping forty feet, must certainly have looked to the early settlers, as they look today, to be the one place along the Willamette to found an industrial city of the first importance. Portland's site could offer nothing in comparison, except for level ground on both sides of the river. Oregon City had a steep hill. Yet hilly ground, as Seattle and Tacoma were soon to demonstrate, will not prevent the rise of a metropolis.

No, it was something other than level ground that made Portland. A weatherbeaten deep-sea skipper who wore thumping great earrings had something to do with it. "To this very point," said Captain John H. Couch, late of Newburyport, Massachusetts, "to this very point I can bring any ship that can get into the mouth of the Columbia River. And not, sir, a rod further."

Captain Couch was a man of no halfhearted opinions. He was much respected in the Oregon of the 1840's, for he had been everywhere, and he knew the Columbia River bar as perhaps no other captain of the time knew it. When he spoke so forthrightly for the new site twelve miles below Oregon City, there were many who listened and believed not only in Oregon, but back in New England. Yankee merchants and speculators were already coming around the Horn, looking not for a placer mine, but for a place where they might exercise their native talents. Brand-new Portland turned out to be the goal of many of them. They had heard what Captain Couch had said.

When Captain Couch was making his influential statement, he was speaking of a site on the west bank of the Willamette in which, for the sum of twenty-five cents, Asa Lawrence Lovejoy from Massachusetts had just bought a one-half interest. His investment of a quarter of a dollar was for the filing fee. His partner in the enterprise, who was Francis

Pettygrove from Maine, had to pay "$50 in store goods" for his half. The entire site was covered by an unbroken stand of immense old Douglas fir. The two optimists felled a few trees, went ahead to plat four streets, then considered a name for the future metropolis. Pettygrove won the toss of a coin, and called the place Portland for the principal city of his native state, thus perpetrating the most notable opportunity in the United States for the misdirection of mail. It might even have been worse. Lovejoy, who possessed no more of soaring imagination than his partner, was set on making it Boston.

It is clear that these two men, for all their pioneering ability, had little feeling in their souls for the poetry of names. They had it in their power to make the future metropolis a musical Willamette or a distinctive Multnomah. But Portland it became, in 1845, and four years later an all-wise Post Office Department approved the choice with an office and a big round postmark. By 1850 the village was bragging of its eight hundred citizens, its steam sawmill with a whistle that could be heard in Oregon City, its log-cabin hotel, and its *Weekly Oregonian*.

Even so, Oregon City was growing too. Captain Couch had given the newer town its first impetus, but something more was needed. Portland merchants and businessmen provided it. By a cooperative effort of herculean size they turned to, felled trees, sawed planks, and laid them to make a glorious road of the rough trail which had led over the West Side hills to the Tualatin Plains. The Plains were already northern Oregon's great farming country. The nearest places for sale and barter were Oregon City and Portland. Portland wanted the back-country trade enough to lay fine thick planks to it. And Portland, no less than the Tualatin Plains, went wild on the day in 1851 when what the press referred to as the Great Plank Road was formally opened. Heady oratory took the breeze. Copious amounts of liquor were downed. Everybody spoke to everybody else of Progress—everybody, that is, except the citizens of Oregon City.

Captain Couch and the Great Plank Road did not make Portland the city it is in 1951. They did combine, however, to give it impetus at the most critical times during its first hundred years. As for the good captain, he did not speak and sail away. He took a claim next to the Lovejoy-Pettygrove tract, and built a house where from his porch he could shoot ducks, and from whence, too, he could view the tremendous fact of Mount Hood, a peak which even then could not be resisted by mountain climbers. In 1859, after several futile attempts, it was first climbed to its top by Thomas J. Dreyer and companions.

The flow and ebb of wild-eyed men to and from the gold strikes east of the Cascades marked the sixties in Portland. So did agitation for a bridge across the Willamette to the distinct city of East Portland. But the ferry interests prevailed for another quarter of a century, prompting a local printer named Stephen Mabell to inspired verse about a lad who sat on the riverbank through boyhood, through middle age, and into senility, chanting endlessly:

> "They're going to build, I feel it yet,
> A bridge across the Will-a-mette."

It was locally the most celebrated doggerel ever penned, and the very scan of it added to the confusion caused by the visible conflict between the spelling and the pronunciation of the name. Usage calls for accent on the second syllable.

Like virtually all cities, Portland had its Great Fire, in 1873; and its Big Flood, in 1894. Neither was so important as the arrival of the first transcontinental train, in 1883, its locomotive decked with flags and roses, its welcoming committee decked with plug hats and Prince Albert coats. Four years later the first of many bridges crossed the Willamette, and presently the two towns merged.

A great deal of money had been made by early and alert settlers, much of it from river transportation, and their mansions began rising along the Park Blocks, displaying M. Mansard's roofs, cast-iron deer in dooryards, and rubber plants that cast their shade over cuspidors fashioned especially for the American trade at Limoges in France. A few victorias made their appearance; and one Portland matron possessed a carriage robe that was greatly admired and envied. It was made of the breast feathers of 144 canvasback ducks. There were other elegancies, too, for the gorgeous Saint Charles Hotel was at last finished. It had a lock on every door. Every floor had a bathroom. Every chamber had a bellpull of red plush, and a handpainted chamber pot complete with knitted husher. Gaslights glowed and flickered in the Saint Charles, and all over the town.

Now came Ben Holladay, called the Duke of Oregon, who operated steamship lines and was building the Central Oregon

Railroad, to promote the city's first streetcar line. Surely
Portland was a city now. Everybody said so. Yet the savage
frontier was not far. One day a white-faced young Army
lieutenant came hurrying to the Montgomery home, at
Seventh and Madison, to ask Mrs. Montgomery please to
notify her good friend, Mrs. Canby, that she was a widow.
The general had been butchered by Modocs while attending
what he believed was a peace treaty with the tribe. Kindly
Portland quickly raised $5,000 for the widow of the gallant
soldier; but she declined, and much of the fund went to help
the city's Library Association.

One of Portland's glories almost a century after its
founding is the Public Library. It is fortunate that it has been
a continuous heir to the notable collections of books brought
around the Horn by many of the city's early settlers. As
these literates aged and died, their books went to the library,
often accompanied by substantial amounts of cash. Mr.
Carnegie's help was never needed to make Portland's the
incomparable public library in the Northwest.

Meanwhile, the city's many sawmills whined and droned
day and night, and their planing mills screeched and clattered,
all to the end that Australia and China and the British Isles
might have deals and timbers. Upriver and downriver the
refuse burners of the mills cast their glare on huge rafts of
logs towed to town from camps at places named Scappoose,
Eagle Cliff, Stella, and Clatskanie. And to Portland from
these and a hundred other camps came the boys of the
woods, the lumberjacks, the long-loggers, to blow their stakes
along the Skidroad, which centered on Burnside Street. Fully
as important to the city as any bank or mercantile house
was August Erickson's immense drinking establishment.

The ironies and incongruities that attend pioneering were
perhaps never more marked than in Portland. It had the
biggest and best-known saloon in the Northwest. It had the
biggest and finest public library.

From the very first, too, which is to say 1850, Portland
has had an outstanding newspaper in the *Oregonian*. No
other paper in the Northwest has matched its influence. It
had much to do with forming Portland's character, which
many of us who live here think of as conservative, and which
visitors damn as stodginess. Most of our well-to-do citizens
live without ostentation, an attitude that may stem from
such early settlers as William S. Ladd, a Vermonter who
became Portland's most eminent businessman. Though Ladd

was called, rightly enough, a magnate of commerce, he answered his voluminous mail in his own hand, using slit-open envelopes, or by turning the letters received upside down and writing between the lines. He lived well enough, but with no pretense. Another early Portlander, Simeon Gannett Reed, saved his money and bequeathed his fortune to found Reed College, now one of the outstanding liberal-arts colleges in the United States. These men, and others like them, are important because they had something to do with forming Portland's character.

Then there was another local magnate, Henry W. Corbett. His big home stood on a full city block that came to be surrounded by tall office buildings, while on the Corbett lawn still grazed the Corbett cow—a Jersey—and chewed her cud. It was a sight made to order for the roving reporter of a national magazine, who featured the Corbett cow as a symbol of Portland. Both the Corbett home and the cow have disappeared, and the delightfully bucolic scene has been replaced by a bus depot, blazing with neon, noisy as the sheet-iron roof of hell, and smelling twice as bad. This is Progress.*

The strange chemistry of time has somehow preserved memory of the cow on the lawn in the center of Portland's business district. It has all but completely obliterated memory of Captain Couch's famous and influential remark that the hamlet in the tall timber was the true head of navigation. It has also obliterated all echoes of the pounding hoofs on the Great Plank Road to Tualatin Plains. I lived in Portland many years before I heard of either. Most of the old settlers told me the city had grown great because of the Lewis and Clark Exposition held in 1905. This fair, patterned after the Pan-American of 1901 in Buffalo, though much smaller, seemed, in the memories of my informants, the one really great local event since the first city lots were surveyed. Doubtless it did attract many people to the city and the state, though census figures reveal, in their typically cool and detached way, that whatever the impetus to Oregon's growth

*While this small book was being written, our Chamber of Commerce progress was making enormous strides. I stopped work on five occasions, simply to attend the obsequies of the Kamm and the Knapp mansions, the Kamm and the Kraemer buildings, and the magnificent old Hotel Portland. Replacing three of these noble structures are the ugly modern gold mines called parking lots.

the fair may have had, it was much larger on the population growth of neighboring Washington. So far as Portland is concerned, the two most influential events in its history, I believe, were Captain Couch's forthright statement, and construction of the Tualatin plank road.

In mid-twentieth century Portland presents a civic character of complexities. This is due to the fact that though many of its leading men have wanted the place to become another New York or Chicago, just as many others have been quite content with its status of the moment, whether the moment was 1850, 1900, or 1950. In contrast, the history and the character of Seattle is simple and crystal-clear. Seattle is a place of singleness of mind. The idea is always a Bigger and Better Seattle. I think the two adjectives have merged in the Seattle mind, and now mean the same thing. Here is the perennial boom town. I can think of nothing more indicative than an event of the holiday season of 1950 when, determined to outdo any and all Christmas trees anywhere in Christendom, a Douglas fir, 212 feet long and weighing 25 tons, was brought down from the mountains and erected with guy lines in Seattle's Northgate district. Holes were bored in the immense trunk, and limbs inserted in the holes. Then it was draped with "miles of decorations" and hung with 3,500 lights. I am certain it was the *biggest* Christmas tree ever seen.

Seattle is blessed by nature with a fine harbor, blessed again with fresh-water lakes, wooded hills and glades, with mountains to the east, south and—at considerable distance—west. And its citizens developed into the greatest home-town boosters in all the Northwest. They bragged, and they brag still, of the Seattle Spirit, a metaphysical condition fit to accomplish the several tasks of Hercules, and to move mountains. Indeed, in a civic engineering feat still talked about with emotion, the people of Seattle cut off the tops of their monstrous hills and sluiced them down to the waterfront to make new land. This was only one of many wonders they performed to prepare the difficult terrain for the big city they meant to build.

Seattle is *the* metropolis of the Northwest. It did not become so simply because of favorable location. Despite the professors of economics, whose union does not permit them to admit the workings of human intelligence, or even of human urges, Seattle outdistanced all its rivals largely because of the single-mindedness of a large majority of its citizens, early and late. For one thing, they had to build a railroad. The Northern Pacific transcontinental had ignored Seattle and selected Tacoma for its terminus. The enraged citizens of Seattle raised funds and started construction of the Seattle & Walla Walla Railroad. The Northern Pacific, impressed by such spirit, quickly put Seattle on its main line, and much later moved its offices there from Tacoma.

The same single-minded citizens kept the Territorial legislature in an uproar until Seattle was chosen as the site for the University of Washington. When, in early days, they discovered the town had few marriageable young women, one of their number, Mr. Mercer, went to the East Coast with the plan of shipping out whole cargoes of spinsters and widows. That the idea was only partly successful does nothing to dim the spirit of the idea, which was superb.

Seattleites were quick to raise money to encourage shipyards, street railroads, and public utilities. One of them, Henry Yesler, noting the lack of a road over the Cascades, put up his steam sawmill, with no strings attached, as first grand prize in a Territorial lottery to raise funds for such a road.

The Seattle Chamber of Commerce was a hair-trigger outfit from the first, reaching out for any industry, large or small; and the city fathers were most generous with sites and conditions of taxing. It was probably the go-getting Chamber that was responsible for the visit to Seattle of the one and incomparable Andrew Carnegie. That was as long ago as 1892. It is significant that although the king of steel spent a full day and two nights in Seattle, he did not get out of his private railroad car as he passed through Portland.

It was the first visit to the Pacific Coast of America's wealthiest man of the era. Carnegie's coming was sufficient to raise the civic pulse even of San Francisco. His visit to Seattle was sensational, the more so because he completely ignored the smug and then much larger Portland. But "sensational" is a weak word to describe the event as it was seen by Seattle eyes.

"A Man of Millions, Andrew Carnegie Is Pleased with Seattle." That is the way the *Press-Times* announced it. The *Post-Intelligencer* hailed him as "King of the Vulcans." It was not every day that Seattle entertained a man who readily admitted to being thirty times a millionaire, and who was known to have given enormous sums for libraries and museums, though, most regrettably, not one copper cent for churches. The gentlemen of the Seattle press obviously felt constrained to write with unusual elegance.

The party arrived on Sunday morning, March 13, in the steel king's private car Iolanthe. With Carnegie were his wife and her sister, Miss Whitfield; Henry C. Frick, the king of coke and Carnegie's partner; Charles S. Smith, president of the New York City Chamber of Commerce; and Professor Andrew D. White, variously referred to in the Seattle press as "a savant" and president of Cornell University. There were also a Mrs. King and a Miss Brown, weaklings both, who were "much too fatigued" to essay the Seattle hills. They probably knew how it would be, anyway, for Carnegie and his party saw the city on foot, as a reporter noted with wonder, "even disdaining the assistance of the cable to take them to the top of the hills which no one denies are to be found in this city."

Mr. Carnegie was patently full of oats. Despite his fifty-six years and white beard, he looked at the terrible hills as nothing at all. "I will walk," said he. "I learned pedestrianism on the Scottish moors. There's nothing so good to stimulate appetite as climbing a hill." And away they went, while one reporter reflected with amazement that "very few persons who noticed the pedestrians knew that one of them was a man who had made $30,000,000 without speculating, and had also found time to become a thorough political economist."

This lack of ready recognition, so a man on the afternoon paper could not resist remarking, occurred because the morning paper had run an alleged picture purporting to be that of Mr. Carnegie, though the steel king's wife thought "it was Mr. Blaine's likeness palmed off on an unsuspecting public." Which showed you the true character of morning newspapers.

Mr. Carnegie was clearly out to show Seattle that though he might travel in a private car, he was still pretty much a common man. He hadn't lost his touch. He stopped his party, which included the press and his local guides, who were Judge Cornelius Hanford and D. H. Gilman, in front of a clothing store. He pointed out that his own suit was "of the same texture as that of one in the window." The suit in the window, as the reporter marveled, "was marked $21."

Both reporters must have found Carnegie good copy. He had an opinion on any subject they cared to bring up. The people of Seattle, he had discovered after less than four hours among them, were enterprising and industrious. They were generous and more hospitable than people in the East. Here, however, he sounded what may have been a guarded criticism: the people out West were "not so frugal." And when the Seattle press asked the favorite question of all Western questions, Little Andy was ready. "Has the young man of the West," he was asked, "a better opportunity to secure wealth and preferment than in the East?"

"Ah," replied the baron of steel, "you wish me to encourage immigration." Mr. Carnegie was not encouraging emigration to the Northwest. "The young man of brains," he told the Seattle press, "will rise anywhere." Having thus parried neatly, Carnegie saw an opening to speak of the nobility of hard labor. "We have," he said, "some 23,000 men on our payroll. I think I have taken every one of them by the hand, and as I have seen them at their toil the thought has come to me that kings were not more noble than they, and that honest toil and humble poverty were the crucible in which men's souls were tested."

One wonders if Mr. Henry Clay Frick of the party did not choke a little as he heard Carnegie emit that little homily. He hated labor unions no less than Carnegie did, and was not backward about saying so. And what the reporters heard Mr. Frick say of honest toil and humble poverty was, "We have regained control of the labor in our region since the great strike of last summer."*

With these things out of the way, the gentlemen of the press wanted to know what Mr. Carnegie planned to do with his "vast fortune." He replied with what one reporter said was "quiet sarcasm": "Sorry I left my last will and testament at home, or I would show it to you." But he readily understood the implications in the query. "I suppose you want to know," said he, "whether I will endow a university or church here. We have enough universities at present." As for religion, one of the reporters heard Andy say, "Ingersoll and I are very much in rapport so far as religious convictions are concerned." (Robert Ingersoll was America's best known agnostic.) Another reporter heard Andy say that he was "an agnostic and an admirer of Herbert Spencer."

*Three months after Mr. Frick made this remark, the Carnegie Steel Works at Homestead, Pa., was the scene of the bloodiest riot in all American history, before or since. Frick got the blame, for Carnegie had sailed away to Scotland just prior to the shooting, leaving his partner in charge.

That cleared up nearly everything except the subject nearest Seattle's heart: Was Carnegie planning to extend his empire of steel and coke into the Pacific Northwest, meaning Seattle? The multimillionaire parried this question again and again while he and his party were ranging all over the city, even as far as Queen Anne Hill. But at last they were led to the fount of things, the Seattle Chamber of Commerce. Here, with their backs to the wall, the Messrs Carnegie and Frick could no longer shift and side-step. The boosters had them cornered. Mr. Carnegie rose, or rather sank, to the occasion, and told the assembled patriots he much regretted he did not have time to investigate the iron mines of Washington. He was too old anyway, he said, to embark on new enterprises.

This was bad news, a cool wind on the hot Seattle spirit. Nor did Mr. Frick say anything to alleviate the blow. A Chamber of Commerce man thrust a piece of Seattle-made coke under Frick's nose. That gentleman glanced at it. "It is of very good quality," he remarked coldly, then quickly passed it back to the Chamber's expert as though it had been some hideous and unnameable thing. I fancy Frick dusted his hands, too.

Then the handsome Iolanthe was coupled to a train, and the Carnegie party left for Tacoma, where, as Seattleites were pleased to know, they were to stop only a few moments before starting East over the Northern Pacific. In Portland, as related, the party never left the depot. It was clear that Carnegie had come to see Seattle.

It was typical of the era that the member of Mr. Carnegie's party referred to vaguely as a savant of, or the president of, Cornell University received no attention beyond bare mention of his name. Andrew Jackson White was merely the man, more than any other, who was responsible for the founding of Cornell, where the School of Architecture was his especial favorite. He was already one of the best known writers in the world on the then live subject of the war of science with theology. He was soon to be named United States Minister to Russia, and later our ambassador to Germany. He was also one of the outstanding founders of the Hague Peace Tribunal. It was White who inspired the generous Carnegie to found what is now the Carnegie Institution.

Yet the Seattle press and the Seattle Chamber of Commerce were justified in ignoring Mr. White in 1892. It was an era and a place when and where men who dabbled in intellectual matters were to be seen, possibly, but not heard. The State of Washington had a university, anyhow. What Seattle wanted was a thundering big steel plant, and uncounted acres of smoking coke ovens.

The Seattle Spirit soared again quickly after the cruel disappointment furnished by the Carnegie party. The place was doing well enough; and in 1897 a wonderful stroke of luck—nay, of Providence—sailed into the harbor. This was the *SS Portland,* fresh from the north, with more than one million dollars' weight of gold dust from the Klondike River region of the Yukon. This was the event that touched off the biggest rush since the days of Forty-nine. The news went out that a ton of solid gold had arrived in Seattle, and for the first time in its history that city was advertised throughout the nation and the world. On came the seekers by the thousands, and they were outfitted by the competent and dollar-happy merchants of Seattle. Industries sprang up to meet the demand. Ships were hurriedly built, or chartered, and Seattle went into the Alaska shipping business, which it has dominated ever since. Gaudy hotels went up. So did theaters and honkey-tonks of all kinds.

Between 1880 and 1900 Seattle grew from a population of 3,500 to one of 80,617. It had not yet overtaken Portland, though it was well on the way to doing so, for it continued to boom. In 1910 it passed the Oregon city. In mid-century it is our only Northwest city of truly metropolitan aspect and outlook. It did not arrive at this position through sheer modesty.

What struck me most, when I first saw Seattle, was a bold and blatant sign, a bronze plaque, at the base of its tallest building. It is still there in 1951, and it tells all who care to read that this amazing structure is the "L. C. Smith 42-Story Building." The preposterous plaque is as significant as it is amusing. It is the perfect symbol of the Seattle Spirit which, more than geography, more than the fortunate accident of the ton of gold, more than anything else has made Seattle the first city in our region. Seattle worked hard to get and to hold its first half-million people. It deserves the position it holds.

The difference between the first and the second cities in the Northwest is beautifully epitomized by the perfect symbols of each: At about the same time the bronze plaque was being affixed, in order to call attention to the forty-two stories of a Seattle building, the Corbett cow grazing in downtown Portland was indication that this overgrown village cared little whether or not it ever had a forty-two story building. I don't think it cares much to this day, which, incidently, is one of several reasons why Portland is my home.

Railroads had no influence whatever on the beginnings either of Seattle or of Portland. But the sites of Tacoma and Everett were arbitrarily selected by interests closely allied, on the one hand with the Northern Pacific, on the other with the Great Northern. They happened to be pretty good sites, too, and there was never much doubt that the settlements would become sizable cities, even though neither has yet achieved the monstrous proportions visualized by their founders.

Tacoma was virtually a child of the Northern Pacific, though a full thirteen years before that road arrived on Commencement Bay, General Morton Matthew McCarver was there, waiting. General Tacoma, as he came to be known, was a typical town planner in the best tradition of the West. Breezy, cheerful, and filled with as much energy as imagination, he was there, in on the ground floor, before the Northern Pacific rails had hardly pushed beyond Minnesota, eighteen hundred miles off. He was buying land, too, shouting glory, naming streets that did not exist, staking out "extensions," wondering aloud if the many miles of waterfront would be equal to the titanic demands of Tacoma's future industries; damning the killjoys who mentioned fog or steep hills, both of which the place had in plenty; and calling upon all to "Watch Tacoma grow." It was a day of rejoicing, in 1870, when General McCarver got Tacoma's name on a state map. Three years later the first train arrived. For the next forty years Tacoma pressed Seattle hard for first place among Washington cities.

There was no cut-and-dried pattern as to how a city might take hold and grow. Everett was planned for one thing, yet became something else. It was the place where Jim Hill's Great Northern rails were first to meet tidewater. A group of eastern capitalists, including John D. Rockefeller, had the ground floor in Everett. It was to be their smelting headquarters for the untold riches of Monte Cristo, a mountain of more or less solid gold and silver some forty miles distant in the Cascade mountains. The great smelter was built, too, and so was a railroad that wound its tortuous way up impossible canyons, along a route hacked around sheer cliffs, or drilled through ledges, to come at last to the hole in the ground named for the novel of Dumas *père*. The novel was great fiction. So was the mine. I do not know how much the Frenchman made from his novel. It was far more than the Rockefellers got from the mine which, with excellent judgment, they abandoned after their experts had given the first few loads of ore a thorough working-over at the smelter.

The smelter was soon abandoned, and Everett went into the business of making lumber. Great dreams, however, die hard, and to the bewilderment of many tourists Everett's leading hotel is the Monte Cristo. It is a good name for a hotel. If I were running it, I should try to indoctrinate the help to explain how the hotel came by the name. I have stopped there many times, and have always asked one or more of the help whence came the name Monte Cristo. Few of them have had so much as a vague idea.

During a period of some forty years after 1880, a main-line railroad was generally believed to be the right foundation for a future metropolis. All along the lines of the Northern Pacific, the Union Pacific, the Southern Pacific, the Great Northern and, lastly, the Milwaukee, men with visions but without influence platted nobody knows how many scores of cities. A few of them grew into flag stops. The rest wholly disappeared.

Occasionally a town, already settled and doing business, picked up and moved when a railroad came near but did not touch it. Wenatchee did, in 1892, when the Great Northern was seen to be by-passing it. Yakima was an incorporated city with a population of four hundred, a newspaper, and a post office when the Northern Pacific selected a site four miles northwest for its depot. Yakima moved forthwith, and the original town became Union City. Both Yakima and We-natchee survived in their new locations, and have flourished modestly ever since.

It did not do, in the seventies, the eighties, and the nineties, for a town to be arrogant or grasping toward a railroad. Railroads themselves had sufficient of those qualities. When the Northern Pacific announced, or seemed to announce, that Washington's Territorial capital of Olympia would naturally be on its line, a local sharp-shooter bought several thousands of acres of land which he had good reason to believe the railroad would be obliged to cross. This was, in that era, one of the accepted methods by which one made money quickly. The Northern Pacific, however, had not built halfway across northern United States and remained naïve to the ways of land sharks. It simply ignored Olympia. In later years it did build a branch through the town, but the capital was never to be on a main line of the Northern Pacific or any other railroad.

The roaring old mining town of Jacksonville, Oregon, founded in 1852 on a gold strike, grew to importance in stagecoach days, and was made county seat. It was directly on the projected line of the Oregon & California Railroad, which later became part of the Southern Pacific. But local politics, plus what appears to have been a right grasping attitude of the town fathers of Jacksonville, angered the railroad builders, so they left it a good five miles from their tracks, to build Medford, which prospered from the first.

A different story was the modest though genuine epic of Prineville. Dating from 1868, when Barney Prine erected a saloon of willow logs and opened for business with his sole stock a case of Hostetter's Bitters, this Central Oregon town became headquarters of what wool growers called the Crook County Sheep-Shooters Association. Prineville was a *cattle* town, and proposed to remain a cattle town. It grew slowly. Its citizens were sure the reason for its lack of growth was the lack of a railroad. For the next forty-odd years, first one railroad, then another, which were tapping the region, failed to reach or to come anywhere near Prineville. The by-passing was not due to the greed of Prineville's people, who had consistently offered every inducement. Prineville just didn't seem a likely place for a railroad.

After repeated disappointments, the desperate citizens bonded themselves and set out to construct and operate the eighteen miles of track necessary to connect with the Oregon Trunk at Prineville Junction. The line was completed in 1918. One of the first incoming freights included several boxcars filled with automobiles—a truly terrible cargo in respect to the City of Prineville railroad. Yet the road continues to operate in 1951, even though it failed to make a metropolis of the "city."

There was at least one city and region in the Northwest whose development was retarded greatly by Indians. They were present Klamath Falls and its surrounding County of Klamath. It was Modoc country. The Modocs were by all odds the most savage and competent fighters of all Northwest tribes. In early pioneer times they wiped out two wagon trains. After settlers came, they continued to burn and massacre, and often clashed with Federal troops. As late as 1872, the tribe was not only still resisting, but managing to carry on a bitter local war as well. The result was to saddle the region with a reputation that did not encourage further settlement. It began to break down only as late as 1900, when a large irrigation project opened much desirable land. It broke down even more in 1909, when the Southern Pacific tapped Klamath Falls sawmills with a branch line. The city boomed. It boomed again when, in the 1920's, the Southern Pacific built a new line over the Cascades. This became in effect the road's main line between Portland and California. In a decade and a half Klamath Falls's population increased more than sixfold.

Of all Northwest towns and cities, none has had a stranger life than Port Townsend. It was the heartbreak of them all, early and late. Its story is like that of nothing else in our region. It has known the most and worst setbacks. For more than three-quarters of a century, one misfortune after another was its common fare. Its survival and present healthy condition is a classic happy ending, a sort of Truth Will Triumph, to a long story of calamities.

Port Townsend is one of the oldest settlements in Washington, older by six months than Seattle. It dates from April, 1851, when Alfred A. Plummer, from Maine, and his friend Charles Bachelder staked claims on Port Townsend bay, so named by Captain George Vancouver on his voyage of discovery and exploration in 1792. The two young men liked the look of the fine harbor on a point of land where the Strait of Juan de Fuca becomes Puget Sound. They were soon joined by Francis Pettygrove, the same restless man who already had named Portland and sold his claim in that town. He was still searching for the site of Metropolis.

Fishing and logging began. More settlers came in. Within a year the townsite plat was drafted. Application for a post office was made. Jefferson County of Washington Territory was formed, and Port Townsend was made its seat. The local boosters thereupon declared the place to be the Key City of Puget Sound. The Federal Government listened and apparently was impressed; Port Townsend was made a port of entry, and customs headquarters were removed from Olympia and established in the newer town. Citizens had reason to believe their city was to be the great port of the Northwest.

Now came a mad rush of California prospectors heading for the Fraser River placers in British Columbia, thousands of them in ships that called at Port Townsend. When the mining boom quickly collapsed, many of the miners returned no further south than Port Townsend. The population more than doubled.

The first of the succession of civic blows came from a new customs collector appointed by President Lincoln. He was Victor Smith, and in his opinion the only proper place for a customhouse was the come-lately hamlet of Port Angeles, fifty-odd miles to the West. He soon had his superiors in his way of thinking, and was ready to move when he discovered that the city fathers of Port Townsend had "stolen and secreted" all of the customs office's records. He tried moral suasion to no effect. Then he ordered the lighthouse tender *Shubrick* to stand off the port and to clear her decks for action with her three twelve-pounders. The threat brought results. The records were surrendered, and the office was moved to Port Angeles. (Six years later the customs office was returned to Port Townsend.)

This blow was much more than simply the loss of the office. The news of the removal was spread enthusiastically by the newspapers of Seattle, Olympia, Steilacoom, and other competing settlements; and the inference was drawn that Port Townsend, which up to then was probably the busiest place in the whole Territory, was already fading into insignificance. Removal of the customs was a sore wound, though not quite fatal.

During this period a proposal was made to move the Territorial capital from Olympia to Vancouver. For the promised aid of Port Townsend votes, that city was to be allotted the penitentiary; and for a like reason the university was to be allotted to Seattle. But the proposal failed to pass. Seattle, however, did get the university. As for the penitentiary, it was established not in Port Townsend, but in Walla Walla, on the east side of the mountains. Whether or not this was a blow to Port Townsend, its citizens considered it so, and so did the newspapers of other Puget Sound settlements, happy to see the Key City humbled again.

More blows were in store. As the transcontinental line of the Northern Pacific approached the West Coast, there appeared at Port Townsend an agent for the railroad. He said it was planned to extend the Northern Pacific line from Portland to Port Townsend Bay. What the railroad wanted, said he, was free land in Jefferson County for right of way and a terminus. Citizens were highly elated, and most generous. They came forward, with little urging, to donate the lands wanted. Nothing more happened—that is, nothing except that the Northern Pacific built a line to Portland, and another line to Tacoma, leaving Port Townsend right where it had always been, on an isolated peninsula far from a railroad.

This, one must remember, was the Railroad Era. Holy writ was no more devoutly believed than was the proposition that no town in the Northwest could achieve eminence without a railroad. The stouthearted citizens of the Key City of Puget Sound felt that the time had come when they must bestir themselves and take the initiative. Businessmen thereupon incorporated the Port Townsend Southern Railroad, with the plan of building a line some 250 miles down through the Territory to connect with the Northern Pacific at Portland, thus connecting the Oregon metropolis with the future metropolis of Washington. Considerable capital was raised locally. More was promised, or seemed to be promised, by outside capitalists. The idea was to start construction simultaneously at both ends of the proposed railroad.

There was to be no lagging at the Port Townsend end. The entire population, including a brass band, was present when the first spadeful of railroad dirt was turned; and work went ahead furiously until a mile of right of way had been cleared. Then it ceased, for it was learned that nothing whatever had been done at the other end of the projected line. For another decade nothing happened at either end of the Port Townsend Southern. Alder and fireweed grew high along the cleared right of way. Doldrums gripped the key city.

Now there appeared a new gleam of light in the form of something called the Oregon Improvement Company, a subsidiary of the Union Pacific Railroad. This outfit proposed to build and operate a line from Port Townsend to Portland. The by now dim though still legal Port Townsend Southern was to turn over its franchise and real estate to the new group. In addition, citizens of the terminal city were to raise a bonus of $100,000 as a contribution of good will. Optimism took over again. The bonus money was raised, the deal made. Within another sixty days a crew of mere than one thousand five hundred men was clearing land, laying track, and generally creating the noises of Progress.

Port Townsend soared again. Within a short period three streetcar lines were chartered. What was more, they were not just projected. One after the other the three concerns actually laid tracks, brought in rolling stock, and put up the trolley poles to touch the new wires of the newly chartered Electric Company, which turned its dynamo by steam power generated from slabwood. The bells of three lines started to jangle with the sweetest music imaginable to city builders. A telephone company was organized. Six banks set up in business. Block after block, many of them of concrete or stone or brick, was going up, and each had a waiting list of customers for store space or offices.

The *Weekly Register* could not find room to report all of the tremendous doings and at the same time speak of the heady future. When it did have room, it could and did report the steam railroad to be making swift headway. Trains were running as far as Lake Hooker, some twenty miles from the city—the Key City—and their smoke was as attar of roses.

Every ship to dock unloaded new settlers, and on them the oldtimers began unloading real estate. The "values" were enormous. Tom Bracken sold his farm for $16,000. Fifty-five front feet of Water Street fetched $27,500. Lots in the quaintly named subdivision of Saints Rest brought a total of $100,000. Half a dozen Chinese laundries had opened, sure sign of great things. There was a saloon on every corner, several more in between, and a livery stable in every block. Hail to the Key City. The year was 1890. Real-estate transfers in Port Townsend, for twelve months, reached the all but incredible figure of $4,594,685.93.

Nothing could stop the Key City now. The Port Townsend Nail Works was incorporated with local capital. Up went a factory. Tons of machinery were unloaded at the dock and installed. More sawmills were built. So was a fish cannery, then another. The Fire Department ordered new equipment. When the Port Commission said what the city needed was a hell of a big drydock, the glory-mad citizens of Port Townsend rallied round, cash in their hands, to put thousands of dollars into the enterprise. It was not a projected drydock, either. Work promptly began on one large enough to handle a battleship.

The first faint feeling of unease began to appear when it was seen, even with starry eyes, that construction at the northern, or home, end of the railroad had lessened noticeably. Worse, a persistent rumor had it that no work whatever had been done on the southern, or Oregon, end. A committee of citizens went to investigate. They returned, much sobered, to report that the Oregon Improvement Company was patently more of a land-shark outfit than it was a builder and operator of railroads. No sign of tracks, or even of a grade, was to be found in Oregon.

Port Townsend hardly had time to get this bad news down before the Panic of 1893 reached the West Coast. The Oregon Improvement Company went down and out. Four of Port Townsend's six banks shut their doors tight. Somebody came and towed away the immense drydock, completed but still unusued. Somebody else came to the closed factory of the Nail Works and took away the machinery to be sold for junk. Every local sawmill closed. So did the canneries. The three streetcar lines operated a while longer, and their business was the carrying of thousands of citizens down to the docks where they might get a steamer for Seattle, or Tacoma, or Olympia, or almost anywhere. Then even the car lines halted. The tracks were pulled up. So were the few miles of steel laid by the late Oregon Improvement Company. Deep melancholy settled over the Key City of Puget Sound.

Here was more than a deserted village, more than a mining camp gone to seed after the placers had been washed out. Here was a solidly constructed city, laid out and built for a population of 35,000, perhaps 50,000 people. Little of it was jerry-built. Most of the business blocks were staunch affairs, built for a century. Between six and seven thousand townsmen had walked away and left everything where it stood. Only a few hundred remained.

For the next quarter of a century those who stayed in Port Townsend lived in a dream atmosphere of suspended animation. One who was there said it was a strange experience. There in front of your eyes every morning, and on all sides, was the shell of a substantial city, much of it boarded up—waiting. Meanwhile, the few residents moved about in the echoing warrens, on the decaying streets and sidewalks, and somehow or other managed to make a living. Then, in 1917, came a whiff of new life. Nearby Forts Warden and Flager bustled with troops. Things looked up for a while, as the long-closed sawmills revived to meet war's demands. Bored soldiers came into town to spend a little money. It didn't last, of course. With war's end, most of the soldiers disappeared. The mills closed again.

Things now grew worse than they had been right after the great exodus of the early nineties. Even the city's water system failed. There was no money to repair it. I was there once during this period, and found the place a fantastic sight, almost eerie. It was as if some movie outfit had erected not just a street of store fronts, but a whole city, block after block of sound buildings, complete with signs, and had then gone on to other things elsewhere, leaving the stupendous "set" to the elements. One immense building of five stories stood up, scarred and soiled, like some late Victorian Acropolis, its scores of windows made sightless by boards, a brooding hulk throwing its shadow on lesser hulks around it. I felt like walking as quietly as possible along the crumbling sidewalks. The toot of an automobile horn seemed magnified, and was almost too much for the ear. One waited expectantly for Gabriel. . . .

Port Townsend remained much as I saw it until 1927, or some thirty-five years after its worst debacle. In that year a handful of die-hard local businessmen, who had never ceased to believe in the Key City's natural advantages, put forth one more heroic effort. They managed to convince officials of the Crown Zellerbach Corporation, makers of pulp and paper, that the Key City of Puget Sound was the proper place for the large kraft mill the corporation was planning. The plant was built there at a cost of about $7,000,000. And for once, at least, the citizens of Port Townsend were not asked for a bonus, or even to invest in a new industry. All capital came from outside. One can readily understand how the older townsmen, who had put money into railroads, streetcar lines, drydocks, sawmills, canneries, and nail companies, only to see them dissolve one after another in bankruptcy, were now prepared to believe in civic miracles.

Crown Zellerbach's Port Townsend plant employs more than five hundred men and women, and it has an annual payroll of $1,000,000. But it has meant much more than that. It brought life to a town that had been beaten, and beaten again, until it was close to death. Since 1927 the revived city has known a quarter of a century of stability. It has also enjoyed a steady growth. Metropolis passed it by, yet Port Townsend has long since passed many a town that was built close to the main-line tracks of the railroad.

2. Cities of Illusion

THERE WERE ALSO CITIES WHERE GASLIGHTS FLICKERED AND went out, or perhaps never emerged from the hopeful conditions described by the town-boomers' favorite adjective "projected." The latter were the cities of even less substance than cardboard. They were cities of paper, illusions on a map. Occasionally a few props were added to the scene, though these were not absolutely necessary. Just as good as props, and much cheaper, was an extensive town plat, bolstered with pen-and-ink sketches by an artist of riotous imagination.

But there were really no rules. My favorite city of Bourne, Oregon, already mentioned, came into existence and a brief prosperity on the strength of one printing press which emitted two separate and distinctly different newspapers. Bourne was a mining venture. It never troubled itself with a fanciful city map, for Bourne's promoters were not selling lots. They were selling stock in alleged mines.

The promoters of Bourne styled themselves The Sampson Company, Limited, and listed offices at London, New York City, and Bourne. It was one of Oregon's biggest and best swindles, conducted almost wholly by mail. The swindle started in 1900 and blew up in 1906. For six years the hard-worked printing press, brought in by wagon because Bourne never had a railroad, groaned for days, and many nights. It turned out one paper strictly for local consumption; the other, with a gigantic mailing list, covered much of the known world of suckers, to tell them, wherever they might be, of gold strikes that never happened, of ore mills never built, and

of bullion shipments never made. At one time Bourne doubtless held three thousand citizens, including actual miners,
parasites of all kinds who preyed upon the miners and, of
course, the tireless gull catchers employed by J. Wallace
White, genius of The Sampson Company, Limited.

What might be termed the Country, or Sucker, edition of
the Bourne paper never ran out of good hot stories concerning progress of the mines, but it did in time run out of
suckers, and the mirage evaporated. Citizens started moving
out at once, leaving everything where it stood. A handful
of incurable hopefuls stayed on a while, but most of them
moved after a cloudburst in 1937 removed almost all of the
old shacks.

Strictly speaking, Bourne does not belong in the city-
promotion story. It was selling stock in holes in the ground,
not house lots and industrial sites. The champion promoters
of gigantic nothings in the matter of mythical cities—not
mining camps—were the men who whelped two mirages
called Ocosta and Boston Harbor. There was no connection
between the two frauds.

Ocosta was the first to appear above the horizon of
imagination. On May 1, 1890, according to the press of a
goodly part of the new State of Washington, there ". . .
sprang into being a city that will challenge the great ports
and industrial centers of the Atlantic coast. . . . Three
hundred city lots were sold on the day Ocosta threw open
her gates to the world."

For at least three months before her gates were thrown
ajar, Ocasta's name had been constantly in those daily and
weekly papers which were, as the opposition papers had it,
creatures of the Northern Pacific Railway interests. Such
papers reported quite truthfully that Ocosta had been selected
as the terminal city of the nearly completed Tacoma &
Grays Harbor Railroad, a subsidiary of the Northern Pacific.
The site was described as being "as logical as it is beautiful,"
and on the south shore of Grays Harbor on the Washington
coast. This was truly a terrible piece of news to the citizens
of Hoquiam and Aberdeen, both also on Grays Harbor;
furthermore, both were going concerns, complete with may-
ors, police and fire departments, and schools. Both were
doing a big business making lumber and shipping it to China
and the Antipodes by seagoing vessels which could dock at

any or all of the score of sawmills and shingle mills. Yet neither Hoquiam nor Aberdeen had a railroad.

Now came this new, this only railroad (in which, incidentally, a number of Hoquiam and Aberdeen citizens had purchased stock on the assumption that it was to tap their towns), and elected to pass up, or by, those established cities and build its own metropolis. Wickedness could go no farther.

After three months of typical build-up, the promoters of Ocasta-by-the-Sea, as it was officially known, invited their friendly newspaper editors to visit the place "on the inclosed pass from the City Committee of Ocosta." Cut-rate transportation was offered to "all interested parties," by which was meant everybody who wanted to get in on the ground floor by buying a city lot or two, now, while prices were at rock bottom.

More than a thousand people arrived at Ocosta on that delirious 1st of May. (For months to come there would be other excursions.) Most of them must have noticed that while prices might be low, they could not be said to be at rock bottom. There was no rock bottom to Ocosta. It was all marsh, a wild, desolate expanse of reeds, coarse grass, seaweed and kelp, dotted, at low tide, with barnacled boulders. There were hundreds of acres of swamp. Indeed, Editor McDonald of the (unfriendly) Snohomish *Eye* declared the place should have been called the Great Dismal Swamp, and called it such in an editorial as soon as he returned to his sanctum.

The visitors to this metropolis saw that the swamp was lined and crossed with miles of raised plank walks. Starting near the end of the railroad, the planks seemed to stretch out to the horizon, and beyond. But what struck them more was that the wooden walks were lined, and most symmetrically, with handsome fir and cedar trees, not great trees, to be sure, but all of them ten or more feet tall. They looked mighty pretty. To skeptics, however, who were impressed less with the beauty of the saplings than with the fact that they should be there at all, in such terrain, and took the trouble to look, saw that the trees had been firmly spiked to the wooden stringers of the sidewalks at graceful intervals of about sixteen feet. They had been cut elsewhere than in swampy Ocosta, toted in by team, then raised and spiked one by one to the boardwalks. The trees were symbolic of Ocosta. They were rootless.

Yet more than three hundred of the visitors on that May day in 1890 believed in Ocosta as the City of Destiny, as advertised. They bought one or more city lots, or industrial sites, and went away, happy to be in on the ground floor, marshy though it might be. More gulls came later, by the cut-rate excursions, and they too bought Ocosta property. Men who described themselves as industrialists arrived to say they planned to build, respectively, a sawmill, a shingle mill, a brewery, a business block, a livery stable, a streetcar line, a gasworks. Man alive, it was wonderful the way Ocosta-by-the-Sea was going ahead. . . .

Whether or not Ocosta would have grown into Metropolis is to be doubted. In any case its fate was sealed presently by the he-men of Aberdeen, one of the two established towns which the railroad had by-passed. These stouthearted pioneers of Aberdeen set out to build their own one mile of railroad to connect with the Northern Pacific at a place they called Grays Harbor Junction. To do it, they salvaged rails from the wrecked bark *Abercorn,* which had providentially sunk in the harbor; and though the steel was pitted from six years in salt water it was still usable.

The spirit was cheering to behold. Pioneer Samuel Benn donated a city lot in Aberdeen to every man who helped clear the right of way and lay the rails. Pioneers Charles Wilson and A. J. West donated the ties. Pioneer J. M. Weatherwax salvaged and donated the rails. Citizens turned out by the hundreds and labored like beavers. Their wives fetched food, set up camp, and fed their men as the grade proceeded. And on went the rails. The one mile of track was laid without hitch, and at record speed.

By then the promoters of Ocosta were ready to quit. They dropped their paper city and were glad to run their trains to Aberdeen, and a little later to Hoquiam. The rails to Ocosta rusted a while, then were taken up.

Thirty years later, when I first saw the place, the wind swept wildly across the wastes called Ocosta-by-the-Sea. The only gulls there were sea gulls. Two hulks of battered frame buildings leaned and shook to the blasts off the harbor. There was not even a windbreak of spiked trees to soften the ordeal. Complete melancholy blanketed the City of Destiny.

The mirage wildly heralded as Boston Harbor appeared near the turn of the century. Its site was on Budd Inlet,

an arm of Puget Sound near the capital city of Olympia,
Washington. It was perhaps the highest-powered attempt in
the Northwest to create a city out of paper, plus a few
props.

The promoters of Boston Harbor did not have to bring
in and set up trees. They had, on the contrary, to clear
several million feet of big old Douglas fir that grew almost
down to the very shore of the inlet. Between and around
and over the monstrous stumps they platted lots and parks
and streets and boulevards; and through the deep forest
around the main site they platted Additions that ran back into
the hills, well out of sight of the blue waters of Puget
Sound. These promoters were truly ambitious men, men
who planned for the centuries, farseeing men who meant to
assure a plenty of breathing space, as it was called, for the
citizens of the metropolis of Puget Sound, if not of the West
Coast.

Quite in keeping with the new city's name were the
thoroughfares. The main stem was Tremont. The great boulevard was Commonwealth. The several parks were designated
Concord, Lexington, Brookline, and Harvard. These were
not just names on a map, either; at every intersection were
neatly lettered signboards. No wanderer amid the stumps of
Boston Harbor need wonder where he was, if he could
read.

An immense jerry-built wharf ran out to deep water in the
harbor proper. Facing the steamboat dock, where no visitor
possibly could miss it, was half a mile of the most stupendous
signboards ever erected on Puget Sound. In black and red
letters large enough to be read at two hundred yards, even
by the astigmatic, one readily learned of the Future Home
of Boston Harbor Smelter, of the Boston Harbor Lumber
Mills, of the sites reserved for Boston Harbor Iron & Steel
Corporation, and the Drydock of Boston Harbor Shipbuilding
Company. Only slightly smaller signs, scattered along the
waterfront, told of other industries that even then were
hurrying thither.

While the signs were going up and the streets and boulevards being surveyed, the promoters of Boston Harbor
prepared their seductive literature. I have in my time studied
no little amount of the literature devoted to civic mirages,
and I must admit that none of it surpassed the stuff put out
in praise of Boston Harbor. The chief exhibit, a handsome
pamphlet, charmed as it stunned. It featured a panorama of

the metropolis as envisioned by an artist of unimpaired potency. You saw a dock fully a mile long that was clogged with vessels, many of them true Leviathans. The sky above was darkened by clouds of smoke billowing up from a gigantic smelter, from the steel works, from the sawmills. At the Boston Harbor Shipyards hundreds of men were busily engaged whacking up a big vessel obviously almost ready to slide down the ways. The whole waterfront, in fact, was a hive.

Then your eye turned to the city proper. Buildings higher than any I had seen on Tremont Street in Boston, Massachusetts, reared up fifteen stories. Streetcars, hansom cabs, delivery trucks, and a couple of primeval automobiles combined to make a chaos of traffic. But it was different out on broad Commonwealth Boulevard. Here were victorias and broughams rolling leisurely along between rows of deciduous trees set in landscaped acres. Little children, properly accompanied by uniformed nurses, rolled hoops and flew kites in the gorgeous parks. Well back on a ridge were mansions gaudy with bay windows, towers, plenty of gingerbread, and mansard roofs.

You turned the pamphlet's pages to find what life was like in the many Additions to Boston Harbor. Here grass to shame the pampas grew twelve feet tall, if the man shown happily smiling in its midst was a six-footer. On another page was a fat little girl of tender years. She was smiling too. And why not? In her chubby little hands she held perhaps half a dozen strawberries, each piece of the luscious fruit clearly drawn; and the reader could tell by the ten-quart pail that stood by the little one's feet that a couple of dozen of these monstrous berries would fill the pail to overflowing. Such was the fruit to be raised in Boston Harbor's Additions.

The running text with these and many other pictures was in character. In those days advertising men were poets, licensed to sing of things seen or unseen, to paint structures and landscapes beyond the field of common vision.

How many of these pamphlets went into the mails I could never learn, but I do know they went as far afield as Massachusetts, and were also distributed along the intervening 2,800 miles. Their greatest concentration, however, was in the general area of Puget Sound.

Boston Harbor's promoters were masters of timing. A few days after the pamphlets had been mailed, and when they had reason to believe the seductive poison was flowing madly in the veins of congenital suckers, the masters used large advertising space in Seattle and Tacoma newspapers to announce free excursions. They chartered two big steamers to carry the thousands who would want to see the new star in the Northwest.

Thousands did hasten up the gangplanks, while brass bands played, and away they went. Though the voyage was to be less than two hours each way, the bighearted promoters were no men to attempt to unload real estate on the famished. Hot dogs, coffee, and ice cream were served, free as the air, to the pilgrims, and they arrived well fed and cheerful at the city, or rather the site, of Boston Harbor. There was no obligation to buy a lot. The visitors were taken in tow by experts who expanded on the opportunities of buying now. After an hour or so, all hands went back up the gangplanks and were returned to Tacoma or Seattle, the bands still beating the daylights out of "Over the Waves," the hot dogs still free.

Sunday after Sunday, and sometimes on weekdays, the two vessels carried capacity loads to Boston Harbor. How many in the hordes purchased lots, nobody knows; but, they were many, a large number of whom soon came to believe they had been rooked. They raised their voices in the loud wail of the sucker taken, and it was heard, at last, by state and Federal authorities, who thereupon closed in on Boston Harbor's promoters.

I could not learn that anybody ever got his or her money back. I know of only one person who bought a lot and actually went to live in Boston Harbor. She was an old lady who had bought one house lot during the excitement. She moved to Boston Harbor about 1906, when the noise had died away, and there she built a little house. Twenty years later, when I called on her, the total population of the place was perhaps a dozen, surely not more than twenty.

I found Boston Harbor to be a delightfully restful backwash tucked away on an arm of the Sound some eight miles from the roaring traffic of the Olympia-Tacoma main stem. A few small houses, little more than huts, were scattered in disarray along the shore. The tide lapped gently along the beach. Sun glinted on the mild waves of the harbor, and brought out the handsome driftwood tone in the weatherbeaten siding of the dwellings.

Exploring in the alders and other brush, I came across a length of sewer pipe, obviously unused, lying fair on top of the ground; then another, and another. There must have been half a mile of it in the brush. I learned it had been there since the last brass band had piped aboard the last horde of gulls who came to look at Boston Harbor. Nothing else, however, remained of the artifacts of the great mirage. I had hoped to find a street sign, but was told they had long ago been cut into kindling.

The old lady, who so far as I could learn was the only person who had lived there since the great days of civic promotion, was curious about me, even eager. It was some time before I came to realize why: She believed that I was the advance guard of the untold thousands of long delayed lot owners who at last were coming to build and live in the city on which she had gambled to the extent of $150. Her questions, her manner, the obvious excitement that a stranger who asked about Boston Harbor had aroused, finally made me comprehend what had seemed incredible. Here was blind faith such as is given to few. From a cupboard she brought forth a cherished copy of the Boston Harbor pamphlet, and urged me to read its prophecies, its glowing words, the wonderful illusion which had sustained her for more than two decades. Were the big mills coming, she wanted to know. What about the great foundry, the steel plant, the shipyards? True, there had been long delays, but now. . . .

For a moment I felt I should lie to her, lie enthusiastically. But I didn't, and pleaded ignorance of any "developments" for the city of the old lady's dreams. I fancied she faded a bit at my lack of knowledge of any bright news, and the sudden animation I had noted in her quickly died. "Well," she said when I bade her good day at the door, "if you hear any news I wish you would let me know." I promised I would. When she said goodbye she seemed to be looking past me and down toward the shore. I felt she could see the great belching stacks of the Boston Harbor Iron & Steel Works, blotting out the sun and the fleecy clouds, blotting out the blue waves; and I felt less sorry for her. She did not know how fortunate she was, for she had never seen South Chicago, or Youngstown, or McKeesport.

As much a favorite place for paper cities as Puget Sound was the Columbia River, which divides Oregon and Washington. During the nineties both banks of the big stream were witness to the Merlins of the mythical town plat. In 1891, for instance, the mists that hung over Grays Bay, near the river's mouth, were wafted aside momentarily to reveal what a promoter and his artist were pleased to call Mighty Frankfort-on-the-Columbia. (They liked long hyphenated names in those days.)

In press and pamphlet the Frankfort illusionists declared their city was to be the "terminus of three transcontinental railroads." The usual billboards were erected to mark the future site of this or that great industry. Many lots were sold. Then the mists again enfolded Grays Bay, and when the sun had cleared them Frankfort had evaporated into the salt-washed air.

Farther up the Columbia, about where North Bonneville is today, there was a considerable tumult and shouting about a city called Lower Cascades, seat of Skamania County, Washington, until a band of muscle men stole the county records and removed them to Stevenson, which then, as the rules were understood, became the county seat. Lower Cascades had been platted for four miles in every direction before quick disintegration set in.

Nearby was Garrison City, with "streets" until you were dizzy, but the promoters forgot to dike, and the flood of 1894 washed Garrison City down the Columbia in the direction of mighty Frankfort. Umatilla Landing and North Dalles were two other riverside towns that never got beyond the plat stage.

Still farther up the Columbia, and later in time, was Bridgeport Bar. This was less a town promotion than it was a singularly inept attempt to get rich quick, or fairly quick, by the honorable method of growing apples. It also happened to be one of those absentee-ownership affairs, or largely so, and thus had an appeal that is most attractive to many people: All you did was to put some cash into the Bridgeport Land Company and its subsidiary Hudson Water Company. Somebody then planted the apple trees, irrigated and cared for them, picked the apples, sold them at a huge profit, and then, one fine day in autumn, sent you a whale of a check. Like all such schemes, before and since, it was simplicity itself.

The two companies were formed in 1908 for the purpose of planting 1,600 acres of apple orchards at Bridgeport Bar, a terrace extending along the Columbia not far from the mouth of the Okanogan. Less than eleven inches of rain fell here annually. The temperature extremes were 110 degrees and —23 degrees. In its native state Bridgeport Bar was sand, sagebrush, and bunchgrass. It was, and is, usually thought of as desert country. But irrigation was to make Bridgeport blossom. The water was to be pumped from the Columbia by a plant fueled by driftwood. This was the subsidiary Hudson Water Company.

There was to be no fake about this promotion. Both the land company and the waterworks had been incorporated and had made motions of getting under way when a Chicago traveling man named Charles N. Crewdson became interested. Because his own firm was the Outcault *Advertising* company, Mr. Crewdson was of necessity a man of vision. He seemed to have sparked at once to the unlimited possibilities of Bridgeport Bar, and lost no time in taking over the existing if halting land and water companies. He himself purchased a 70 per cent interest. Among his associates were J. F. Pershing, a brother to the general; H. P. Kinsley of the Associated Press; a Mr. Morris of the System Company, Philadelphia; W. C. Watrous, a high official of the Great Northern railroad; M. R. Brown, private secretary to James J. Hill himself; L. M. Herman, of the Kuppenheimer clothes people; Frederick Starr, University of Chicago, noted anthropologist and author of *The Truth About the Congo* and many other works; Mr. Dunn and Mr. Hardenbrook, of Mandel Brothers, Chicago merchants; Mr. Morgan of the Morgan Envelope Company, and no less a celebrated American than Richard Felton Outcault, who practically invented the funny papers.

In 1909, when he joined the Bridgeport Land Company, Outcault was still drawing Buster Brown, which he had originated in 1902. Before Buster, he had originated the Yellow Kid, a brat of Hogan's Alley who, with his many imitators, was responsible for the term "yellow journalism." Buster Brown was probably the most famous funny-page character of his era. From him stemmed Buster Brown haircuts, clothes, shoes, even bread. Outcault made a fortune from Buster. then founded the advertising agency in Chicago for which Bridgeport Promoter Crewdson was the star salesman.

Things now started to move at Bridgeport Bar. In 1909 the company began to plant its 1,600 acres of apples. The pumping plant was built. Canals were laid through the orchards. Although most of the orchards remained in company ownership, several investors preferred, and were per-

mitted, to purchase land and water rights, and to develop
their holdings themselves.

Few of the land-company investors took the trouble to
look at their orchards until three years had passed. What
they saw caused several to abandon their interests at once.
What had happened, according to Edward C. Whitley,
Bridgeport Bar's sole historian, included a number of unto-
ward things. To begin with, the amateur orchardists had
planted their trees in great blocks, without consideration for
necessary polinization. Large sections had been set out in the
poorest soil. The irrigation canals had not been lined, and
they lost much of the water pumped by the rather erratic
works of the Hudson Water Company.

Still, not all the investors were fainthearted. In 1917 they
enlarged the pumping plant and installed electricity. The increased flow was still inadequate, and owners of individual
orchards dug wells and installed pumps of their own. Con-
flicts arose over the company water. Soon the company plant
ceased to function at all.

Spring frosts came to plague the growers, and the heating attempts accomplished nothing but adding to expense. Year after
year, too, the lack of polinization resulted in chronically low
yields. The color of the apples was consistently pale. This made
them difficult to market. Then along came the coddling moth.
Heavy lead sprays were applied. It soon turned out that the
local packing sheds lacked equipment for removing the
poisonous residue. The fruit had to be shipped across the
Columbia, at extra cost, to more efficient sheds in Brewster.

By this time still more of Bridgeport's orchardists had
given up and gone away, or stayed away. Empty and decaying farmhouses studded the district. The dead or dying orchards were felled like so much timber, and cut into fire-
wood. The still standing trees increased the orchard pests. By
1935 much of the original project had been reclaimed by
the desert, and was marked only by stumps and battered
houses in the shifting sands. By 1950 the original 1,600 acres
had been reduced to less than 100 acres.

The survivors of Bridgeport Bar's rainbow age turned to
soft fruit and juice grapes without much success. Dairying
proved worse, largely because incessant spraying had resulted in a toxic topsoil in which many crops could not be
grown.

I visited Bridgeport Bar but once, in the 1930's. It then

looked desolate. The addition of a few whitened skulls of cattle or bison would have made it a classic scene. But Historian Whitley had been there recently and was encouraged by what he found. The construction, a few miles upriver, of the Chief Joseph Dam, has given the surviving· orchardists hope that the dam will soon supply gravity water to the thirsty acres of Bridgeport Bar. Already experimental plantings of grapes, apricots, cherries, and prunes have been made, and early success has given encouragement to growers of these crops.

Many homes for construction workers on the dam have been erected at and near Bridgeport Village. Land that comparatively recently was carried on the county tax rolls for many years now brings premium prices. The hard-bitten citizens of Bridgeport Bar are beginning to talk much as the original boosters did almost fifty years ago. They believe that as cheap water becomes available, the area will see great agricultural expansion. Others visualize in Bridgeport Village fine factory sites for industries that will use the hydroelectric power to be generated at Chief Joseph Dam. Either thing, or both things, could happen.

Though Mr. Whitley is happy at the new life of Bridgeport Bar, he is also a good historian, and as such has a word of warning. "While these new possibilities cannot be ignored," he said recently, "the region should not lose sight of the danger that this boom may collapse as have those of the past." Even with the best of good will, the creation of Metropolis, or of Eden, is not assured.

3.   The Edens of Erewhon

IN CONTRAST TO THE STANDARD TYPE OF CITY BOOMER, talking shrill and fast of gaslights and streetcars, the Northwest attracted an unusual number of settlers who were seeking not the conventional metropolis, but the ideal community symbolized in the anagram of "nowhere," which Samuel Butler used as title for his philosophical novel. Erewhon had no slums. It had no poor. It had a great deal of milk and no little honey. Everybody lived on the sunny side of the street.

That's the way it was in Erewhon. The best place to establish Erewhon in the United States, or so it seemed to several thousand Americans in the eighties and nineties, was surely somewhere in the Northwest, a new region not yet wholly corrupted by materialism.

Butler's book alone was not responsible for the idealists who came in large numbers to found Erewhons here and there around the shores and on the islands of Puget Sound. The publicists who emitted a thousand books and pamphlets on the Rochdale Cooperative had a hand in it. These were the idealists affiliated with Equitable Pioneers Society, founded in England in 1844, and most influential. The English reformer John Ruskin had something to do with it too. So did the Frenchmen Cabet and Fourier. Perhaps the greatest stimulus of all appeared in 1888 as a book called *Looking Backward*, by Edward Bellamy.

The earliest of the Northwest Erewhons was established before the powerful urge of Bellamy's utopia had been loosed, and it was incorporated in 1887, under Washington Territorial laws, as the Puget Sound Cooperative Colony. A Seattle attorney, George Venable Smith, seems to have been the leader of the enterprise. His photograph occupies the center position in a page of thirty-five portraits of men and women present at what was called the Incorporating Convention. They are good faces, too, these thirty-five idealists, and the glow of good will seems to shine forth from the mustached or gorgeously bearded countenances and is to be seen in the steady gaze of women in boned collars and tight waists. They must have felt themselves to be participating in a historic event, too, for the portraits are obviously set pieces taken expressly for the occasion of the Incorporating Convention, to show how looked the pioneers who already had crossed the hideous plains of Materialism and were now about to found the Model Commonwealth.

That was the name on the masthead of their official organ, the *Model Commonwealth*, and in it one read of what the group aspired to do; namely, to "find the solution of Entire Co-Operation." This was to be achieved by "a separate Community of Collective Industry, means, utilities, public & private, and of persons, under a single management, and responsible for health, usefulness, individuality and security for each and all." Brave words those, and they were to have splendid backing, for the corporation was capitalized at $1,000,000—at least, that's what the instrument said. Shares were $10 each, payable in labor, services, property, or cash.

The over-all plan was that this Puget Sound colony should be only one, and the first, of a group of affiliated cooperatives that were to be organized by people in Tacoma, Portland, and in Greeley, Colorado; and probably, too, by other people in various towns of Wisconsin, Illinois, and Ohio. Somewhat later, when all groups had got under way, the several units were to exchange products with each other. Success of these pioneer groups would attract and convert the materialistic or fainthearted elsewhere, the units would multiply until—until, bless you, the United States itself should be bound together not only politically, but by the common sense and decency of "Entire Co-Operation." Poverty would automatically disappear.

This was heady air to whiff. Once they had whiffed it, the Puget Sound colony lost no time. A site was elected and purchased along Ennis Creek in the bustling and otherwise typical frontier community of Port Angeles, Washington Territory. A steam sawmill was the first requirement. It was erected by colony artisans while other members felled gigantic firs, then brought the logs to be sawed into boards and timbers. All hands turned carpenter and put up a rambling big building to house office, store, the printing plant, and to serve as colony hotel. At this period, for reasons not now clear, Leader Smith retired in favor of Thomas Malony, who appears to have been a levelheaded man of good managerial ability.

Individual homes were built. So was a dock. All was humming in the community. It was lively with the noise of members sawing and hammering to build a fine sixty-ton schooner, which went down the ways as the SS *Angeles* and was put into colony service to carry freight and passengers.

The colony organ began, and continued, a war against all trusts and robber barons, who were quite numerous at the period, and came out for the single tax and free trade. The paper said, too, that the wage system must go, and outlined the plan adopted by the Puget Sound colony: All work done was credited in hours. Foremen could grade men at their discretion, that is, credit individual workers with more hours or fewer hours according not to the actual time worked, but in respect to the energy and ability displayed. This was apparently an unusual quirk in cooperative bookkeeping, and it shows that the colonists knew that many communities in the past had been wrecked by free riders. Hence, they would penalize the shirkers. Four times a year the whole earnings of the colony were to be divided by the total number of hours worked, and individual members paid off for the number of hours credited to each.

Colonists also accepted "outside" work. They submitted the lowest bid to build a public schoolhouse for the town of Port Angeles, and went ahead to build it. Members appear to have more than dabbled in real estate, for a group of them presently advertised lots for sale in "Second Addition to the Townsite of Port Angeles."

One of several grandiose plans, set forth in the colony's prospectus but apparently never put into effect, was that of Associated Homes, by which domestic help was to be paid by colony funds, thus releasing talented housewives from the kitchen.

The Puget Sound cooperators seem not to have been bedeviled by the subject that has troubled so many communities. I could find nothing in their literature about free love under any of its several names, nor could I find that they were ever charged with "sex orgies," or even with the unconventional domestic arrangements that have brought scandal to many such unorthodox groups.

Yet other troubles appeared, and they seem to have stemmed chiefly from lack of finances. The million-dollar incorporation goal was probably just something to talk about. Although Manager Malony reported, in April of 1889, that colony resources exceeded colony liabilities by the healthy margin of $79,569, these alleged resources were made up largely of real estate; and colonists, even as other men, are notoriously prone to optimism in the matter of their speculative real estate. In any case, things within the group were on the downgrade. In the columns of the *Model Commonwealth* one begins to note bitter recriminations. Schismatic tendencies appear. Colony cows are sold at auction.

The colony, however, continued to function as such, and in 1891 members erected a whopping great hall called the Opera House, where they might have more room for their almost continuous debates. Entertainments were also staged. But conditions gradually worsened, and in January of 1894 the Puget Sound Cooperative Colony was declared bankrupt. Not until ten years later was the receivership discharged.

What the failure cost creditors isn't to be known, though one can form an idea from the last item settled by the receiver. It was a bill for $36.30 from the Yankee Baking Powder Company. It was paid off at $2.72.

Many of the colonists, including George Venable Smith, remained to become esteemed citizens of Port Angeles. A few of them still lived there in 1950, nursing, as a local historian wrote, "advanced old age as tenderly as may be while the shadows gather, glad and grateful that their lines were cast in pleasant places." On the site of the colony now stands a big plant of Rayonier, Inc., and manufactures dissolving pulp. The Opera House of the colonists stood until 1923, in which year I saw it, an authentic relic of complicated frontier elegance, battered and stained by the suns and storms of a quarter century. It was the last visible evidence of the Puget Sound Cooperative Colony, capitalized at $1,000-000. With and in it died what William D. Welsh, then a Port Angeles newspaperman, termed "a noble and ill-starred venture."

Other noble ventures were afoot before the Port Angeles colony had quite breathed its last. One of these labored under the style of the Brotherhood of the Cooperative Commonwealth, which its members sensibly ignored in favor of Equality, taken from the title of Bellamy's sequel to *Looking Backward*. Equality Colony was a child of the American Socialist party, which in 1897 had come to believe the time ripe to demonstrate by concrete example the benefits of cooperative effort in the building of communities. The Socialists thought it best to select a comparatively new country for the experiment. Puget Sound appealed to them, and a pioneer group went forth to choose the spot. This turned out to be deep in the big timber near the village of Edison, in Skagit County.

No community since the times of Robert Owen's New Harmony got under way with better financial support than Equality. Some 3,500 Socialists throughout the United States assessed themselves ten cents a month each for the enterprise. When William McDevitt, secretary of the Brotherhood, arrived there in 1898, he found the pioneers to have accomplished great things. A majority of the advance group had come, strangely enough, from the State of Maine, never a notable breeding ground for Socialistic experiment; and its leader was Ed Pelton, a capable and energetic woodsman who directed members in clearing the immense timber, putting up a sawmill and turning the logs into material for houses.

McDevitt, fresh from an office job in the Smithsonian Institution, was much taken with Equality. The primitive buildings were not quite finished, yet they were already habitable, and of generous proportions. Except for a few families, who lived in small houses, the nearly three hundred members were living, "in true communal style," in refectories and dormitories. Although young McDevitt was filled and running over with Ruskin and Butler and Bellamy and William Morris, he was still youthful, and not so far gone in complicated theories that he failed to notice the waitresses in the main refectory at Equality. In later years he recalled how taken he was with these "several very rosy-cheeked and affable beauties." He even remembered that one "was a lovely and becomingly buxom blonde, and another was a gracefully lissom brunette." But McDevitt's cooperative instinct was strong, and so he was pleased to know that these handsome young women also were teachers in the Equality school. What harm if Athene looked something like Venus?

There were, however, serious things to consider. Every night, naturally enough, there was a hot debate in the community hall, and the subject was often: Shall Equality Be a Practical Democracy, or Shall It Be Wholly Anarchodemocratic? So long as Ed Pelton lived, the answer was in line with the practice outlined in *Looking Backward,* which was "a subordination of individual liberty to the will of the majority."

But one day Pelton was struck by a falling tree, and killed. With the passing of this dominant and prudent character, McDevitt remembered, the colony became like a ship with a bad rudder. It was at this period that the Ault family arrived from Newport, Kentucky. Young Harry Ault was fourteen, and the big woods, the clear streams, and Puget Sound, with its clams and fish and ducks, made Equality a heaven for him. Many years later Ault looked back on the experience with pleasant nostalgia, and also with no little humor concerning the deadly serious cooperators. "There were some three hundred of us," he recalled, "man, woman and child. There were about sixty heads of families, each and every one of whom knew the only way to achieve the cooperative commonwealth. All other ways were wrong. The women had come along mostly because their husbands were sold on the idea of cooperation, but they did find there their first experience as equals, and most of them became ardent equal-righters."

For two years the bright vision of the Cooperative Commonwealth shone brave and clear. In 1900 the colony's paper, *Industrial Freedom*, was still speaking in strong voice. Pilgrims were coming to Equality from many distant states. Yet there were departures, too, and total membership dropped to 120. Misfits, disgruntled free riders, and the merely curious had been leaving the community. And perhaps *Industrial Freedom* had been overly enthusiastic in describing the colony. At least one large delegation from Dayton, Ohio, arrived with the intention of settling in Equality, but one look at the utterly primitive settlement amid the towering firs was enough. They were so repelled that they pulled out overnight, to settle in the orthodox community of New Whatcom, later a part of Bellingham. McDevitt remembered that this happening was a serious blow to Equality's morale, which steadily grew worse.

For the next few years the colony continued to go to pieces. Many reasons have been cited for the failure. Probably all of them are correct. The free riders surely were well to the front among the causes of defeat. Worth W. Caldwell, who interviewed several survivors of the colony, said that they told him many of the pseudo-members, who never had any intention of subscribing to Equality principles, lived there until they had stocked up with a large amount of clothing and supplies, bought cheaply at the colony store, then moved away. All such community efforts have found free riders a major curse, unless the Puget Sound Colony at Port Angeles, already cited, was an exception.

Just when the Brotherhood of the Cooperative Commonwealth that was Equality breathed its last is something lost in the mists. All that seems certain is that no trace of it was to be found after 1906.

At almost the same time the Equality Colony was getting started, another and smaller band of experimenters set out to establish Erewhon in Pierce County. The place was an arm of Puget Sound called Burley Lagoon. The organizing group called themselves the Cooperative Brotherhood, with no "Commonwealth" attached. Exactly what theory of cooperation they favored is something I wouldn't even try to set down on paper. To do so, even now, so many years after the Burley adventure faded, would be to invite "corrections" and hot, argumentative letters from survivors. Indeed, there are two things about which I long ago learned to be cagey in print: quoting any veteran of any war or campaign against American Indians, and stating flatly that this or that Socialist or cooperative colony believed so-and-so.

I have read reams of pamphlets and whole bundles of newspapers put out by social experimenters of the eighties and nineties, wading through a dense and often dark forest that was variously named the Social Democracy of America, the Brotherhood of the Cooperative Commonwealth, the Rochdale Cooperators, the Social Democratic Party, with subsidiary clauses relating to the aforementioned Cabet and Fourier, to say nothing of William Morris, Robert Owen, Laurence Gronlund, Ruskin, Albert Brisbane, and Eugene Debs. So thin, yet so precise are the intramural lines dividing these groups, and so fanatically held by true believers, even those who have long since become resigned to capitalism in its most brutal forms—so sacred still are these worn-out theories, that one might better attempt to qualify the Virgin Birth than to indicate that a Rochdaler was a Full Cooperator.

All I'd care to say of the theories held by the Burley experimenters is that they *seem* to have believed in Erewhon as a place where colonists would operate a sawmill, a shingle mill, and a cigar factory for the common good. At least, those are the things the Burleyites did operate on a communal basis. They bought such supplies as they needed from "the Rochdale Wholesale House in San Francisco." They also had a colony paper, a monthly called simply the *Co-Operator*. This was first issued in 1898; the last issue I could find was that of December 7, 1901, though I think the paper was continued for a while longer.

A year after its founding, Burley had a combined office, store, and hotel building of two and a half stories. There were also the shingle mills and the sawmills, a barn, harness shop, and cigar factory, a school building, and "a kindergarten building in the course of construction." Sixty acres of heavily wooded land had been cleared. The whole Burley site had cost $5,917. A knitting machine had arrived.* A few months later the Burley paper was advertising Co-operative Brother-

---

*I have often wondered if this machine was inspired by the Shakers at Canterbury and Enfield in New Hampshire, whom I had visited as a youth, and who did famously well knitting sweaters and socks for sale. The Shakers and the Burley group are the only communities I know of that had knitting machines.

hood Cigars. These were handmade and cost from $1.50 to $3.00 for a box of fifty.

Though I could find nothing to indicate the banning of coffee, the Burley paper carried a standing advertisement for Equality Cereal Coffee, which was made and sold by the Brotherhood of the Cooperative Commonwealth at Edison, already mentioned.

The Burley paper also carried advertisements of Bellamy's book *Equality,* offered to "Brothers and Sisters at the Special price of 35 cents a copy." The Burley group addressed each other, at least in print, as Brother and Sister; but Kingsmill Commander, a former Burley member, and now of Tacoma, told me these salutations were not used in conversation.

The Burley group appears to have had a loose sort of association with the Equality group. The Burley paper also spoke well of something called the Twentieth Century Improvement Society of Buena Vista, Colorado, which in 1901 was trying to sell stock at $100 a share. I don't know what for.

In 1901, too, the Burley colonists could listen "to the busy clipping of our shingle machine, as it converts the blocks of cedar into roofing material, and makes pleasant music to our ears." In June of that year the colonists cut and packed a bundle of select shingles which they forwarded for exhibition to the Pan-American Exposition at Buffalo, confident it would be "a silent witness to the skill of our workers."

Yet colony conditions left something to be desired. "There must be a change this winter," warned the Burley paper, "from the backwoods accommodations now prevailing here." It went on to cite a lack of social intercourse, and said the great need was for a good meeting place, or main building of some sort, and proposed one that was to cost $100,000. Burley was never to have such a hall. It did have a fire or two, but these did not wreck the experiment. There does not, in fact, seem to have been any wrecking, or blow-up. Burley just faded. In 1908 its population was thirty, and of these only seventeen were members of the Cooperative Brotherhood. How long those hardy seventeen held out I could not learn.

While Burley and Equality were being born, a somewhat different adventure was going forward on Whidby, one of the larger islands of Puget Sound. This was officially the Free Land Association, and the colony site at the head of

Holmes Harbor was named Freeland. No wild ideas' emanated from Freeland. It was not a Socialist community. In
the words of one who was reared there, Freeland was simply
a community of socially-minded individuals grouped about a
Rochdale mercantile establishment, who "hoped through the
instrumentality of the Rochdale to provide themselves with
homesites, and a pleasant environment." In the vernacular,
Freeland hoped to do away with middlemen.

Fifty years afterwards, Marvin Sanford, who has lived in
a number of more or less idealistic communities, defined
Freeland pretty well. To him it was "a settlement of farmers
buying their own goods from their own store, selling their
products through it, and shipping on their own vessels." The
profits of the cooperative store were to be applied on the
purchase of land for members of the cooperative. Freeland's
early years were quite successful. Its newspaper, the *Islander,*
had a little trouble with the Post Office Department, and
was barred from the mails briefly, seemingly for its stout
defense of the self-styled anarchist members of Home Colony, of which more presently.

The Freeland colonists also had a piece of bad luck in
1902, when their boat was wrecked. The salvage and repair
bills came high. In spite of this, the annual report for 1902
showed members "to have been paid 4 per cent on their investment."

Though the red-hot Socialists at Equality took occasion to
sneer in print and to refer haughtily to the Freelanders as
"a profit-sharing, interest-paying outfit," the latter seemed
not to mind. And the Freelanders themselves were not immune to the snobbery of doctrinaires. In a colony statement,
they spoke of Freeland as having "no saloons, slaughter
houses, or *cigar factories.*" Neighboring Burley Colony, it will
be recalled, did have a cigar factory, and was thus, one sup-
poses, beyond the pale—as the pale was understood by decent, honest, staunch Rochdale people.

Like so many community enterprises, the Freeland colony
did not end with a crash, or with a detonation of any sort. It
simply, as a former member put it, petered out. He set the
demise as "around 1905."

By the time Edmond S. Meany, Washington historian, got
around to writing (in 1909) of the unorthodox communities
of Puget Sound, all except one had disappeared, or were at
least moribund. Professor Meany obviously felt somewhat
apologetic that his beloved Puget Sound country should have

harbored such packs of assorted radicals. He admitted that any future historian, coming upon "a bare recital of so many attempts at more or less socialistic colonizing" would be justified in believing that Puget Sound was a favorable place for "originating new schemes to change the social order." Then he set out to guide the "future historian" into proper channels of thought. All of these colony efforts, said he, were exotics. "Nearly every member," he went on, "was recruited and brought to Puget Sound from some other State." This statement is comical, for at the time the good professor was writing, a majority of all citizens of Washington had been born elsewhere.

Professor Meany remarked, comfortingly, that what he called the "normal citizen" of Washington had looked at these colonies "with equanimity, heedless of any taint such schemes might cast on the reputation of the State, and perfectly willing that the plans should succeed if, the promoters' hopes could be realized." This statement is far from the truth. Every one of the colonies he wrote about had met, first, coolness, then downright hostility, then even persecution at the hands of "normal" neighbors, many "normal" county officials, and most of the "normal" newspapers of the region. A casual study of Puget Sound newspapers of the time reveals constant ridicule and often savage attacks on the several colony experiments.

The professor came nearer the truth in his guess as to why the Sound attracted so many exotics. "The mildness of the climate," said he, "and the ease with which the necessities of life could be obtained from the soil, the forests, and the waters of the Puget Sound Basin are the main reasons why such experimenters have directed their efforts toward this region."

Professor Meany was wrong again when he spoke of these colonies as things of the past. There still remained, as he was writing, a community of anarchists called Home, a few miles south of faded Burley in Pierce County. Home, at the time the professor was writing, may have been quiescent, but it was only a brief lull. Less than a year later, Home was front-page news on Puget Sound and in Los Angeles, Chicago, Boston, and way points.

Like the others, Home Colony was a child of the hard times and idealism of the late nineteenth century. It was founded on the shores of Joe's Bay on Puget Sound by three families from a short-lived Socialist colony called Glennis, near Tacoma. They were thoroughly disillusioned in regard to Socialism and cooperation of any kind, except in the matter of land, which they thought should be owned in common by a group or society, and portions of it rented to individuals. So, in 1897, the Mutual Home Colony Association came into being.

As soon as the Home pioneers had shelter over their heads, they naturally founded a paper, first named the *New Era,* which castigated Socialist communities. A year later James F. Morton, Harvard, 1892, and Phi Beta Kappa, arrived to look at the place. He told the colonists they were anarchists, and thereupon founded an organ destined to make considerable noise. In a moment of genius he named the paper *Discontent, Mother of Progress.* A close reading of this paper's brittle files shows that *Discontent* was more interested in sex than in economics. Every issue contained at least one article, and often several articles, concerning "the rights of Woman in sexual relations" and other aspects of this interesting subject. The paper quickly attracted to the colony all sorts of offbeat characters. Soon the paper was coming out boldly for what it termed "free love."

Meanwhile, the individualistic Home colonists were logging, their hens were laying well, their bees busy in the fireweed. Up went Liberty Hall, a forum where presently Emma Goldman came to lecture. Home's population rose to one hundred, as more reconverted Socialists arrived to rent a piece of colony land for ninety-nine years, and to erect homes. All went swimmingly until September, 1901, when a self-styled anarchist shot and killed the President of the United States in Buffalo, New York. Patriots in Tacoma suddenly thought of the other self-styled anarchists living on Joe's Bay, just across the Sound. They chartered a boat to take them, three hundred strong, to Home, where they planned to apply the torch. Cooler heads prevailed, however, and the anarchists were not disturbed in their homes. But the editor of *Discontent* was arrested (charged vaguely with printing "obscenity"), the paper was barred from the mails, and the post office at Home was closed—for good. The colonists' mail henceforth arrived at Lakebay, two miles away.

The colony continued to grow slowly, and around 1905 received a number of Russian Jewish families to settle on Mutual Association land. Elbert Hubbard, the sage of East Aurora, New York, came to stay a week and to write a favorable piece about Home in his immensely popular *Philistine*. Other noted, or at least notorious, characters visited the place, among them Harry Kemp, the tramp poet; Big Bill Haywood, the Wobbly; Dr. Ben Reitman, who taught the Home school for a while; and Emma Goldman again. A new and larger Liberty Hall echoed to the eloquence of vegetarians, single taxers, birth-controllers, pantheists, freethinkers, monists, Mormon missionaries, and exponents of Esperanto and Koreshanity. All were listened to at Home, and everybody had a wonderful time.

The great activity at Home Colony did not go unnoticed around Puget Sound. Stories of horrible sex orgies there became current and popular with the "normal" citizens in the area. Much of this talk stemmed from articles in the uninhibited *Demonstrator,* which had filled the void when *Discontent* fell under the Post Office ban. Complaints of neighbors came to Pierce County authorities: certain anarchists of Home were given to bathing in the nude, men and women together. The charges were true enough. The simple Russian peasants who had come to Home many years before had brought their custom of mixed nude bathing. It had been going on at Home for a decade, and without a comment.

Pierce County deputies arrested one man and four women. They were convicted on charges of indecent exposure. The trials made excellent news copy throughout the West, and in many Eastern papers.

At this period Home had a new paper, the *Agitator,* edited by Jay Fox, an old-time labor organizer who dated back to the Haymarket bomb affair in Chicago. Editor Fox wound up and came forth with a sizzling editorial, "The Nudes and the Prudes," which got him into jail, charged with advocating disrespect for law. He was convicted and sentenced to two months in Pierce County jail. On appeal, the state supreme court upheld the verdict.

The I.W.W. and other radical groups the country over took up the case and made it a *cause célèbre* in all liberal circles. The Free Speech League, forerunner of the Civil Liberties Union, and headed by such well known persons as Lyman Abbott, Brand Whitlock, and Lincoln Steffens, joined the battle. Money was raised for an appeal to the United States Supreme Court, which found the verdict to have been proper. Fox went to jail for six weeks, and was then pardoned unconditionally by Governor Lister of Washington. He returned to Home, and there he lives in 1951, mellow now, perhaps the last of the gospel anarchists.

In retrospect, Home Colony would seem to have been the most successful of all the social experiments on Puget Sound. This is probably so simply because Home had no ambition to change the world. The people at Home cared nothing for what the world might do so long as it did not interfere with affairs at Home. The Mutual Association was dissolved many years ago, and the land parceled out to members. Yet the ties of the colony must have been strong. In southern California, late every summer, the Home Colony alumni hold a picnic which is attended by as many as forty persons who come from as many as six states to talk over the days when idealists and cranks of every kind and degree made the place on Joe's Bay the widest known Erewhon in the United States.

It seems odd that scarcely a writer on the political and economic atmosphere of present-day western Washington has paid any heed to the possible influence of the unorthodox colonies. There is almost nothing about them in print. Yet they preceded the left-wing unions of the shingle-weavers and the revolutionary Industrial Workers of the World which for two decades kept much of the Puget Sound country in a state of nerves. What is more, these labor organizations discovered the Puget Sound region to be far riper for unionism than any other section of the Northwest.

The Socialist and other colonies also preceded the so-called Seattle Revolution of 1919, a general strike which tied that city tight as a knot for five days. Both the later C.I.O. and Technocracy found a special welcome around Puget Sound. The proponents of Dr. Townsend never discovered a softer spot than Puget Sound. The ablest edited and most successful labor daily the West Coast has ever known was the *Union Record*, of Seattle, whose editor was Harry Ault, whose boyhood was spent in the Brotherhood of the Co-operative Commonwealth at Equality.

The first strike in the Northwest by the Newspaper Guild took place on Puget Sound.

The bloodiest battle the I.W.W. ever staged in the Northwest was the so-called "massacre" at Everett, a Puget Sound city.

Although it was a wholly unfair remark, and was made in

the heat of political debate, it is perhaps of some significance that a congressman once referred, on the floor of the House, to "the forty-eight states and the Soviet of Seattle."

One of the favorite pieces of apparatus of professors of politico-economics is the assembling of enormous charts showing the percentage of Republican and Democratic and "other" votes by years. These are supposed to prove something. Yet one can study these charts and still fail to find any connection between them and the economic and political atmosphere patently to be sensed in a given region, such as, say, Puget Sound. I believe the temper of Puget Sound to be conditioned in some part by the Erewhons of the Puget Sound Cooperative, the Equality Brotherhood, the Freeland Association, the Burley group, the Glennis Socialists, and the Mutual Home Colony Association.

PART FOUR

HAMLETS

1.   The Wheat Field

WHILE THE RAW NEW CITIES BUSTLED WITH ACTIVITY AND
fought for attention in the Northwest, and prayed their noise
would be heard in the monied and supercilious East, life of a
sort continued at the whistle-stops and at crossroads that
were never even to hear a locomotive. Life in these hamlets
might be serene, but there was nothing exciting about it. The
passage of a railroad train, or the arrival of the mail in the
Star Route man's buckboard, was the marker of time.

Then, perhaps once in the age of man, and never oftener,
it seemed the vagrant fancy of Fate to select one or another of
these outposts to become, for a brief instant, the outstanding
place in the whole region, a place to dim the gaslights of
Portland, to drown the clangor of Seattle's cablecars, to be
talked about and sometimes to be looked at in pictures, in
such distant parts as Chicago, New York, and Boston—even
in London and Paris.

There was no rule for these things. Man could not plan for
them to happen. They happened in spite of man, often to his
great sorrow, and almost never were they of any advantage
to the community. For a moment, however, they lifted some
peaceful or merely dreary crossroads into the white heat of
newspaper headlines to make its affairs of equal importance
to a mass murder in Chicago, a graft exposé in New York, or
a parade of the Ancient and Honorable Artillery Company in
Boston.

It so turned out, in the summer of 1902, that the tiny
village of Creston, in the wheat country of eastern Washington, was to be one of these headline makers. On August 3 of
that year, a rancher I know named Oscar Lillengreen drove
into Creston to get shaved. He found George Dodd's barbershop fairly seething with talk, not, as usual, about baseball,
prizefighting, or wheat prices, but about Harry Tracy. Word

149

had just come to Creston that Tracy was hiding out on a ranch near the village.

In August, 1902, Harry Tracy was as notorious throughout the Northwest as Jesse James had once been in Missouri. In the sixty days before Oscar Lillengreen's visit to Dodd's barbershop in Creston, Tracy had escaped from the Oregon penitentiary, had evaded a thousand or more militia troops of Oregon and Washington, and numerous posses of deputy sheriffs and their bloodhounds, and had made his way, on foot, by stolen buggies and commandeered boats, from Salem, Oregon, north across the Columbia River, on to Olympia and Seattle, and so—or such was the news at Dodd's barbershop—and so to the wheat fields near Creston. The Oregon badman had covered not far from five hundred miles. On the way he had found it necessary to shoot and kill seven men, four in Oregon, the others in Washington.

Like everybody else, Oscar Lillengreen was excited. "Soon as I got shaved," he told me years later, "I looked up the town marshal, an old friend of mine named Charlie Straub. He said there was sure enough a reward of $4,000, out for Tracy. We talked about it. Some other men were there too, including Dr. E. C. Lanter, Maurice Smith, attorney, and Joe Morrison, a section foreman on the Northern Pacific. Straub remarked that there was none of us couldn't use a piece of that $4,000.

"Well, I tell you, nobody argued that statement. The wheat crop was poor enough. Squirrels had been eating what little there was. We also knew about Tracy—and those seven dead fellers. We weren't cowards, but any man is likely to think a couple of times before he gambles his life against one-fifth of $4,000. We dallied."

The five men dallied all night, but by morning they had made up their minds to tackle the Oregon badman. "We didn't form a dashing posse, the way it goes in the movies," Lillengreen remembered. They just hired a rig at the local livery stable, piled into it, together with their guns, and struck out.

"We got to the Eddy ranch where Tracy was supposed to be hiding about four o'clock in the afternoon," Lillengreen recalled. "We saw one of the Eddy boys working in a field quite a piece from the barn. We went up to him. We could tell he was mighty nervous. Scared-like. Acted queer. Charlie Straub asked him if he had seen any stranger around there. Eddy didn't even look at us. Muttered something about a man having been around there but had gone away. Just then I saw a man come out of the barn. He saw us too, and ducked back inside. Right off quick he come out the other end of the barn and started running for the wheat field, fifty yards off. He had a rifle, and he started shooting at us as he ran.

"We didn't just stand there. We scattered, and all hands hit the dirt. The bullets were dusting all around us, but nary a hit. We got into action. All five of us were shooting. And one of us got him in the right leg. He stumbled. That's when he was hit, as we found out later. But he kept on, and plunged into the wheat, which was probably three foot high. We could follow his progress as the stalks waved. We kept on shooting into the wheat for quite a while. Then we quit. Everything was quiet."

Well, here he was, the Oregon badman, in the wheat. The five men who had set out to get him were in no hurry. They wanted to divide that $4,000 five, and not four ways, or two ways. The sun had now gone down. Twilight settled over the wheat field. The five men spread out around, the better to watch all sides; and by now other manhunters were gathering. Lillengreen said they numbered more than a hundred. All hands took places around the grain.

"Pretty tedious night," Lillengreen recalled. "The only break in it came about half-past ten. We heard a single shot somewhere in the wheat. All was quiet again, and it remained so the rest of the night. By morning the crowd around the field was better than four hundred men.

"Soon after daylight, a bunch of us moved into the wheat, our guns ready. About seventy yards in we found the outlaw. He was dead enough. His body was covered with blood from head to foot. He was lying on his back, a Winchester across his chest, and a Colt .45 in his right hand. There was a big hole over his right eye. It was clear he had shot himself in the night rather than bleed to death from the leg wound. He had tried to plug the wound with a handkerchief, but it wouldn't plug good."

In the big crowd around the field were newspapermen from the major cities of the West Coast, and from Chicago and New York. There was at least one photographer, and the first piece of business after discovery of the body was to pose the dead thug neatly on his left side, gun in hand, finger on trigger, with the tall wheat as background, to make a picture that was to sell in postcard size by the hundred thousand.

Creston, population 216, was in the headlines across the nation, and up and down the Atlantic coast. A Tracy cocktail soon made its appearance. A passably good five-cent cigar was named for the late outlaw. Ten or more women suddenly appeared, each to claim she was the widow of the great man. Within thirty days a melodrama with Tracy as the leading character had taken to the road.

One is not to think, however, that the five brave men who ran the outlaw to earth were to get their $4,000 without further effort. The Lincoln County sheriff put in a bid for it. But when Tracy's body was shipped by rail to Salem, Oregon, three of the purposeful posse went right along with it, guarding it every moment, until they saw it buried deep in the prison graveyard. One is glad to know that the five men got the reward. "For my part," Oscar Lillengreen told me, "for my part it come in very handy. The wheat crop hadn't got any better."

For one hectic day the population of Creston rose by well over 500 per cent, and almost as quickly returned to its normal figure of 216. The tremendous affair of Harry Tracy seems to have had no material effect, other than related, on Creston or its citizens. The town remains today about what it was in 1902. Yet Tracy did not die wholly in vain. He supplied a most interesting topic of conversation that has lasted into the present, and bids fair to last at least another half-century. Meanwhile, Tracy, variously described as King of Bandits, the Lone Bandit, and the Oregon Outlaw, has been appearing regularly, first in the dime novels, later in the true-crime magazines, and now in the comic books.

2. Disaster in June

EXCEPT FOR HARRY TRACY HIMSELF, THE AFFAIR AT CRESTON was a most enjoyable occasion, a sort of Fourth of July in August, complete with notable fireworks. It wasn't to be that way, almost a year later, with Heppner, which the vagaries of chance were preparing for headlines of a most tragic kind.

It had been a long sweltering day, the 14th of June, 1903. The sun traveled across the Oregon sky in a steady blaze that shriveled the wheat and sent thousands of sheep to find such shade as they could in the creek bottoms. Since dawn the windmills on the ranches had stood motionless. Heat blurred the vision as it shimmered in waves up and down and across the sides of the barns.

It was even worse in the village of Heppner, county seat and trading center of a vast sheep-and-wheat region. Set in a narrow valley along tiny Willow Creek, Heppner was hemmed by stark hills. Not a breath of air moved all that interminable Sunday. Tar oozed from the seams of papered shacks. Clapboards curled on the better homes. Dogs slunk under porches and panted. The children couldn't go swimming, for there wasn't enough water in Willow Creek to cover their knees.

But four o'clock brought welcome signs of relief. The sun abruptly disappeared. A breeze came up, fitful yet strong. The sky turned gray, then black. Heppner people began to feel better. They could tell that a cooling shower was about to break the hot spell, just as hot spells had been broken time out of mind.

A few big drops of rain splattered the parched roofs. The leaves of the cottonwoods along the creek rustled nervously, and turned to the rising wind. Then the sky, as black now as midnight, was split by a bolt, followed by thunder that sounded in the close valley like the crack of doom. And the rain came down.

Heppner folks were used to quick, violent storms. This one seemed to be particularly violent. Water poured down in volume such as the oldest inhabitants had never seen. Hail came intermittently, but so thickly it began to pile up in dooryards like so much snow. The valley and the village were lighted every few moments by savage flashes in the dark sky. Thunder rolled in continuous volleys. It was a wonderfully exciting time for the youngsters. They stood at windows and saw Willow Creek rising as they watched. Fathers and mothers were unworried. The creek might fill its banks. It might overflow. It had done so in the past. But there could be no danger. There were no dams upstream to give way, either on Willow Creek or on Balm Fork, which joined the creek just above town.

The cloudburst continued for perhaps twenty minutes, and

with it the hail, the wind, the thunder and lightning. Then the clatter of the tormented elements was wholly lost in a new and sudden roaring. It wasn't a noise that grew. It was a noise both mighty and full-blown when it struck the ear, and it brought men up out of their chairs and women out of their kitchens.

This strange and new noise was the meeting, just above the village, of two monstrous great torrents rolling down Balm Fork and the main creek, merging into one thunderous wave of water bearing trees, ranch houses, barns, horned cattle, sheep, fences, and baled hay. The two torrents made one flood, not of Old Testament size, but sufficient to wipe out the village of Heppner.

The new steam laundry, filled with heavy machinery, held out for a few minutes, long enough to dam the waters twenty feet deep, and long enough for a few people to see what was upon them and to start running. Then the dam gave way, loosing the rush of a lake into the streets. Carrying children, a few of the running men managed to get out from under; but not many of the women. Skirts were long in 1903, and the muddy water quickly made them unbearably heavy. The women sagged, stumbled, then disappeared.

George Conser, cashier of the town bank, and his wife were at home. They heard the noise. Just then the first tremendous wave struck. The windows and doors caved in. The Consers started upstairs, water at their heels. The whole house groaned. It wrenched. It reeled, and then its lower portion collapsed. Away went the Consers in their ark of an upper story.

August Lundell had an instant in which to run out of his house and to climb a big cottonwood tree, dragging two youngsters with him. Just then the Lundell house caught the full force of the wave. It left its foundations, keeled over, and came rolling past, Mrs. Lundell clinging to the top side. Her husband reached out and caught her, like a sack of mail at a way station, pulling her into the God-given tree, where the Lundell family lived it out while Heppner was being destroyed.

At the fine Palace Hotel, three stories of staunch brick, Mrs. Phil Metchan, wife of the owner, who was absent, saw her two Japanese houseboys run out of the hotel toward the flood, a block away. She couldn't tell which way the flood was going to move next, nor how fast. She picked up Dorothy, her two-year-old, and ran for the nearest hill. Back at the hotel the waters were already trickling into the cellar.

Meanwhile, the two Japanese lads were performing heroically in pulling women and children from the water and débris; and one of them gave his life in the effort.

Now the wallowing houses, the cattle, the sheep, the mud, hail, and human beings were being piled up in a hideous jam against a row of stout trees; and another dam was formed, to hold just long enough to make and loose a second lake. It struck the little hand laundry and ground it instantly into a mass of kindling, killing the seven or eight poor Chinese within. Then the wave went on to leap at the Mallory home, picking it up entire, with Gus Mallory, postmaster, bedridden in an upper story, and sent it on a careening voyage halfway across the village, to come to rest on Main Street, facing the front doors of the Belvedere saloon.

In the Belvedere a quiet poker game had been in progress; and between interest in the cards and the terrific din of the storm the players did not know that Heppner was already under water. Then the flood hit Main Street. Frank Roberts, owner of the Belvedere, ran out to look for his family. The other players left too, and old Dick Neville, Civil War veteran and bartender, waved them on their way. "I'll stay with her till she floats," he cried, and turned down another jolt.

At the Heppner railroad station Agent Kernan and family got a look at what was coming from the upper part of town. They ran for the hills. Kernan, however, had forgotten something, but whatever it was, it was scarcely worth the effort, for when he emerged from the depot this time, Time had caught up. The rush of water tore him off his legs and whirled him into the dreadful hodgepodge of bodies, timbers, and other débris.

Meanwhile, two young men of Heppner had set out on a heroic mission. They were Leslie Matlock and Bruce Kelley. They saw the first big wave when the steam laundry gave way. They knew it was too late to do much for Heppner. It might even be too late to warn the hamlet of Lexington, ten miles down Willow Creek, and the hamlet of Ione, eight miles beyond Lexington. But a man, two men, could try.

While Kelley hurried to get horses at the one livery stable not in the path of the waters, Matlock ran to Bisbee's hardware store for wire cutters. They would have to ride overland, and between Heppner and the lower villages were fence after fence of taut, well strung barbed wire. The store was locked. Matlock kicked in the door, got two pairs of cutters, then ran for the stable. He and Kelley mounted and took off, heading over the big bare hills in order to get out of the Willow Creek Valley, now running high and fast with damnation.

It was tough going, overland. All downhill or uphill, and no road. Dark, too. Every half-mile or less was a fence to be cut, a dangerous business, with the sky flashing and every strand of wire potentially an electrode, ready to burn a man to a crisp. And down came the rain, while the great hailstones beat and frightened the horses.

The animals responded well for speed, but they were hard to manage at the fences; and the cutting took time—true, only a few seconds here and a few seconds there, but they began to add up when racing a flood tearing hell-bent down Willow Creek. The two riders came in sight of Lexington to find that the waters were going to beat them by about two minutes; but no lives were lost, though several houses were destroyed. At Lexington the waters were damming up just as the two horsemen pounded past on the hillside above the settlement. "We can beat her to Ione," Matlock yelled to Kelley. On they went.

There were more fenecs to cut. Both animals were tiring. The riders urged, praised, cajoled, demanded, using every trick known to experienced horsemen. The animals responded, too, and presently came galloping into tiny and unsuspecting Ione. Matlock looked over his shoulder to see what Willow Creek looked like down here. It was bank-full, swift, mean-looking, but the flood hadn't come yet. It wasn't in sight.

The sudden appearance in the hamlet of two men on wind-blown horses brought people running out of their houses. "Get to the hills!" Matlock cried. Ione's total population went into action. Driving such stock as they had at home, and carrying such household treasures as they could, they moved to the hills on either side of the settlement. The flood waters hit the village within minutes after the horsemen arrived, but not a life was lost.

Back in tragic Heppner the worst had happened. Within half an hour—some said twenty minutes—after the steam-laundry dam gave way, the flood had thundered and boiled through town, and the waters had receded until they no more than filled the banks of Willow Creek. It had been as quick as that.

The worst was bad enough. When Phil Metchan rode into the stricken village early next morning, he saw a sight he recalled vividly almost fifty years later. It was a big, long two-horse farm wagon moving slowly up Main Street to one of the several emergency morgues. On it were bodies piled one upon another, twenty, thirty of them, with the long mud-matted hair of women hanging out over the wheels. All over Heppner Death was moving in somber processions, riding in wagons, carts, hayricks, even in rubber-tired buggies.

Here and there, like the Palace Hotel, a few buildings still stood—the Odd Fellows Block, the courthouse, the Fair Store, and the Belvedere saloon and its upstairs Opera House. The latter structure's two big floors were covered now with bodies laid out under blankets and pieces of canvas.

In between these few larger buildings was the ghastly débris of the deluge—the barns and houses that had become mere piles of jackstraws in which searchers looked for, and found, still more bodies. Before night two companies of Oregon militia had moved in to help.

All day and all night, by the light of flaming torches and dim farm lanterns, an army of men dug graves while another army of carpenters sawed and hammered to make coffins. Many would be needed. The death count rose steadily throughout the day: 180 at noon, then 200, and finally 225 bodies were recovered, among them that of the brave Japanese lad who had lost his life in saving others. (In 1951 his was the only Japanese grave in Heppner Cemetery, and a granite marker tells of his courageous deed.)

Two hundred and twenty-five people had died in Heppner between half-past four and five o'clock. Nearly all were killed, not by drowning but by the dreadful battering. The number of dead amounted to nearly one-quarter of the population, for Heppner's wildest booster in 1903 claimed no more than 1,100 citizens, men, women, and children. Not even the larger and far more celebrated Johnstown Flood took so proportionately great a number of inhabitants.

Heppner in mid-century is still a small place, little larger than in the times of its Deluge.* Old survivors walked with

*It does not like being referred to as a village. It is an incorporated municipality, and within its borders is a building whose façade has in bold letters the legend "City Hall."

me over the site of the disaster, pointing out where the
Conser house had stood, and the site of the steam laundry
that had held to form the first fatal dam. (Other survivors
say it was a small hospital building and not the laundry
which made the dam.) They showed me where the Lundell
home had stood, the house that became an ark. The Mallory
house yet stands. So does the stone building that contained
the Belvedere saloon and the upstairs Opera House. This is
now a drugstore, with apartments above. Old-timers said that
neither saloon nor opera house could survive their use as
morgues; the association in the minds of townspeople could
be dissipated neither by alcohol nor by dramatic and musical
art.

Heppner's local history naturally divides into two periods;
one before, one after the Flood. Still among living survivors
of that tragic day is Leslie Matlock, now a patriarch, pointed
out to strangers, and most properly so, as the Heppner Paul
Revere, the man who rode out the Flood on horseback. It
required some persuasion to get him to tell me of the ride,
about which he was modest. When walking the streets, however, the old hero is likely to be carrying a gold-headed cane,
on the brightly burnished head of which is an inscription, dim
but still legible: "Leslie Matlock, Presented by the People of
Ione in grateful remembrance of Heroic Ride during Flood
at Heppner, June 14, 1903." (The late Bruce Kelley got a
cane too.)

The flood and the ride made a front-page item in the press
all over the country. Young Kelley and Matlock received
telegrams from two circus outfits, offering them featured
jobs. They declined. Heppner went promptly to work to clear
the flood damage, then to rebuild along the banks of Willow
Creek as before, and to carry on as a trading center and
rail-shipping point for sheep and wheat.

When I was there last, I stood and looked long at the creek
where it enters the village, trying to imagine how this piddling
stream could have desolated even so small a place as Heppner, and filled a graveyard. In places the water was perhaps
six feet across, never more than ten feet, and very shallow.
Survivor Frank Roberts was with me. "It was the damming
up behind the steam laundry that did it," he said. "When
she let go—well, that's all there was to it."

In June, each year, the Heppner *Gazette-Times* runs a re-
minder of the Flood; but the event is little remembered out-

side of Morrow County, whose somewhat weird courthouse stands on a hillside at Heppner. An alleged event concerning the town clock in this structure is proof of the wondrous magic worked by Time on what men like to think are their memories. It is worth setting down here in some detail, for what we are obviously dealing with is that threshold over which fact passes to turn instantly into fancy. It is the threshold of the imagination which processes some dull or meaningless item to bring it into accord with the love of the marvelous. It is the threshold to the manufacture of myths often called folklore.

No piece of folklore is more immune than that a watch or a clock stopped miraculously at some particular moment of great drama. In sober accounts of events, no less than in fiction, we have a timepiece stopping at the instant of some eminent man's death, often miles away; or stopping at the very moment of some tragic or historic event, as so many Southern clocks did when General Lee gave his sword to General Grant. It is the same romantic notion so immortally ensconced in the verses, "It stopped short—never to go again —when the Old Man died."

Well, that was exactly what happened to the town clock in the courthouse tower at Heppner, according to several residents; its hands had halted at half-past four on the afternoon of June 14, 1903. I had fully expected this piece of misinformation, for I had been exposed to a good deal of similar folklore. And so, when I came to contribute an article on the Heppner flood to the *Oregonian,* I mentioned that the stoppage could hardly have occurred, because the works of the clock had not then been installed. I got this information, I think, from the late Phil Metchan, already mentioned in this chapter.

Letters of protest and abuse rolled in from flood survivors living in all parts of the Northwest. Many were heated, several almost incoherent. The writers termed my article fiction. What the writers meant, of course, was that my account, based on careful research, did not jibe with their memories of what had happened forty-seven years previously. It is most instructive that no two letters quite agreed on the clock or anything else concerning the day of the Flood, except that there was a town clock. Two correspondents remembered that the clock stopped "at 4:15." Others held that the hands stopped at varying times from 4:45 to 5:15. Half a dozen more were just as sure that the clock did not stop at all, and of these one remembered how "it tolled the weary long hours of that terrible night." Incidentally, the courthouse then stood, and still stands, well up a hillside, far beyond the highest waters of the flood.

The Heppner *Gazette-Times* was most courteous in helping to clear up the business for me; and in good time I received a letter from Mr. O. M. Yeager, a Heppner native who has lived there for the past sixty-seven years. "There *was* a clock," Mr. Yeager was good enough to write to me, "*but it was not running.* The tower of the courthouse had settled a little, enough to stop the works. Many weeks after the flood, Judge Ayers had me take a carpenter to the tower and put in some new supports. Then a watchmaker came and got the works to running smoothly."

This would seem to correct the memories of those who had heard the weary hours of the night marked by the striking of the clock, and of those who were just as certain that the clock had stopped at the instant of disaster. I wish that I could believe this would settle the matter. But I don't. I feel sure that in all oral tales of the flood, the clock in the Morrow County courthouse will either continue to stop, or to toll the weary long hours, so long as a survivor has the power of speech.

Yet the supporters of this and of other myths are not to be charged with fabricating. They are merely poets, poets seeking to fasten a measure of that mysterious thing we call art to an event or a thing that is graceless without it.

3.   The Affair at Copperfield

THE UGLY BLOT ON THE MAP OF OREGON THAT WAS COPPER-field no longer exists. It was removed by Miss Fern Hobbs, who was twenty-five years old and weighed exactly 104 pounds when fully dressed and wearing her gold pince-nez.

The Copperfield affair was one of those happy combinations that no newspaper can resist, and no reader either. For a period of several days Miss Hobbs and Copperfield were known and discussed all over North and South America, in the British Isles, Holland, France, Germany, and in the Antipodes. It seems only reasonable to assume they were discussed also in Mongolia and in Madagascar.

There was no copper in Copperfield. The town grew suddenly up among the rocks and sagebrush of a grim, narrow canyon of the valley of the Snake River on Oregon's eastern border. That was in 1909. It had one purpose; namely, to cater to the uninhibited appetites of more than two thousand men who were engaged on two nearby construction projects, the one a railroad tunnel, the other a power plant. The town was near the far end of a tortuous sixty-mile branch that left the Union Pacific's mainline at Huntington. A mixed train came and went three times weekly.

Within a month from the day the first stake was driven, Copperfield had blossomed like some evil flower of the desert into a long street of false-front buildings which contained saloons, gambling joints, a big dance hall, and several places of easy or no virtue. There were also a couple of general stores, a tiny railroad station, and warehouses.

For three years or so the town thoroughly enjoyed vice and debauchery undisturbed by any sort of law, city, county, state, or federal. Remote from all other communities, and so situated as to discourage visitors from "outside," it grew fat in the manner of parasites. It was anything but dull. Gang battles between the two construction crews took on epic proportions. These were fought mostly with rocks and beer bottles, and thus resulted in many casualties, though few deaths. Drunken men lay on occasion strung out like railroad ties, both in the snow and in the dust under the blistering sun.

There were no arrests, ever. Copperfield bragged that it had no peace officer and no jail. The county seat and sheriff were at Baker, 150 miles by railroad.

Then, early in 1913, the construction jobs began to peter out. Fewer men were employed. Competition for the remaining trade became stiff. The saloonkeepers began feuding. One night the joint operated by a Montenegrin named Martin Knezevich burned to the ground. He and his wife narrowly escaped cremation. Pretty soon another saloonkeeper, William Wiegand, discovered his place to be on fire, and found the blaze to have been carefully prepared with oil-soaked kindling.

Then, rather suddenly, the faction to which Wiegand belonged decided to incorporate Copperfield as a city; and in a dubious election H. A. Stewart, saloonkeeper, was named mayor, his partner Tony Warner made councilman, along with William Wiegand. Just to fill out the ticket, Wiegand's bartender and handyman, one Charles Kuntz, was made third councilman. The first official act was to issue city liquor licenses to all saloons except that of Martin Knezevich.

Mr. Knezevich then made the grave error of appealing to the county prosecutor in distant Baker. The prosecutor made his weary way to Copperfield, remained between trains, then returned to his base. He said that Copperfield was so filled with wrangling and threats he could in no manner get at the bottom of the trouble.

Mr. Knezevich, a glutton for trouble, next appealed for protection to the county sheriff, who was Ed Rand, six feet six, and well over two hundred pounds. Sheriff Rand dutifully went to take a look at Copperfield, and so back to his office. He reported he could make neither head nor tail of Copperfield's troubles.

The new saloon of Mr. Knezevich again caught fire, and was saved from total destruction only by the quick work of the proprietor and his friends.

Such was the condition of affairs in mid-1913. At about this time Governor Oswald West, in Salem, the state capital, 450 miles across the mountains from Copperfield, began to hear of Copperfield and its troubles. Letters from ranchwomen complained that their sons were being debauched in the hellholes of the Gomorrah on the Snake. Presently, the governor received a petition signed by some fifty actual citizens of Copperfield, including the teacher of its only school, asking that the State of Oregon step in to do what needed doing, and which Baker County authorities had refused to do.

Governor West notified Baker County authorities to clean up Copperfield. They advised the governor that Copperfield was a city with its own government. West replied that Copperfield had no government, that it was being run by and for a collection of underworld characters. He named Christmas day as the deadline; if the place had not been cleaned up by then, the state would take steps.

Copperfield celebrated Christmas in its usual style, which was to say, in drinking, fighting, gambling, and whoring.

Os West was, and is, a man of his word. He was by all odds the most brilliant governor Oregon ever had. He was also a Democrat in a commonly Republican state, a militant

Dry in a Wet state. Although absolutely incorruptible, he was a shrewd politician with an extraordinarily fine sense of drama as a part of the fitness of things.

So now, on the first day of 1914, he called his private secretary, Miss Fern Hobbs, and told her to prepare resignations for the signatures of the city officials of Copperfield. He also dictated to her a proclamation of martial law. Then he instructed her to board a train for eastern Oregon, and proceed to Copperfield. In order to save time, he suggested, she might wire ahead to the mayor, saying she wished to meet with officials and citizens at the city hall immediately on her arrival.

"At the meeting," the governor went on, "you will call upon city officials who are in the saloon business for their resignations. If they refuse, you are to declare martial law, disarm everybody in town, close the saloons, and ship all liquor, bar fixtures, and gambling equipment out of Copperfield."

Miss Hobbs got aboard the train. With her, and in civilian clothes, were Lieutenant-Colonel B. K. Lawson and five soldiers of the Oregon National Guard, and Frank Snodgrass, chief of the penitentiary guards. All seven men were veterans of the Philippine Insurrection. All were large, rugged, and bold fellows.

With Miss Hobbs and her delegation on the way, Governor West called the press. He had just dispatched his secretary, he said, to clean up the mess of Copperfield. He pointed out that though Sheriff Ed Rand of Baker County was six feet six and weighed over two hundred pounds, he had admitted he wasn't big enough to handle Copperfield. "My secretary Miss Hobbs," the governor thoughtfully added, "is five feet three and weighs 104 pounds." The papers and the wire services got the idea, and at once shared it with their readers.

The news even reached Copperfield, and Mayor Stewart of that city replied with what he considered fine humor. "We are decorating the city with ribbons," he told the Associated Press, "and will try to have some flowers for Miss Hobbs."

Informed of this sparkling repartee, Governor West remarked that he thought flowers appropriate. Weren't they traditional at funerals?

While these amenities were being exchanged, Miss Hobbs and the Guards rolled on over the Cascades, then into the desert country of eastern Oregon. Years later, when I asked what her thoughts had been while heading for Copperfield, she admitted to a few qualms at the outcome; but apparently it never occurred to her to be frightened.

Miss Hobbs is obviously a self-reliant person anyway, and she had made her own way since high school. Born of New England parents on a Nebraska ranch, she had come to Oregon in 1904. While acting as governess in the family of a Portland banker, she had learned stenography. While working as secretary to the president of a title guarantee company, she studied law. In 1913 she was admitted to the Oregon bar. Governor West hired her as chief stenographer, and soon made her his private secretary.

And here she was on the way to what an Oregon clergyman had just termed "the poisonous toadstool of the badlands," a description, commented Governor West, of pure whitewash and arrant flattery.

On the bitterly cold morning of January 2, Miss Hobbs and guard changed from the Union Pacific's mainliner to the creaking mixed train for Copperfield. Four hours later the train wheezed into the stark white canyon, coming to a stop in front of a board shanty labeled Copperfield. Massed around the depot and strung out along the single street was the entire population. Three saloonkeepers and a bartender, comprising the mayor and city council, gave cheery if cynical welcome to Miss Fern Hobbs as she stepped down from the coach.

Miss Hobbs, demure enough in any garb, was dressed in a modish blue suit, and wore a muff and neckpiece of black lynx. She had on black shoes, and a black hat with two Nile-green feathers set rakishly at one side. Which was very good reporting for a male of the Associated Press. She carried a businesslike briefcase. Her grave blue eyes looked out from behind gold-rimmed glasses. She was escorted forthwith to the barn of a dance hall and took her place on the platform. The place was soon crowded with the citizenry, a good many of whom were patently wearing holsters under their jackets. Colonel Lawson and two Guardsmen stood at the back of the hall beside the one door.

This was one occasion when the speaker of the day really needed no introduction from the toastmaster; Miss Hobbs came directly to the point. She opened the meeting by saying that it was the governor of Oregon's hope that Copperfield officials would resign at once. One who was there recalls that she spoke clearly and precisely, unhurried, with neither undue aggressiveness nor apology in her tone. When she had finished, she passed the prepared resignations to the four saloonkeeper-officials.

Those gentlemen considered the documents briefly, then each rose, one after another, to say he had no intention of resigning.

The crowd grew tense. Miss Hobbs looked out over the audience of several hundred, which included a few women. There was no booing; there were no smart cracks or remarks. Only silence. At the door, Colonel Lawson held his breath, wondering. This was the moment when the situation could turn into a bloody riot.

Miss Hobbs stood for a long minute as though transfixed. Then she took the proclamation of martial law from her brief case. She called to Colonel Lawson. He came forward. He read the message to the still silent audience. Then he placed the mayor and the three councilmen under arrest.

"You will now disperse in an orderly manner," Colonel Lawson announced in closing the meeting.

Both citizens and their officials seemed stunned. Lawson had another message for them. "Attention" he called in the booming tones fit for a colonel. "As you leave the hall you will turn over your revolvers and other weapons to my men at the door."

One after another the citizens of Copperfield meekly passed their many revolvers and a few long knives to the Guardsmen at the door, who piled them in an anteroom. There were more than 170 revolvers turned in.

As they filed outside, weaponless, Copperfield citizens found more bad news. The Guardsmen had been busy. Every saloon and gambling house on the street now had a bold and official *Do Not Enter* sign tacked to its closed door.

The mixed train was at the depot, ready for the return trip to civilization. Colonel Lawson escorted Miss Hobbs to the coach, which she boarded and waved her goodbye. As they pulled out of deathly silent Copperfield, the twilight of approaching night touched the stark canyon, and Miss Fern Hobbs suddenly recalled some verses in the Fifth Reader of her schooldays, and wondered if curfew really had rung in Copperfield that night.

Miss Hobbs returned to spend the night in Baker, county seat, where she reported by wire to Governor West. Colonel Lawson and men continued the process of instilling virtue and sobriety in Copperfield.

The attorneys of Copperfield's embattled saloonkeepers

were getting busy in Baker; and now the telegraph instrument in the little depot began clicking out threats of lawsuits, injunctions, and other legal hocus-pocus. Colonel Lawson ignored them, and stationed a guard to prevent the sending or receiving of messages. Two other Guardsmen, rifle at shoulder, patroled the street after dark, keeping an eye on the closed joints. But nobody attempted to enter the posted premises. Copperfield's badmen seemed to have lost heart.

After dark, however, there was a moment of excitement near the depot. The guard at the telegraph office heard a noise and saw two shadowy figures leap aboard a speeder, which began to snort and chatter. Before it could get under way, the guard took into custody Councilmen Wiegand and Warner, who had had the idea of breaking arrest. They were confined in the depot.

But Copperfield was really stunned at its first meeting with the law. The citizens remained indoors throughout the night, and drinkless, too. It must have been a desolating experience. And although Colonel Lawson and men had no further trouble, next day brought ten additional National Guardsmen to the scene, sent by the governor as an added precaution. They went to work rolling barrels of liquor and beer to the depot, where they were loaded into a commandeered boxcar, along with cases of wet goods and an imposing collection of faro tables, "twenty-one" tables, birdcage games, roulette wheels, cards, chips, and dice.

Meanwhile, Colonel Lawson staged a meeting in the dance hall to form a provisional government, and appointed Sam Grim, a carpenter, mayor.

Despite threats of lawsuits, Colonel Lawson shipped all of Copperfield's liquor and gambling devices to Baker, where they were placed under state bond in a warehouse. Then he and his men returned to the state capital, where Miss Fern Hobbs had already resumed her usual duties in the governor's office.

Miss Hobbs was also being startled at what can happen when the hot glaring rays of limelight are focused on a prim and genuinely retiring soul. The Copperfield incident got a tremendous press, in Oregon, in the United States, in the Western Hemisphere, and in foreign parts.

In provincial New York City, for instance, and for three days running, the Copperfield affair crowded the Becker-Rosenthal case for front-page position. In far-off Salem,

Oregon, Miss Hobbs received wires from the *World, Journal,* and *Times,* asking for "I was there" stories, all of which she ignored.

The *Literary Digest* devoted pages of comment to the affair. The organized Dry forces in all parts of the United States sent messages to Miss Hobbs, referring to her variously as a modern Jeanne d'Arc, as a latter-day Carry Nation, or at the least a womanly knight on a white charger, banner unfurled, a challenge to the forces of evil. Even a part of the press saw her in relation to mythical or historic women of the ages. The Brooklyn *Eagle* ran quite a temperature, comparing Fern Hobbs to "Jael the Kenite woman," to "Zenobia defying the army of Aurelian," and to "the great Catherine of Russia in all her glory."

Miss Hobbs's mail was flooded with homemade poems written in her honor by total strangers; and laced with letters from other total strangers asking her hand in marriage.

In Oregon a group of militant suffragettes erupted and started a boom of Hobbs for Governor.

Vaudeville agents in Chicago and New York offered her contracts to appear on the circuits they represented. A San Francisco impresario wanted to star her in a stage play.

The trade press of the liquor industry banged away with much heavy-handed satire.

In England, the Copperfield story escaped all bounds. One read that Miss Hobbs took off for the hellish place in command of a full battery of field artillery, plus machine gunners, in a special train; that she snapped commands to her troops, and had them unlimber and train the heavy pieces on the doomed city.

On the heels of the daily press, magazines in the United States carried articles on the subject.

The alumni secretary of Massachusetts State College, Division of Agriculture, at Amherst, suddenly showed great interest in locating Miss Hobbs's father, J. A. Hobbs, an alumnus who had apparently dropped from sight. Mr. Hobbs was now the father of a famous daughter.*

As to Copperfield, it was dying by the moment after

---

*It will amuse residents of Oregon and Washington to know that despite the publicity attending the secretary of the governor of Oregon, the alumni secretary of the Massachusetts college addressed his query, typically enough, to Miss Hobbs at Olympia, the capital of Washington. That was in 1915. Most Easterners still have the same difficulty with the geography of the Northwest.

January 2, 1914. I believe it was killed no less by Governor West, Miss Hobbs, and the Oregon National Guardsmen than it was by shame and ridicule. It scarcely breathed or moved an eyelid after the raid. It had surrendered without a shot. Its vaunted lawlessness had turned to meekness within two hours, or between Miss Hobbs's arrival and departure.

Copperfield was dead, and it disappeared altogether a few months later when fire, again of unknown origin, destroyed a block or two of the jerry-built structures. No saloon ever reopened. Citizens drifted away. The doors of the few remaining buildings fell from their hinges. Windows were broken, or removed. Curious coyotes dodged in and out of the old joints, while owls went in the windows to perch and sound their melancholy notes.

The railroad depot was closed. Copperfield for a time was a flagstop, then wholly ignored. Sagebrush grew up and over and through the rotting plank walks. The everlasting winds blew, and sand covered and at last buried deep the last remnants of Copperfield.

Ex-governor Os West is my neighbor in Portland. I often talk with him. He is as alert and as energetic as most men of forty, and though he pretends to be retired, his occasional letters to Oregon newspapers are the joy of editors and readers who like sharp and sometimes blistering comment on local and state affairs.

I often see Miss Hobbs, who lives in Portland in a modest home as neat and tidy as the Curfew of Copperfield herself. She still weighs 104 pounds. Her eyes are clear and blue behind her glasses. There is not a gray hair in her trim head. She lives as quietly as she has always lived, except for those dreadful few days so long ago when duty required otherwise. I doubt that the Copperfield affair had the least effect on her as a person or on her career. She practiced law in Portland, and later became secretary to the business manager of a local daily, from which occupation she not long since retired.

The subject of Copperfield bores her. She had much rather talk of her two years with the Red Cross in World War I, in France, and with the American Army of Occupation in Germany. *That,* she says, and her eyes light up, was a real adventure. One gathers that she considers the affair at Copperfield to have been a deplorable incident.

PART FIVE

MYTHS

1. "Whitman Saved Oregon"

EVERY REGION PLANTS AND CAREFULLY TENDS ITS MYTHS. It finds others already full grown, usually in the demonology of native aborigines. But there would seem to be no standard and reliable recipe for the manufacture of a good, satisfying historical myth that will stand the test of time. That most of us believe the Pilgrims to have lived in neat log cabins a full century and more before that admirable type of house was introduced in New England was due to a misunderstanding of an archaic term, used in their memoirs, by the Founding Fathers at Plymouth—that is, an error.

On the contrary, the myth that the first battle of the Revolutionary War was not an American rout but a victory for the farmers of Lexington grew from a series of accumulated fictions, both in text and in pictures, that were composed over a period of approximately a century by purposeful men —that is, unconscionable lying.

Then there is the myth erected on the proposition that a monstrous lie not only can but should be used as an effective instrument to discourage untruth. A classic example of this method is the mythical cherry-tree-and-hatchet story concocted for his best selling *Life of General Washington* by the Reverend Mason Locke Weems.

There are many other myths, now firmly enshrined in history, so far as a majority of Americans are concerned, which were composed partly through error or mischance of some sort, and partly by conscious invention. That the conscious invention is often a pious or patriotic fiction does nothing to make the myth a historical fact, though its perpetrators are usually excused on those grounds.

In the Northwest we have accumulated a fair number of home-grown myths. Among the more popular and harmless of these are that Stanford White himself drew the plans for the Union Station and Hotel Portland in Portland, and for the late Hotel Tacoma in the Puget Sound city; that the terminal morraine near Tenino, Washington, is really an abandoned city of prehistoric mound builders; and that the Lewis and Clark Centennial Exposition, held at Portland in 1905, actually brought to Oregon an immense number of new settlers.

Not in the class of the minor aberrations cited above is the Reed College myth. This is downright harmful, though less so than it was twenty and more years ago. To expose the myth properly calls for a bit of background. Now one of the outstanding liberal arts colleges in the United States, Reed was founded in 1911 at Portland, on a bequest from Simeon Gannett Reed and his wife Amanda, natives of Massachusetts who had been among Oregon's pioneers. To be its first president came William T. Foster, a Harvard graduate who was discontented with American colleges. Reed, he announced, would not be hampered by hallowed traditions, most of which he termed petrified errors.

The good people of Oregon were presently aware of something new and disturbing in their midst, when President Foster remarked that intercollegiate athletics had no place in Reed's program, and that fraternities or sororities would not be tolerated. The effect of these distinctly un-American heresies in the Northwest, where football and fraternities were held in greatest esteem, was profound. Perhaps "shocking" is the word.

Gathering a faculty of brilliant young men as discontented as he with the attitudes and methods of conventional colleges, Foster went ahead to set Reed well on its rocky and forthright way; and his successor, Richard F. Scholz, of the universities of Wisconsin and of Oxford, where he had been among the first group of Rhodes Scholars, raised Reed's standards still higher. And now began to great Reed myth.

The myth was based on two wholly unrelated names which were conjured up out of the recent past to plague the college as nothing before or since. Indeed, no writer of fiction would care to try the credulity of his readers by inventing a fantasy of coincidence such as was used, most savagely, to discredit Reed College.

A native of Portland named John Reed had died a Soviet hero in Russia, and had, moreover, gained such popularity among communists that he was buried, with titanic ceremonies, along with Lenin in the wall of the Kremlin. That neither John Reed nor any of his family had any connection by blood or act with Reed College mattered not at all. The myth was born, and in time became so adamant that there are Oregonians who still believe that John Reed founded and supported Reed College for the express purpose of training young commissars. Lesser canards have ruined institutions.

The John Reed myth got the stoutest kind of support from the fact that an obscure labor leader named William Z. Foster had just headed a tremendous and violent strike, and had thus become a national front-page menace. Well, wasn't he the same William Foster who had trained young communists at Reed College, of which he was the president? One and the same man—that was the way the story had it. It was made to order.

Nobody connected with Reed College at that period, or since, has ever doubted the sinister effect of the John Reed and William Z. Foster myth. From it stemmed the scandalous trinity of "communism, atheism, and free love" which was so firmly attached to Reed College that a quarter of a century has not wholly dissipated the libel. Yet the school has persevered. In the Northwest today Reed is either quite wonderful or simply dreadful; it has never been charged with mediocrity. In Portland it has finally achieved almost as high a reputation as it has long since enjoyed in such foreign parts as Harvard, the Massachusetts Institute of Technology, the University of Chicago, and Oxford in England.

The John Reed myth belongs somewhere between the myth of our alleged mound builders and our one great outstanding illusion; namely, that "Whitman saved Oregon." Here we are no longer dealing with local antiquarianism, or even with regional history, but have a notable myth of international stature. Courageous and honest Marcus Whitman had nothing whatever to do with the myth, which began to take shape not long after his tragic death in 1847. The manner of his death, which was that of a Christian martyr, doubtless has had a good deal to do with the persistence of the myth for nearly a century.

Stated briefly, the facts are that Marcus Whitman, educated as a physician, and engaged as a missionary by the American Board of Commissioners for Foreign Missions, went to the Oregon country in 1836, and with his colleagues established Indian missions near Walla Walla and elsewhere in the region. In the fall of 1842 he suddenly resolved to "return to the States." His reason for going on this hazardous journey, just when winter was about to settle on the Plains, was to plead with his board to annul its order to discontinue three of the four mission stations established. Dr. Whitman believed that closing of these stations would be fatal to the Lord's work in Oregon.

Dr. Whitman made the journey, much of it in the dead of winter. After nearly six months of truly Spartan travel, he arrived in Boston, was successful in having the mission order annulled, and returned to the Walla Walla mission in 1843, coming much of the way with the first of the great covered-wagon migrations from Missouri to the Oregon country. Four years later Dr. Whitman, his wife, and some fifty of his people at the mission were set upon by Indians and massacred. They thus became martyrs in the Christian tradition that began when the Romans burned early converts at the stake, or tossed them to lions.

There is no historical question as to the founding of the Whitman mission, nor of the massacre, nor of anything else in the Whitman story except in regard to the famous Ride, and the reasons for and the results from it.

The myth apparently began to take shape some twenty years after Whitman's death. By 1895 it was in fullest flower. By then, too, it had become so strong and so romantically beautiful that Harvey Scott was beginning to rumble and protest in the *Oregonian* of Portland. Even earlier, Edward Gaylord Bourne, a professional and brilliant historian, had started hammering away at the myth; and he was later joined by a colleague, W. I. Marshall. As for the rest, both professional and amateur historians held fast to the myth, defending it and attacking the "cynics" with savage enthusiasm. The Whitman myth was essentially that the good missionary-doctor had saved the Oregon country for the United States.

In 1842, when Dr. Whitman started his famous Ride, the sovereignty of Oregon was in some doubt. It was then occupied both by Americans and by British subjects, the latter mostly men of the Hudson's Bay Company. The myth has it that Whitman, at Walla Walla mission, overheard Bay Company men exulting that Great Britain had already won Oregon because its subjects there were the most numerous. It pictures him as thereupon determining to journey to Washington, no matter the winter fast approaching, to inform

President Tyler and Secretary of State Webster of the danger, and to organize and to lead back to Oregon, in the spring of 1843, a mighty caravan of thousands of American settlers sufficient to hold the region against the worst Great Britain could do.

The myth portrays Whitman exacting from Tyler and Webster the promise to delay negotiations with Great Britain until Whitman should have arrived on the ground with the huge pioneer train of American settlers. It goes on to throw Whitman into a furious round of activity, writing pamphlets, making speeches, and otherwise agitating throughout the eastern United States, trying in every manner to electrify the country to the danger, as well as the opportunity, for patriots to act. The myth shows Whitman as a modern Moses leading his people over the mountains, supervising everything, and at last bringing the pioneers into the promised land, there to hold staunchly against the horrible machinations of the British Empire as represented by the Hudson's Bay Company. "Wonder grows," wrote Leslie M. Scott in 1911, "that in these days of enlightenment, of writing and printing, the story could grow to such absurd proportions and to so many fiction details, and that it could gain such wide credence."*

Now for the facts of the Ride: Whitman did not see either Tyler or Webster. He did not make any speeches. He did not write any pamphlets. As for the emigration to Oregon in 1843, that was being planned, mostly by restless Missourians, even before Whitman had left Walla Walla; and the wheels of the so-called Great Migration were rolling over the Oregon Trail before Whitman joined the emigrants, who, incidentally, had never, until he joined them, even heard of Marcus Whitman. On the journey West, if leading members of the train are to be believed, Whitman's services as physician were valuable but not indispensable, and his aid as guide was small and unneeded. Able guides were in the train.

Meanwhile, the acquisition of the Oregon country by the United States was going forward steadily on a basis of horse trading, called diplomacy by historians, and not wholly or even chiefly because of settlement and occupation.

Who were the mythmakers and why did they concoct the myth? On the findings of Professor Marshall,† who de-

---

*In *Oregon Historical Quarterly*, Vol. XII, pp. 375–384.
†See his *Acquisition of Oregon*, 2 vols. (Seattle, 1905). It is dreadfully hard to read, but it is the definitive work on the Whitman legend, and it has never been seriously challenged.

voted twenty-five years to the job, they were the Reverend H. H. Spalding, the Reverend Cushing Eells, and W. H. Gray, all of whom had worked with Whitman at the missions. They were patently seeking an indemnity "of between $30,-000 and $40,000," from the United States Government, for destruction of the Walla Walla mission by Indians. To this end they used the actual martyrdom of Whitman and his pretty wife, together with many of their comrades, to gain sympathy. This surely was right and proper. But they also manufactured the political embellishments to show that Whitman was no less a martyr to Christianity than he was to patriotism to his country. Combine these two items and you have an appealing, an almost indestructible myth, a myth for the centuries.

Almost as an afterthought, the mythmakers also injected into their account a piece of anti-Catholicism; namely, that the Whitman Massacre was instigated by the combined efforts of Roman Catholics and the Hudson's Bay Company. That this charge was as false as it was terrible was made clear by Professor Marshall.

Marcus Whitman's fame in the Northwest is secure without the he-saved-Oregon myth. An imposing shaft to his memory has stood for fifty-odd years. It is something of a historical shrine. A small and excellent liberal arts college also honors his name. So does a county of Washington. No history of the region fails to cite his courage and the purity of his character, as well it should. Fiction is not needed to add stature to the earnest and honest man who fell a sacrifice, with his family, to "the noble effort to change a savage wilderness into a seat of civilization."

2. The Dead Stacked Like Cordwood

THE MYTHS ABOUT DR. WHITMAN'S RIDE APPARENTLY DID not begin to take shape until some twenty years after his death, and another thirty years passed before any determined effort was made to combat them. Thirty years is a head start difficult to overcome; and although the Whitman myths no longer appear in a majority of school texts, past generations to whom the myths were as Holy Writ have passed them along by word of mouth as a part of Northwest history. It is to be doubted that the Whitman-saved-Oregon story will ever be wholly laid. It is the kind of thing too many people want to believe.

All I know of the Whitman myths comes of necessity from books. But it has been my fortune to watch while another myth was being manufactured on the spot, under the eye, so to speak; and to see it grow and burgeon to monstrous size even while my colleagues on Portland newspapers, and the men of local radio stations, worked like Trojans to beat it down. Despite their labors, and some work of my own to the same end, the myth has survived, at least in most part, and bids fair to outlast all of us who combatted it.

Perhaps I should use the plural, myths. They are many, and have to do with a tragic event of Memorial Day, 1948, which any history of disasters will list as the Vanport Flood. Vanport was a typical wartime housing project, built hurriedly in 1942, to care for the 40,000 workers in Columbia and Willamette River shipyards. It was situated at Portland on low ground between the two rivers. People continued to live in its low-rent houses after the war's end. In May of 1948 residents numbered approximately 18,500.

The spring months of 1948 brought fairly high, though not record, waters in rivers all over Oregon and Washington and Idaho; and more than a few Vanport residents had begun to fear for their safety during the last week of May. The Federal Housing Authority reassured them, pointing to the "indestructible" dikes around the project. The authority announced also that if Vanport should appear to be in any danger, which was a remote possibility, a blast of the Vanport siren would be sounded in ample time to permit everyone to leave the place.

Well, on the afternoon of May 30 water surged through a dike almost simultaneously with the blast of the "warning" siren; and minutes later Vanport's thousands were fighting out of the trap, through one inadequate exit, to higher ground. The water was coming from no mere leak. A whole section of dike suddenly collapsed. The backed-up waters of the Columbia rushed through in deluge volume. Within a few minutes Vanport was inundated to its roofs.

The mythmaking started promptly. At the height of the excitement, while scores of houses were careening wildly in the boiling waters, with men, women, and children clinging to roofs or perched in the tall cottonwood trees, people in the employ of the City of Portland and of Multnomah County gave statements to the press and radio that a century later may be related as sober truth. These statements were to the effect that the lower stories of the Vanport houses "were clogged with hundreds of bodies," and that "so many people have been swept out into the main stream and down to the ocean that the number will never be known." One voice from this vaguely identified source was heard to estimate the dead at three thousand persons.

These inexcusable and dreadful falsehoods were sufficient to unleash the mythmakers and set them in full cry. Then and there these psychopaths started to manufacture the legendry or myths of the disaster. They picked up the wild statements of the city and county employees and conjured them into an even wilder collection of marvels, several of which were ingenious to an irrational degree, and should take rank in any collection of truly monstrous lies.

The first of these myths to take root, and one which newspapermen began to batter immediately, was that 457 bodies of Vanport victims had secretly and in the dead of night been put aboard a ship in Portland Harbor for transportation to Japan. At a later time, so went the story, the bodies would be returned to the United States in the guise of Army dead, the coffins draped in flags to support the imposition. The reason for this elaborate subterfuge, of course, was that "they," meaning the officials of Vanport Housing Authority and the Army engineers concerned with Vanport, wanted to cover up the tragic results of their criminal incompetence. For good measure the Portland Chamber of Commerce was quickly added to the "they." This was on the assumption that the Chamber feared the lasting effects of a great disaster on the reputation of Portland, and would go to any extreme to minimize the number of casualties.

While this fantasy was going the rounds, and making good progress despite denials in the press and over the radio, another got under way: A presumably adult woman phoned to all her friends, who appear to have been both many and gullible, to say she had seen, with her own eyes, a room in a cold-storage plant in Portland that contained "at least 600 bodies" of Vanport victims. "They were stacked in that room like cordwood," she said, and the story was distributed as fast as phone numbers could be dialed. This female liar went on to explain that the stacked bodies in cold storage were being held, in sort of escrow, until after Portland's annual Rose Festival, due in early June, in order to hide the true size of the disaster until the festival crowds should have come and gone.

Then, while 457 bodies were on their way to Japan, while 600 more were safely in cold storage locally, and while uncounted other corpses were floating down the Columbia, while these horrors were in progress, still another myth was started: A big school bus, loaded with children fleeing the waters, had been caught by the first wave through the dike and wholly engulfed. Half a dozen, then half a hundred people had seen the bus, later, when the waters had subsided a little, still submerged, pathetic little arms and legs protruding from the windows.

These are fair samples of the myths that were circulated as God's truth within twenty-four hours after the dike gave way. It was naturally difficult for reporters to run down the original sources of the hideous falsehoods. But at least two women and one high-school youth were put on the spot by police and reporters. The youth admitted his prevarication and said he had wanted to impress his friends. I could not learn that the women admitted anything beyond the mild retraction that they got the story "from a friend."

For the most part these and other myths still prevail, four years later, in that sizable segment of the population which loves incredible tales above all else. I have been disappointed that I have not yet heard of some little Vanport boy, preferably named Hans, who stayed on the leaky dike all that fateful night, holding his tiny thumb to the hole in the barricade until the waters at last swept him down the river and so into the Pacific, possibly to Japan.

There was a quite understandable resentment locally because the so-called warning came only with the rushing waters. As late as the morning of the tragic day, the housing authority had posted and distributed a memorandum throughout Vanport, saying without qualification that there would be ample time after the alarm, if any, was sounded. Well, there wasn't ample time, or any time. A friend of mine who lived in Vanport, Bob Clark, together with his wife and four daughters, almost lost their lives because the Clarks had believed the 'housing authority. They had expected a warning. Clark, a veteran copydesk man of the *Oregonian,* still resents the lack of any warning, but resents even more the fact that Mama and Papa were shown, indeed, exposed, to their children as not knowing what they were talking about. Like most other parents in Vanport, Mr. and Mrs. Clark had told their children not to worry, that there would be plenty of time to collect and take with them their dolls and bikes and blocks and picture books. Then came the first brown boiling wave through the dike, and everyone fled, doll-less, bikeless.

"The kids," Mr. Clark has related, "knew instantly that Mom and Dad had told them wrong. The youngsters lost all their most cherished possessions. After that experience, Mom and Dad might pass the test as parents, but never again will kids put their whole trust in them. Pop and Mom just don't know the score. I resent that more than the loss of everything we owned."

It is quite impossible to arrive at the grand total of flood deaths reported by the mythmakers. Bob Clark was keeping score but lost count at around 1,800 dead and missing. David Ayre, then news editor of the *Oregon Journal,* recalls the bitter phone calls from readers charging his paper, and the *Oregonian* as well, with foul conspiracy to suppress the truth about the disaster. Again and again he was told that the dead were stacked like cordwood. One woman wrote to the *Journal:* "We can't understand the reports that only a handful of people are missing after the flood. We *know* there are more. . . ." On that same day, Dr. Earl Smith, county coroner, told the press that he had begun to hope "the death list will show less than a dozen," and though his estimate turned out to have been very close, his statement had little or no effect on the consummate liars. Now, years later, one can hear that the press somehow or other had a stake in the business, and that the local papers "never began to tell the truth about the number of dead."

Incidentally, the total dead in the Vanport disaster numbered fifteen. There were no missing, none unaccounted for.

In addition to the mythmakers, there were also the experts, the barbershop bores, the men who knew right off where to put the blame for the high waters of 1948; and they placed it on the heads of lumbermen. "The cutting of timber and the devastation of the huge forests," one of these pundits said in my hearing, "brought erosion and thus permitted a too-sudden runoff of the unusually deep snow and heavy rains of the early months of 1948."

That sounds well enough until you know that in June of 1894, long before any amount of logging had been done, the Columbia River and its tributaries swelled to flood proportions that made the 1948 high water seem inconsequential in comparison. The official high mark in 1948 was 29.9 feet, and came between May 30 and June 1. The 1894 high mark was on June 8, and it was 33.2 feet, or more than three feet higher. The flood of 1894, it should be kept in mind, came at a time when little timber had been cut, either in Oregon or in Washington.

But experts of any sort will have no truck with simple explanations. Otherwise they would not be experts. I prefer to believe that the high waters of 1948 were due to a combination of deep snow, much rain, and a hot sun.

As for congenital liars, the mythmakers, they are probably as immune to psychiatry as they are to police action or exposure by the press. So long as many human beings prefer the miraculous, the impossible, and the preposterous, or even plain romantic hogwash, to anything remotely resembling actuality, the preservers of myths will flourish. A century from now, despite the printed record, such people will still be speaking of the 1,800 lives lost at Vanport, a city of Oregon, a region that was saved for the United States from the greedy British by Dr. Marcus Whitman, who rode across the continent in midwinter simply to admonish the President to gird his loins and set a vast migration of covered wagons to rolling.

And when the multitudes of Vanport dead have been properly stacked like cordwood, and when Oregon is safely American, some other future gull will remark of Reed College, in Portland, that it was founded by the late John Reed, commissar in chief of American communists.

3. "I Was with Custer," He Cried

THE ONLY LIARS OF EXCEPTIONAL TALENT I HAVE MET IN the northwest were a couple of masqueraders who were posing as historic characters; and one other, even more talented, perhaps indeed of genius, who claimed to have taken part in a historic event which I had always believed, and still do believe, to have had no surviving participants —at least, not among white men.

Of the two characters in historic false face, whom I met at different periods, each said he was the one and only Jesse Woodford James, who was shot and thoroughly killed on the morning of April 3, 1882.

I met the better liar of the two Jesses in 1948. It amused him no end, he told me, that people actually believed he had been killed by Bob Ford sixty-six years before. Showed you how cheap newspaper talk got around. Showed you that newspaper fellers would print any old thing that would help peddle their papers. Come to think of it, take one thing and another, we'd be better off without no newspapers. Now, take the way editors put in the paper that the man who shot Lincoln—Booth his name was—you take the way them editors said that a posse caught Booth in a barn and killed him. Nothing but a brassbound and copper-riveted lie. Booth, he hid out some place or other, and got clean away. Lived somewheres down in Colorado for another forty year, and what's more . . .

After another ten minutes on Booth, every bit of it quite wonderful as preparation for the story to come, and related with assured innocence, my Jesse James gradually led up to his alleged killing at the hands of Bob Ford. "It wasn't me Bob shot," he said. "Was another feller, name of Charlie Bigelow." He went on to say that they laid Charlie Bigelow away in the grave prepared for Jesse James. A pleasing footnote to the affair—and one knew it was a footnote by the way the narrator changed his tone from a major to a minor key—the pleasing footnote was to the effect that Jesse James himself attended his own funeral, and sang hymns with the other mourners. My narrator chuckled softly as he delivered this portion of the tale, reveling in the humor of a man singing at his own obsequies, then remarked that in his youth his voice "wasn't bad at all."

The other Jesse James came into my ken in 1936. He was very old, and extremely tall. His voice shook, but he managed to let me know that Bob Ford had never even attempted to kill him, but had shot another man. Good old Charlie Bigelow did not come into this account, but whoever it was that died on this occasion "was given decent Christian burial." As for Jesse James, which is to say, my narrator, he simply hid in a nearby barn and was an interested spectator to the proceedings.

Both of these men were genuine masters of the oral tale. In long and elaborate narratives, filled with complex irregularities that had to be handled expertly if the stories were to hold together, they had me at least half believing, momentarily, in their authenticity. And that, I think, is the test by which monumental lies should be judged. The listener must be dazed, or lulled, by sheer artistry into temporary belief, just as a fine stage play accomplishes the same temporary belief on the part of the audience.

Good as both these Jesse James characters were, my candidate for the post of champion liar is, or was, an ancient relic I knew as Silent Simpson. I haven't seen or heard anything of him in fifteen years, and he may well be dead, but his great art is still fresh in my memory. I like to reflect on him. He was, so he assured me in what I knew were italics and capital letters, *the* Survivor of the Custer Massacre, a newsworthy event of June 25, 1876, when General George Armstrong Custer and his men were wiped out by assorted Indians on the Little Big Horn River.

Silent Simpson had been, said he, a noted scout for General Nelson A. Miles and other Indian fighters. He was a tall, thin, and neolithic old party, creased and wrinkled like the rocks of the Bad Lands. He looked the part of our classic plainsman and Indian fighter to perfection. Sitting on a box in front of his battered tent, which he had erected on the banks of Johnson Creek near Portland, one of his long legs thrown over the other, a pipe in his mouth, the two slits of his eyes peering intently, he was exactly right. I could not detect a false note in his make-up. And his knowledge of the battle on the Little Big Horn was apparently quite sound, if the many monographs I have read were authentic.

"I was there," he told me, "on the morning of the 27th, two days after the Massacre, when Lieutenant Bradley, scouting ahead of Terry and Gibbon, came upon the scene and discovered me to be the sole survivor of that gallant band." Silent Simpson paused a moment for effect. I used it to get my breath. Then I went to work on him. He was ready for my questions. "Where was I?" he lowered his voice but let the words come out with great intensity. "Where was I? I was laying in a slight depression on the field—sore wounded, I can tell you—underneath a dead hoss of the Seventh Cavalry, and I had laid there for two whole days." His gimlet eyes fixed me fast. "For—two—whole—days," he repeated.

That was the climax of his story that had required two hours in telling—two hours of magnificent, inspired, incomparable lying, complete with little asides and digressions, all of them apt, each adding some small refinement, and authenticity, to the main narrative; never a false note; every phrase becoming an integral part of the story; the pace perfect, never hurried, never dragged; the pauses for emphasis expertly timed; the few imprecations given in quiet voice, invoking hate, or sympathy, or horror, or astonishment—whichever was called for—while the old liar's voice rolled on and on in musical cadences most gratifying.

It was a superb performance, done with a gravity that impressed the eye as much as its earnestness impressed the ear. When Silent Simpson had finished, and only then, was I able to gather sufficient wit to question what I dazedly thought might have been discrepancies in the story. I was no authority on Custer's Last Mistake, but I had more than casual knowledge of it; and my queries must have indicated some doubts. Silent Simpson, however, met them with courtesy tinged with just the right measure of condescending tolerance. He displayed the greatest dexterity in disposing of my doubts. Any seeming discordances in the tale were erased by prompt and simple explanation which, although I can no longer recall them, were of the highest quality. My queries did not ruffle him at all. He even complimented me on my "alertness." Said he liked to have people pay strict attention. "It's the only way they can understand what happened on that glorious and tragic field of honor," he said.

Such artistry called for refreshment. I invited the old warrior of the Plains to a beer parlor, over whose bar, I knew, was one of those large colored prints of "Custer's Last Stand," put out years ago by a manufacturer of beer and ever since one of the most celebrated barroom fixtures in the West. It prompted a natural question. When his nose had been wetted, I asked Silent Simpson if he would mind indicating to me just where he had lain, sore wounded, those two days under a dead horse of the gallant Seventh Cavalry.

"Certainly, sir," the old man said. With brisk step the ancient hero moved around and behind the bar, peered intently at the great chromo a moment, then lifted his cane and placed its end smack on the felled horse you will see in the right foreground. "I was there," he said quietly, "right under *that* hoss." Then he returned to our table and blew the collar off another beer.

PART SIX

LETTERS

1. Opal the Understanding Heart

WHEN I FIRST CAME TO THE NORTHWEST, IT STRUCK ME as odd that the only writers in the region who were nationally known in a popular sense were females. One of these was Mary Carolyn Davies, the other, Opal Whiteley.

Within the region, the two writers perhaps best known were Dean Collins and Ben Hur Lampman, both of Portland, both newspapermen, both basically poets.

Where, I wondered, in this still new country, this region of the covered-wagon trains, of Tracy the Bandit, of brawling loggers and miners and fishermen, of the wild Wobblies, of sheep and cattle wars, of anti-Chinese riots, where were the hairy prose writers to chronicle these notable violences or to celebrate them in fiction?

It turned out, just a bit later, that the hairy male prose writers were here, though not quite ripe. The Northwest was in a lull between two generations of writers. The giants and pseudogiants of early and late pioneer days were either dead or had ceased to speak in full voice; and a new group had not appeared. In the early 1920's the latter, in large part, were just finishing the college courses that had been interrupted by the war, or were working in sawmills and logging camps, or on farms and ranches, or earning a living otherwise. Many of this younger generation were only beginning to inhale properly, and required only one safety-razor blade weekly. But they were busy, learning that copy should be double-spaced, that a stamped, self-addressed envelope should accompany all manuscripts, and beginning to believe that all editors were hired expressly for the purpose of keeping anything approaching literature out of their magazines and books.

As for the Messrs Lampman and Collins, they were writing unquestionably the best essays and editorials in the region, and their verse, both light and serious, was not only popular but was getting into good anthologies. But neither man was much interested in writing for a national audience.

Of the two nationally known ladies, Miss Davis was immensely successful with her light verse and short stories in the slick magazines. She was also well known as a contributor to the little or *avant-garde* periodicals that were becoming a rage. She had been born in Sprague, Washington, and lived mostly on the Oregon coast.

Miss Whiteley is not to be described so easily. She was an enigma. She was a one-book woman, too, as it turned out; but the book was actually sensational. It was entitled *The Story of Opal: The Journal of an Understanding Heart*. Nothing like it has since come out of the Northwest, or anywhere else. Nothing likely will. No less a mogul of fine letters than Ellery Sedgwick sponsored Opal's book, and printed large chunks of it in the *Atlantic Monthly*. He wrote the Introduction to the book. How many copies of it sold I do not know, nor does it matter. No other book published in 1920, save *Main Street*, created sufficient noise to be heard in the clamor about Opal's; and twenty-five years later Mr. Sedgwick remarked that the Atlantic Monthly Press was still getting many letters about it.

Not too many facts are known about Opal Whiteley. She was a fey and illusive creature who patently existed in a world of her own making. She could no more distinguish between what actually happened from what ought to have happened than could the late Calamity Jane Blake White Dorsett Dalton Utter, who also wrote a book. Thus was Opal able to arrange an account of her life with the greatest ease, though this was of no great help simply because the "facts" of her life changed from month to month, and sometimes oftener. She was probably born, about 1898, in Colton, Washington, a shameful place that has never seen fit to honor her memory with even a modest plaque. During the next seventeen years the Whiteleys apparently moved several times, and were living at Wendling, Oregon, when Opal emerged from the obscurity of a logging camp. This occasion was a Junior Christian Endeavor convention at nearby Cottage Grove.

The editor of the Cottage Grove *Sentinel* was Elbert Bede, then, as now, one of the outstanding figures in Northwest journalism. He was present at the convention and, hearing that a seventeen-year-old girl had been elected president of the group, he sought her out for an interview. So far as is known, this was the first time Opal's name appeared in print.

Editor Bede remembers Opal as a vibrant, fluttery, exotic, deeply earnest young woman, informed strangely beyond her years. She was olive-skinned, had dark hair and dark eyes, and she told the astonished Mr. Bede she was going forth among the children of Oregon to tell them of God. No gospel preaching, however. Opal said that His work could best be furthered by interesting youngsters in God's fairy creatures of the fields, the woods, the waters, and the air. She planned to give the children messages from flowers and trees, from rocks and streams, from birds and animals, from the very shells of the sea. Editor Bede duly reported as much in the columns of the *Sentinel*.

Whether or not Opal began her Christian crusade seems not to be of record. She did, however, attend the University of Oregon for a year and part of another, then took off for southern California, even then a place given over to marvels. Here, it is known, she first dedicated her life to conducting nature classes for children. The plan failed, and she sat down and composed a book. She called it "The Fairyland Around Us." It was to be bound in genuine leather and sell for $10 a copy. While trying to raise money for its publication, Opal put out a come-on in the form of a prospectus. It carried expressions of the warmest admiration for Opal from Theodore Roosevelt, Queen Elizabeth of Belgium, Nicholas Murray Butler, and the immortal Gene Stratton Porter. It is within belief that Opal herself composed these felicitations.

Yet public response to the prospectus was discouraging. Opal thereupon wrote appeals for money to Andrew Carnegie, John D. Rockefeller, and lesser whales of capital. Nothing happened. But the kindly woman at whose home Opal was rooming lent her money for a trip to the Atlantic coast.

One September day in 1919, Opal arrived in Boston, and went direct to 8 Arlington Street, to see Editor Sedgwick of the *Atlantic Monthly*. Mr. Sedgwick read the manuscript of "The Fairyland Around Us," and was not amused. He recalled later that the book was quaintly embellished with colored pictures pasted in the text by hand, and added with careful Bostonian understatement that about it "there seemed little to tempt a publisher."

Opal Whiteley, however, was something else. Mr. Sedgwick found her "very young and eager and fluttering, like a bird in a thicket." Being an old-line Yankee he naturally assumed that Opal might have kept a diary, too. Yes, she had, always. Then, said the *Atlantic* editor, that was the book he wanted, Opal's diary. The bright, shining countenance clouded. "It's destroyed," Opal replied, "It's all torn up." Tears came to the great dark eyes, as soft as those of a doe. A moment later she cheered. Her journal of many years, she said, was indeed torn up, the work of a jealous foster sister; but Opal still had the fragments, every last one of them. They were stored in Los Angeles.

Mr. Sedgwick brightened too. He had Opal telegraph for the journal fragments, and they came, crammed into an enormous hatbox. When this was opened, the editor estimated it to contain at least half a million pieces of paper. A few were of notepaper size. Others were of grocers' bags pressed carefully and sliced in two. There were wrapping-paper fragments, backs of envelopes, anything at all that would hold a few words of writing. As Mr. Sedgwick looked them over, he noted that what Opal said were her earlier efforts, at the age of five or six, were written with childish clumsiness, but that later entries showed the adult hand gradually forming. They were most convincing.

Now Mr. Sedgwick *was* amused. He installed Opal in the huge Brookline mansion of his mother-in-law. She was to live there while preparing the diary for the printer. Next to Opal's bedchamber was a large sitting room. All furniture was removed from this room, and Opal went to work. On the floor, inch by inch, she pieced and pasted together the countless scraps of her journal. They were of all colors, and so had been the pencils and crayons the young diarist had used. I doubt that the home of the Brookline Cabots ever held a gayer picture than that of this woodsprite from Oregon crawling over the Joseph's coat of her childhood labors. She was thus occupied for more than eight months.

As one by one the pages were assembled, they were typed by an editorial employee of the *Atlantic*. The cards were filed in sequence, and at last the manuscript was ready. Mr. Sedgwick has said that everything was printed just as first written, other than omissions, the addition of punctuation, and the spelling, which was "widely amended." Thus did *The Story of Opal* of the understanding heart go to the printers, and meanwhile Mr. Sedgwick was happy to run six generous installments in the famous New England monthly that still, in 1920, appeared between covers of that favorite old-time bilious hue called saffron.

The Story of Opal was a charming performance, especially so to lovers of Nature and of classic literature. At the age of six Opal was speaking to, and confiding in, a Douglas fir tree she named Raphael, a crow she called Lars Porsena, a woodrat named Brave Horatius, and many other characters who infested the tall timber country where her father —or was he her foster father?—was employed by the Booth-Kelly Lumber Company. Here and there the otherworldly tenor of the diary was broken by reference to a bottle of Castoria ("The colic had the baby today . . . but Pearl and I had drunk up the new bottle of Castoria") and other homely things.

The diary made clear that except for her communion with the creatures of her imagination, Opal's childhood had been most unhappy. Opal was—said the diary—a foster child who had been left with the Whiteleys for upbringing. Here began the mystery, or perhaps confusion, or maybe chaos: While the *real* Opal Whiteley was being taken to an Oregon logging camp with her family, she fell into a stream; and the pseudo Opal, she of the understanding heart, was substituted without Mrs. Whiteley being the wiser, an occurrence without parallel, so far as I am aware, in all Oregon.

But the original Opal was not drowned; she was rescued then and there from the dark rushing waters of the mountain stream. Yet what became of her is still as great a mystery as the name of Paul Revere's horse, though I like to hope that she grew up and lived happily ever afterward as Joan Lowell.

Opal's diary is studded throughout with French expressions. Little by little the story is developed that Opal of the diary is doubtless the daughter of Prince Henry of Orléans, Bourbon heir to the nonexistent throne of France. If the influence of heredity is accepted, then it fits neatly into the narrative, for Prince Henry was a noted traveler and explorer whose published works display his constant interest in flora and fauna. Just how neatly it fits, you begin to comprehend when you come to the acrostic which little Opal set down in her diary at the age of seven: "I did sing it le chant de fleurs," wrote the naïve child of the Oregon woods, "that Angel Father did teach me to sing of Hiacinthe, Eclaire, Nenufar, Rose, Iris, et Dauphinelle et Oleandre, et Romarin, Lis, Eglantier, Anemonoe, Narcisse, et Souci." The first letters spell Angel Father's name. Not for Opal the worn and trite strawberry birthmark method of identification.

I shan't go more deeply into the book. If copies of it are not available in all libraries in the Northwest, then it is time they tossed out their shelves of self-improvement books and stocked a volume that has few peers in the field. Opal's diary carried the fantastic little Oregon girl to England, to France, and to India, where she was soon riding in an open barouche down the streets of Allahabad, with royal outriders clearing the way for H.R.H. Mlle. Françoise de Bourbon-Orléans, which was to say, Opal herself. The day-dreams of a neurotic woman never congealed more pur-posely than this.

Within a few weeks of book publication, both author and publisher knew they were in for a highly popular success. Sales kept climbing for months. A vast circle of enthusiastic readers wrote to express their appreciation, among them foreigners such as M. Clemenceau, M. Poincaré, Lord Cur-zon, together with scientists, men of elegant letters, and other distinguished characters. I was unable to find the names of any notable women in this clamorous applause, and have wondered if the ladies were skeptical or merely catty.

Sir Edward, Viscount Grey of Fallodon, K.G., a con-firmed birdwatcher, was so taken with Opal's book that, be-ing in Boston, he asked to meet the author; and Mr. Sedg-wick, who arranged the meeting, remarked that the two nature lovers had a gorgeous time discussing wrens, pe-wits, and one thing and another. Good Sir Edward also con-tributed a foreword to the English edition of Opal's book, published by Putnam.

There was at least one reader of *The Story of Opal* who was both astounded and cruelly hurt. She was Mrs. Achsah Pearson Scott of Saginaw, Oregon, whom Oregonians believed to be the maternal grandmother of the diarist. As soon as she could assemble her wits, after reading her granddaughter's book, Mrs. Scott told the *Oregon Journal* that Opal "has sold her birthright and slandered the name of a good mother." She said Opal had not begun to keep a diary until she was past fourteen, and had never before that shown any liking for writing. Mrs. Scott added that Opal had been a good child until she "got in with a crew of mind readers in Los Angeles."

Of the hundreds of thousands of readers, none gave *The Story of Opal* closer attention than did Editor Bede of the Cottage Grove *Sentinel* (weekly, subscription rate, $2 per year). To him there appeared to be in it discrepancies, omissions, and *non sequiturs* beyond count. Mr. Bede knew all the Whiteleys, found them to be good, honorable people, and literate, with at least high-school education. He reflected that if Opal of the book were not a blood daughter of the Whiteleys of Wendling, Oregon, then she bore a family likeness that was a coincidence almost too great to accept. On second thought, it *was* too great. Thereupon, Mr. Bede acquired a hobby: While continuing to carry on his duties as editor of Lane County's outstanding weekly newspaper, he devoted his spare time to research.

Mr. Bede's first efforts included many talks with several of the Whiteleys, then they centered on the books Opal had borrowed or used in the several libraries she had haunted, in Oregon, in California, and in Boston. In the Boston Public Library, Mr. Bede learned with much satisfaction, was a copy of the will of Prince Henry of Orléans which, he discovered, contained no little of the intimate information that was also found in the many French acrostics in Opal's diary. He came to believe, too, that Opal must also have looked into the books written by Prince Henry himself. Whole sections of these, almost word for word, appeared in the girl's diary of her sixth and seventh year. In the Prince's volumes parallel passages on well thumbed pages were found to bear faint marks in pencil. Mr. Bede was beginning to think the trail was clearing.

Meanwhile, Opal's book sold enormously, reached its apex, then gradually disappeared from the best seller lists. Mr. Bede continued his hobby. He talked again with the Whiteleys, except for the mother, who, he remarks, was "saved by death from the embarrassment of the diary." He talked with friends of the Whiteleys of many years' standing. Both the Whiteleys and their friends said that publication of the diary was the first intimation they had had that Opal claimed to be a foster child.

Mr. Bede next took up the trail in Los Angeles. There he learned that Opal had possessed no immense box of diary fragments when she arrived, but that after almost two years' residence there she did have such a box. He learned that Opal had spent most of her time, day and night alike, writing by hand on paper. When not at this labor, she was mostly in the Los Angeles Public Library. Library attendants remembered her; she was pure glutton for work.

One of the many things about Opal that fascinated Mr. Bede was the problem of why, if she were born in a foreign land, and at the age of six exhibited a nimble familiarity with French in her diary, she was never known to use a word of that language otherwise. Nor could he, in his wildest moments, imagine a tot of seven who was on casual "speaking terms" with Elizabeth Barrett Browning, Henry James, Aristotle, and Aphrodite, to mention only a few of her shadowy companions of the Oregon woods.

When, in good time, the literary detective of Cottage Grove got around to it, he presented his wonderings, as well as his findings, in an instructive essay. His conclusions may be stated succinctly: *The Story of Opal* is composed almost equally of hoax and plagiarism.*

Getting back to Opal; shortly after her book appeared, she departed for England with letters of introduction from Sir Edward Grey and from our own Secretary of State. A little later she turned up in France, and at this point her trail grows extremely dim. But soon it is plain again, fairly blazing, as related, in India, where she was accepted as genuine Bourbon-Orléans by two of the great maharajas of the empire, and entertained regally by tiger hunts on elephants, stupendous fêtes, and attendance of the Bengal Lancers. News of her doings diminished, and presently ceased. So far as we in Oregon were concerned, Opal had disappeared in the mists of India.

In 1936, being in Boston for a visit, I interviewed Mr. Sedgwick, and took occasion to ask about Opal. "Opal Whiteley was no mountebank," said he. "She was, and is, a remarkable person, a strange person." He said he had taken the trouble to verify her reception in India. In reply to his queries, he had received two letters, each carrying a

*Mr. Bede's essay appears in *History of Oregon Literature*, by Alfred Powers (Portland, 1935).

regal crest, informing him that the royal master bade his secretary to say it had been his great privilege to entertain Her Royal Highness Mlle. Françoise de Bourbon-Orléans. The editor also heard from a British officer who described the turning out of the Bengal Lancers, and the tiger hunt. I asked Mr. Sedgwick if he believed Opal's story. "I believe now," said he, "more than ever I did, that her diary was a genuine thing. Whether or not she is of royal descent, I do not claim to know." He added that "Opal was touched with genius."

Ten years later, when the retired editor of the *Atlantic* published his autobiography,* he seemed still certain of Opal's genius, but he was a bit equivocal as to the truth of her story. "The child who wrote Opal's diary believed in it," he stated. One should bear in mind the fact that Editor Sedgwick was subjected to much abuse because he gave Opal's diary to the public. Letters accused him of being a party, at least of the second part, in perpetrating a monstrous hoax. Proper Bostonians and proper non-Bostonians charged the heir to the editorial chair of James Russell Lowell and William Dean Howells with committing an obscene crime fit only for editors of the more lurid Sunday supplements.

So, when in his sunset years Editor Sedgwick comes in his autobiography to the subject of Opal Whiteley, one senses that his guard is up. He remarks that for those whom Nature loves, *The Story of Opal* needs no explanation. But others, says he, who are forever demanding facts and backgrounds, asking for theories and explanations—well, those people should know that of the honesty of Opal's story he is utterly convinced. And yet, and yet—he goes on to reflect on what can happen to people who have single-track minds. They brood on the single idea. They sleep with it, wake with it. Do they not come to think of themselves as apart from the rest of mankind? Is there any among us so bold as to say where runs the boundary line that separates sanity from something else?

Is it not possible that in the heart of every little girl sits Cinderella? As the child grows to womanhood, Cinderella may be relegated to the background, though always present, ready to take over the mind for brief periods. Witness soap opera. But if the child happens to be Opal Whiteley, Cin-

The Happy Profession (Boston, 1946).

derella is made, is *forced*, to bring about her marvels, just as she did in the old story.

Well, then, once upon a time Prince Henry of Orléans visited Oregon, according to a letter Mr. Sedgwick received from an unnamed Oregonian. The correspondent wrote that his father had served under the prince in the Franco-Prussian War of 1870. This Oregonian of French descent informed Mr. Sedgwick that Prince Henry had paused, in his tour of Oregon, to chat with the old soldier, his comrade of the days when Napoleon III, or the Little, was Emperor of France, and when the poilus fought desperately, though vainly, to keep the Boche out of Paris.

If Prince Henry did visit his old comrade in Oregon, which Mr. Sedgwick thinks quite possible, then was it not likely that the appearance of a prince of the blood should have created a sensation, and word of it spread "through the lumber camps of Oregon?" The Whiteleys were residents of a logging camp. What is more likely than that the legend of the prince should have captivated little Opal, and to have grown until it dominated her life?

What is far less likely is that Prince Henry of Orléans should have commanded a regiment during the War of 1870, when he was but three years of age.

What Mr. Sedgwick seems to be saying is that *The Story of Opal* ought to be true but probably isn't. In one place he remarks of Opal that she was a somnambulist, and that she displayed other symptoms of abnormality. Persons touched with genius, so I have read, are almost certain to be abnormal. Doubtless Mr. Sedgwick was not far from right when he observed to me that Opal was at least touched with genius.

Even the skeptical Mr. Bede grants Opal's genius. Not long ago, when he and I spent another pleasant evening in discussing Opal, he expressed his reflections of thirty years on the subject. Remarking that if Henry of Orléans, who never married, had reason for sending a "natural" daughter to the United States, Oregon had one chance in forty-eight of being the place, and because of its remoteness might well have been chosen. Or, on the death of the prince, the heirs of his estate might have contrived the same thing to rid themselves of an awkward situation. Illegitimate children have made hash of the settlements of more than one estate, and appear to be uncommonly numerous in the families of the princely.

The kindly Mr. Bede grew mellow that evening, and wondered aloud if Opal's story might not, after all, be true; if she herself had not ruined it by her elaborate pains to establish a background with embellishments that simply could not be swallowed. His mind cleared quickly, however, as he recalled one by one the results of his extended research, and he then remarked that while discussion of Opal herself was always worth while, her book was pure Cinderella.

Mr. Bede has one regret. He never thought to ask Mr. Whitelcy, who he believes, as does the rest of Oregon, was Opal's real father, how he happened to name his daughter with sheer genius. "Opal the stone," Mr. Bede observed, "is both transparent and opaque. Nothing could better describe our Opal of the understanding heart."

2. The Flowering

MISS DAVIES AND MISS WHITELEY BEING, AS I REMARKED, the two nationally known Northwest writers of the early 1920's, it was perhaps to be expected that the local Oregon sensation of several years later, or to be exact, 1925, was a book by still another woman. She signed herself Virginia Brooks (Washburne), and her bid for immortality was a small paper-bound volume entitled *Tilly from Tillamook*. The author planned it as a smashing exposé of liquor and vice conditions in the state, chiefly in Portland, the "full truth about which," said she, "is unprintable."

Mrs. Brooks's prose style stems direct from Bertha M. Clay, but she is what Miss Clay wasn't, a crusader with burning eyes, using the sugar teat of fiction to warn all decent Oregonians of the sin of cities. Tilly, a slip of a girl smelling of clover, leaves rural Tillamook County to work in Portland. Here Tilly runs into more pimps, procurers, and bootleggers than I had believed Portland could possibly harbor. Virtue remains triumphant, and Tilly, on the last page, has returned to her native meadows, and to Olaf, a swain. "It's grand to be be back," says Tilly rapturously, "back to the smell of the spruce, to the seaweeds on the tideflats, to the cheese factory."

At least three editions of *Tilly from Tillamook* were needed to supply the demand, which was brisk less because of the message or of the quality of the prose, than because among the book's vilest characters were believed to be certain prominent Portland citizens, there presented under names readily recognizable, and committing sins and crimes of an abominable nature.

Tilly was a favorite for reading aloud at the old Portland Press Club, then housed in a decaying Victorian mansion which had an unusually spacious cellar where uncounted gallons of stout Prohibition-era beer were brewed and stored, briefly, in generous bins. The club's perennial secretary-manager, Charles M. Hyskell, was a retired newspaperman who denied heatedly having served as a correspondent in the Mexican War, or some eighty years previously. It angered him, too, when the wives of members phoned to tell him that the Portland Press Club was a hellhole, and should be closed by police action.

The police, however, were most courteous, and never troubled us in the least. On two occasions they warned us of impending Federal raids on our homey quarters; and members, rallied by telephone at the *Journal, News, Oregonian,* and *Telegram,* soon arrived by streetcar and taxi to remove their precious beer or to drink it on the spot. And on our annual Award Nights, when a committee presented the Guy Bates Post Silver Cup for the best local drama criticism of the year, and the ancient warrens of the old structure vibrated with song and occasionally shook with battle, the cops might drop in, but only to warn us that neighbors had reported riot and murder being committed in our club-house.

Our clubhouse had known better days, and so had our furniture. Grand Rapids golden oak sat next to the Morris period pieces of Elbert Hubbard's East Aurora craftsmen; chair legs were loose, arm rests had disappeared, while the springs of the vast leather-covered couch, in what Secretary Hyskell said was the drawing room, were viciously undependable. The particular place where you chose to sit might let you down with a jolt, while elsewhere the coiled metal would stir uneasily, and even get out of bounds. I recall the evening when Clarence Darrow honored our club with a visit. Just as he let his huge frame gingerly down on the couch, one of the springs struck out like a cobra, though harmlessly. For a moment the old man was visibly shaken, but his iron nerves were still good, and he recovered at once.

It was much the same with all our furnishings. Age and hard usage were bringing them close to the point of complete disintegration. An exception was the immense piece of wood which Secretary Hyskell characteristically referred to as the refectory table. This monstrous thing weighed nigh a ton, and was reputed to have come round the Horn. The broken-down beds in the several rooms on the second and third floors each had an alleged history, commonly ribald; and one was said to have come from the brothel of Madame Fanchon, an enterprising Portland matron of the nineties. The beds, and the club itself, were free to such members of the craft, local or itinerant, as were out of funds, or merely in need of rest.

I doubt that anyone ever knew how many roomers we had at a given time. Tramp reporters, cartoonists, and artists were still moving about the country, and their comings and goings were not to be predicted. We could give them free room, but board was something else. A succession of middle-aged housekeepers was kept on short rations—"Abundance makes for waste," Secretary Hyskell liked to say—and the poor women could spare little from their meager cupboards even to sustain distressed men of letters. If our roomers were to eat, they went to the grocery store around the corner on Burnside Street, fetched their sardines and crackers in a bag, to feast upon them in the gloomy cool reaches of the Catacombs, as our immense cellar was known, along with beer brewed by Deacon Stearns and Joe Goodwin, brewmasters who operated on a percentage, or rather a grist, basis.

Our free roomers presented a special problem when we were having a dinner, for it was Secretary Hyskell's custom to get in advance the names of all who planned to attend, then to victual according—I might say, closely. Then, just as we gathered for grace before sitting down to the boiled potatoes, the stew meat, and bread, which, with moonshine and beer, composed a Press Club banquet, down from the upstairs rookery might drop anywhere from a couple to eight or ten of our temporary and nonpaying guests, often hungry, always thirsty.

Some few of these guests tried to make themselves useful around the club, and there was in truth much to do. The fireplaces were given to smoking. Our several water closets seemed always out of order, and were of an era no living plumber could remember. The club's walls were so high that replacing a burned-out globe called for a crew of at least three men, plus chairs and a table to stand upon. Doors sagged, windows were cracked, mirrors became coated with dust.

Outside, our façade presented to the passing public the idea that although the House of Usher might still stand, it stood none too surely. A relic of the worst taste of the eighties, it rose up three stories, with an octagonal tower still reaching for the elaborate weather vane. There was a full measure of gingerbread, and decorations were set into the outside of the chimneys. The roof molted shingles. Two wide porches and their fancy railings ran two-thirds of the way around the house. They were fearfully warped. The steps to the lower porch tilted and heaved, and threw many a sober man. What we called our lawn was a field of hay, weeds, and nettles, mowed no oftener than twice a year. When taken to task about it, the secretary retorted he would be damned if he would pay fifty cents for the trifling labor of mowing half an acre.

Such was the old Portland Press Club at Northwest Davis and 17th streets, long since a victim of the wreckers, its site now a playground for little children. No visitor, and no passer-by, I fancy, failed to be struck with the old mansion's deep melancholy. Yet this seedy temple dedicated, in a manner of speaking, to Literature, seemed joyful enough inside; and it was the gathering place of young newspapermen and free-lance writers from all over the Northwest. Among them were several who meant to remedy the dismal condition of the state of letters in our region, a region whose contemporary literary scene was dominated by the clever trash of Miss Davies and the endearing hallucinations of Miss Whiteley.

It was time for the flowering. The Northwest's largest bookshop, Gill's, in Portland, had just installed on its ground floor an immense stone fireplace, and a Poet's Corner where local writers might gather to discuss their arcane craft, and to meet on occasion such traveling singers as James Stephens of *The Crock of Gold,* Vachel Lindsay, Carl

Sandburg, and George Sterling. There, too, the writers of verse might meet and talk with Grace Hall and Hazel Hall, whose collected poems had already appeared under New York or Boston imprints. At Gill's the amiable Margaret Ewing had just added to her staff the young and lively Edith Bewley, known to a later generation as Edith Bristol.

It was time for the flowering. At Salem, Colonel Hofer had founded a "Western literary magazine," the *Lariat*. At Missoula H. G. Merriam had started publication of the *Frontier,* the most influential little magazine the Northwest has ever known. All over the region small groups of people, many of them dilettantes, were forming clubs and leagues and societies and associations, all dedicated to turning these literary wastes of the Republic into a rich garden where— as one speaker so aptly said—the tender, halting shoots of fine letters might burst into fullest flower.

The first burst of this hoped-for flowering was a book, *Paul Bunyan,* by James Stevens, whom I had known as a sawmill worker at Bend, Oregon. He had been urged to write it by Henry Louis Mencken, to whose new *American Mercury* Stevens had contributed. *Paul Bunyan* was an immediate and whopping success, both popular and critical, and it made Stevens a national literary celebrity overnight. The book also set off the Paul Bunyan craze, which continues to flourish almost thirty years later. Our Press Club was proud to claim Stevens as a member, and we proceeded to throw three or four prepublication parties in his honor.

A far-roving Cockney, Albert Richard Wetjen, who had arrived in Oregon in a boxcar, which he said was more comfortable than the Press Club beds, soon came out with a book, *Way for a Sailor!,* a rousing sea tale that was made into a movie. Edison Marshall, of Medford, Oregon, who had been turning out pulp-adventure and slick-adventure stories almost as fast as they could be printed, started to widen his scene with historical fiction. Victor Shawe, a hard-rock miner from Idaho, began his Seattle Slim stories in the *Saturday Evening Post,* one of the most popular series the magazine had ever run.

Robert Ormond Case, a good club member, quit his job on the *Oregonian* and turned to fiction in both slicks and pulps, and soon had a successful book, *Riders of the Grande*

Ronde. In Seattle, Kenneth Gilbert was beginning to hit his stride with adventure stories. In Seattle, too, was the most prolific of all, Frank Richardson Pierce, who was an occasional visitor at our club. On a bet, Pierce once dictated two 5,000-word stories in six hours, and sold them promptly to a leading pulp magazine. Jim Marshall, of the Seattle *Star,* quit writing editorials to join *Collier*'s as an associate editor.

At this period Ernest Haycox, often one of our club's vice presidents, was grinding out a pulp Western every two days. He went quickly into the slicks, and several of his serials were made into wildly successful movies. He himself, however, never went Hollywood in any sense. He continued to live in Portland, and when he died, in 1951, was unquestionably the best paid writer the Northwest had ever known. He was a native, too, while most of the rest of us had been born elsewhere.

Another notable native writer was H. L. Davis of The Dalles, Oregon. His *Honey in the Horn* took a Pulitzer Prize for fiction in 1936, and rightly so. It was a piece of outstanding realism about those commonly sacred characters, the pioneers. Davis was working on it in the days when he used to drive in to attend one of the club's evening functions, arriving in a car held together with haywire and rawhide, and appearing at our decaying mansion in a decaying sweater, hair over his eyes, boots to his knees.

Although Archie Binns, a Washington native, had gone elsewhere to live, his first novel, *Lightship,* and a big success, indicated he was still to write of his native region. In Idaho, Vardis Fisher began, with his *Toilers of the Hills,* to dispel the glamour with which most novelists, Davis excepted, had been plastering the life of the pioneers. Dr. Alan Hart, of Gardiner, Oregon, wrote *Doctor Mallory* as an indictment of medical societies. Sophus K. Winther of Seattle came out with the first of several novels about emigrants from Europe in the American West.

Meanwhile, schools of journalism and classes in creative writing were fertilizing the garden that had begun at last to bloom. Among pioneer gardeners at the University of Washington were Leo Arthur Borah and Glenn Hughes, whose labors were carried on and intensified by George Savage; and at the University of Oregon W. F. G. Thacher, George S. Turnbull, Alfred Powers, and Mable Holmes Parsons were performing like services. At Reed College in Portland, Victor Chittick was writing books on folklore characters and urging his classes to investigate that field.

Younger men were beginning to show, and of these none was better received than Nard Jones, whose first novel, *Oregon Detour,* won high acclaim in the Eastern centers. Another was Roderick Lull, a precocious youngster who managed by imposture to become a member of the Press Club, appearing before Secretary Hyskell, who was near-sighted, wearing a minute though compelling false mustache, and swore he had voted for James Middleton Cox in 1920. While still at a tender age, Lull began writing for the *Atlantic Monthly,* then for the *Saturday Evening Post* and *Collier's.* Robert Cantwell made a noise with his first novel, *Laugh and Lie Down,* set in Hoquiam, where the author had worked in a plywood factory. While reporting for a Seattle newspaper, Michael Foster wrote *Forgive Adam,* which started his novel-writing career. Another Seattle reporter, Douglas Welch, began contributing short stories to the *Saturday Evening Post.*

In Tacoma, Norman Reilly Raine conjured up a character famous in magazines and movies, Tugboat Annie, then went away to write scenarios. Raine took time to encourage talented younger writers, among whom was Howard Brier of Seattle, probably the most successful author of boys' stories in the Northwest.

I must mention here the names of three influential books written by men allied by birth or residence with the North-west: Vernon Parrington's brilliant *Main Currents of American Thought,* John Reed's *Ten Days That Shook the World,* and Ernest Sutherland Bates's *American Faith.* Reed was a Portland native. Parrington worked in Seattle, Bates in Eugene, Oregon.

In the slightly younger group was the successful and possibly unique brother-team of John and Ward Hawkins, Oregon natives, who by empirical method worked out a plan of collaboration that put even their earlier stories into the slick weeklies, and several into the movies. Among the group that began to flower in the 1930's, too, was Richard L. Neuberger, of Portland, who started writing in college, and who has doubtless contributed more articles to more periodicals than any other writer in the Northwest, and perhaps in the United States. For the past fifteen years his protean interests have entertained readers of high, low, and middlebrow magazines.

Though most of our writers have practiced and made their varying marks in fiction, our group developed an able and graceful historian in Philip H. Parrish, who also became editor of the editorial page of the *Oregonian*. In his Press Club days Parrish was working on his *Before the Covered Wagon*, one of those rare and happy kind of books that are read alike by adults and youngsters. Much later than Parrish, Joseph Kinsey Howard came out with his fine *Montana: High, Wide and Handsome*, a critical and lively study that brought him both abuse and applause. Glenn Quiett of Portland had time, before his premature death at forty-one, to write *Pay Dirt* and *They Built the West*. In his *And There Were Men*, Russell Blankenship of Seattle brought to light a remarkable and rank individualist, Old Bill Potter, long since my candidate for the most interesting character in our region.

Of writers of verse, the Northwest perhaps has as many as any other region, possibly more, if it be true that surroundings have a perceptible influence on the production of verse. No poets live in grander country than ours. And poets are the only true writers. Discouragement cannot stop them. Success will not ruin them. No matter the weather or the times, they will sing. They will sing just as quickly and just as well for a farthing, or for nothing, as they will for $100, or $1000. They are, surely, the only genuine writers, who write simply because they must impart some truth that is plain to them, though obscure to the rest of us.*

But prose writers like myself are not competent to discuss poets or poetry. That must be left to the poets themselves; or to the professors, who are ready to discuss anything. But I may mention with some pride, and I hope with propriety, my comrades of the old Press Club who have had their verse brought out in covers, such as Ben Hur Lampman's *How Could I Be Forgetting?*, and Dean Collins's *White Crown Singing;* Courtland Matthews's *Aleutian Interval*, and Verne Bright's *Mountain Man*.

*For many years their chief outlet in the Northwest has been the creditable column conducted in the *Oregonian* by Ethel Romig Fuller, whose own poems appear in national magazines and in several volumes.

Getting back to fiction, one should not think for a moment that its flowering in the Northwest of the mid-twenties and later was confined to the men. As early as 1925 Doubleday was happy to bring out Anita Pettibone's *The Bitter Country;* and a year or so later Harper published *The Cabin at the Trail's End* by Sheba Hargreaves. Kay Cleaver Strahan wrote the first of her mystery novels, all laid in the Oregon country. In Montana, Mildred Walker's *Winter Wheat* was hailed by most reviewers. Allis McKay set her *They Came to a River* in the apple-growing district of Central Washington. Helen Hedrick peopled her Klamath River novel, *The Blood Remembers*, with natives, red, white, and mixed. Berenice Thorpe's *Reunion on Strawberry Hill* was set at Camas on the Columbia. Nancy Wilson Ross, long an expatriate, returned to write an excellent novel and to celebrate pioneers in *Westward the Women*. Mildred Masterson McNeilly, a reporter in Seattle, came out with a sound historical novel based on Alaska, *Heaven Is Too High*. Another Washington native, young Elizabeth Marion, showed unusual brilliance in her remarkable *The Keys to the House*. At the end of the 1940's, Ardythe Kennelley of Portland completed her first novel, published a year later as *The Peaceable Kingdom,* and taken by one of the bigger book clubs.

Despite much local-booster talk to the contrary, there never was a Northwest group or school of writers, or an Oregon school, or a Portland school.* The outbreak of letters that began in 1920, and which has continued more or less to the present, was fortuitous. There was no Hollywood here to attract writers. There were no magazines. There was no Emerson, no Bronson Alcott. There was not even an Ambrose Bierce. He who might have become our revered and grand old man of letters, Charles Erskine Scott Wood, had left the Northwest to live in California, and there to write his *Heavenly Discourse*, as amusing a satire as ever came out of the West.

No, there was no lodestone in the Northwest, not even a

*Portland patriots like to point out that within a period of fourteen months, the *Saturday Evening Post* carried stories or articles by Haycox, Lull, Neuberger; the Hawkins brothers; Case; his sister Victoria Case; and Steve McNeill; while in *Collier's* were appearing Haycox, Neuberger, and Margaret (Mrs. Roderick) Lull; and in the *American Magazine,* short stories by Thomas Thompson. All of these writers were living in or near Portland.

beacon. It merely came about that a rather large number of
men and women who meant to become writers, most of them
born elsewhere and within a few years of each other, happened to congregate, a majority of them, in or near Portland. Nature then took its course. Most of their writing, by
the law of literary averages, will probably prove to have been
of passing interest rather than of some permanence. Whatever its value, the male writers did manage to remedy, for
a time, the dreadful conditions prevailing about 1920, when,
as most of my male colleagues agree, there were in our
whole vast region only two writers known from coast to
coast, and those two females.

Yet just when we professional male writers thought smugly
we were at least holding the line against the encroaching
women, there appeared, as recently as 1945, the most
popular book *ever* written by a Northwest author. This was
The Egg and I. Its author was Betty MacDonald. It sold
copies beyond knowing. It was processed into a movie. It inspired thousands of women who should have remained in
their kitchens to take pen in hand and write stupid imitations
of Mrs. MacDonald's lively book. It prompted the editors
of virtually every publishing house in the United States to
blanch every time they opened a manuscript from some unknown, and read the author's letter of transmission: "Dear
sir: All my friends tell me that *The Egg and I* cannot compare with these true experiences of mine, and . . ." The editors, as I say, blanched. Then, with shaking hands, they
quickly rebundled the true and incomparable experiences
and hastened to the Railway Express Agency.*

Mrs. MacDonald's book fathered gags and songs and advertisements. I have heard that it inspired sermons. The book
was pure Northwest, too; its setting was the Olympic Peninsula, its characters stump ranchers. *The Egg and I* made
its author as well known in 1945 as Opal Whiteley had been
in 1920, which is to say, better known by far than any male
author in the region. Literary historians of the distant future,
one feels certain, will be charmed and perhaps a little
perplexed when their labors make it clear that the two most
widely known writers over a quarter of a century, and in

*Two publisher friends, one in Boston, one in New York, told me that
throughout 1946 and much of 1947, almost every other manuscript they
returned to lady authors was patently inspired by Mrs. MacDonald's
work.

what otherwise appeared to have been a he-man's country, should have been females. One can only regret that our great feminist, the late Abigail Scott Duniway, did not live to see this triumph of her urgings and of her prophecies.

PART SEVEN

WOODS

1. The Changing Forest

MY FIRST THREE YEARS IN THE NORTHWEST WERE SPENT wholly in logging camps. For the next decade I was a reporter and an editor dealing much with logging and lumbering. My news beat took in a generous area. It comprised Oregon, Washington, Idaho, and occasionally called for trips into Montana and British Columbia, and less often into the redwood and sugar-pine regions of northern California. At one time, perhaps in 1929 or 1930, I could have said truthfully that I had visited every sawmill and logging camp in that sizable area. I may have missed a small outfit here and there, though not many. I got around. Still later, for four fire seasons during World War II, I was employed by the Division of Forestry of the State of Washington. Thus I have never been far from, nor long out of, the timber.

The forest has changed much in thirty years. It is still the most important single fact in the Northwest. Our statisticians publish figures every little while to say that sixty-five cents of every dollar in our region derives from the forest. Thirty years ago the figure was slightly greater. New industries have cut into the Northwest dollar, yet the woods are still our incomparable source of livelihood. Their influence is felt everywhere.

The city man commonly thinks of the forest as being a remote and savage place where nothing moves, nothing happens.* The woodsman knows better. He knows the forest to be as busy a place as Manhattan at its peak hours of rush, a place of intense activity. No classified page could possibly list its daily births and deaths. No column could begin to record its fires and other disasters. The worst human bar-

*Here and there, in this chapter, I have leaned on a former work, *Green Commonwealth* (1945), privately printed.

barian could scarcely believe the ferocious warfare constantly waged in its shadows.

Though I've never been prone to fancy, I have often thought of what it would be like to edit a newspaper of the forest, specifically a journal of the forest I happen to know best, that of the Douglas-fir region of Oregon and Washington. It would be a forest editor's dream, a scene of staggering headlines of holocausts, of huge and deadly invasions by enemies, some of them armed with powers as mysterious and fearsome and as little understood as the powers of nuclear fission; of individual murders and other crimes on a scale to dismay those who think of nature in terms of pretty birds and cute little animals. Only the blackest of ink would do justice to these news stories of the timber.

There, for instance, in what to the city man seems suspended animation, hosts of armed and armored beetles march a beetle's equivalent of a hundred miles a day, to attack a stand of fine old firs. More than ten thousand trees died under one such recent attack by beetle divisions on a few acres in western Oregon. It was a tremendous happening that would rate a banner headline in any forest newspaper.

Along a creek I know, where the firs grow 275 feet tall, and even taller, and where the sun touches the forest floor only in narrow geometric slants, is the very midtown of this forest, where forest dwellers come to drink and, for all I know, to discuss topics of the day. Here to a wind-felled tree comes the lone cougar to slake his thirst, and perhaps to wait for a deer. The deer come, too, but their noses are sharp, and more often than not they smell the big cat in time. But when deer and cougar *do* meet, there's a headline for you.

The very tree now lying prone across the creek was once a headline. Up to 1921 it stood tall and mighty. It had stood thus for some 450 years, or until the big wind of '21 blew a smaller tree against it, and broke off a limb. Into this wound, a wound as real as any flesh is heir to, there presently crept parasitic fungi, to eat into the middle, into the vitals of the ancient trunk, and leave its heartwood in decay. Not long ago came another wind, and that time the sickly giant went down with a crash that would have startled every living thing in the forest for a mile. Its fall was comparable to the sudden collapse of a skyscraper in a city, a headline across the page.

There is always something going on in the woods. Less

than a mile from the big windfall, on a spring day in 1927, a vast cloud of butterflies swept up out of a glade. They were pretty enough, as they winged aimlessly for a moment; then, almost as straight as so many bees, they flew a course that took them to a wooded ridge of hemlocks. Here they settled as if by plan, though doubtless by some inner compulsion we do not quite understand, and call instinct. They laid their eggs in the hemlocks, and a bit later the green of the needles faded, then turned to brown. All the trees on the ridge were dying, killed by the larvae of these butterflies. Woodsmen call them the hemlock looper.

The devastation along the hemlock ridge was as if some plague had brought death to every human being between, say, Fifty-ninth Street, Sixth Avenue, Lexington Avenue, and Forty-second Street in New York City. Headline: Loopers Lay Whole Province Low. . . . More's the pity, it would be true, too.

Even bigger type would be needed to report the terrible disaster that struck the same woods in 1690. In or about that year fire, probably from a thunderbolt, loosed a dreadful destruction. Thousands upon thousands of acres were left stark dead. All was swept except for some small islands of trees which survived because of the unpredictable vagaries of forest fire. It is in these survivors of the great fire storm of 1690 that we can read of the tragedy which befell their fellows. Cross sections of stumps are accurate books for those who can read the language; and the records in these particular stumps tell also of other great fires in Oregon in 1846 and 1868. Washington forests also were swept by fire in the latter year.

Thus have fire, wind, and parasitic enemies attacked the woods, the forest metropolis. Headlines over a period of almost five centuries would have told of epidemics comparable to the Black Death, of wind devastations similar to Florida hurricanes, and of fires greater than Chicago's.

The trees have always fought back in their own way, their only way: rapid reproduction. Americans have at last come to learn that a forest, given half a chance, will reproduce itself endlessly. Only repeated fires can destroy it by destroying the seeds in the forest floor. In early fall, when warm winds open the cones on the branches, the seeds fall like rain, each with a wing to aid its flight, or rather its glide. How far seeds will glide is not known, though there is good evidence of flights of ten miles. This, however, is an epic flight. Mostly the seeds fall to earth within a quarter of a mile of their parent. Nor can the seed search out, as does a doe, a proper place to reproduce its kind. It glides and falls according to the strict laws of aerodynamics, and there it must thrive or die.

The persistence of the forest is a thing of constant wonder to me. A few years back a timber cruiser and I came across an old log house and barn in what had been a clearing but was then deep in woods again. Maps and records indicated that no one had ever settled on that piece of land, so they must have been squatters. The branches of trees had now grown through the windows of the squatter's cabin. Had they pushed out the small glass panes in their growth? Shattered glass on the floor suggested they had. Other trees grew snug to the door, almost barring it to entry. Still others had felt their strength by crashing in a side of the stout barn.

The cabin was sheathed with newspapers, turned brown and soggy. We looked closely and discovered a front page of the *Oregonian* of Portland. The date of the paper was 1905. The featured story told of the surrender of Port Arthur to the Japanese.

Subsequent research brought to light that this home had been made about 1890 by a man and a woman who must have lived there at least fifteen years, and that they had reared two boys and one girl, then moved away. For fifteen years this family had lived on its industry, making cedar shakes. Now the cedar and fir have taken over again. All is deep woods. It gives a man a sense of permanence which no mass of buildings, no matter how imposing, can bring. The forest will almost always reclaim its own except when idiotic man burns and reburns it.

The dynamic forest soon covers the scars made by the loggers, and even obliterates the symbol of their occupancy of the woods, the logging camp. I can think of no scene more conducive to sadness, to that doubtless irrational nostalgia for times past than that of a deserted logging camp. Perhaps this is so because I can so readily call up the scene that was: the bunkhouses alive with familiar sounds and sights, the cookhouse with its glowing range, the smell of fresh bread; the blacksmith shop and its reek of coal and iron; and the sidetrack where a locomotive drowsed the nights away.

I used often to come across one of the relics. The one I recall most vividly was in the Grays Harbor country of western Washington. It had been deserted for less than three years, when I chanced upon it, and it was already a place of deepest melancholy. Window holes stared blankly from the shacks. Many a door was off its hinges. Not far from the cookhouse stoop was a pile of rusty fruit and vegetable cans. Curling like an anaconda through the underbrush was a hundred yards or more of wire rope.

Fireweed, that strange and lovely flower of boundless range, grew close to the plank walk, and up through cracks in it. More fireweed choked and almost hid a few rusting rails of the sidetrack. Great ferns shaded the remains of the pigpen. There was moss on the roofs of the bunkhouses, from a few of which a length of stovepipe arose, and leaned.

It was not a scene of desolation. That is too strong a word. It was more as if life had suddenly been arrested, not destroyed, as in death, but held in abeyance, perhaps like the life of a hibernating bear or woodchuck, ready to stir again when the warmth of spring told of a winter gone.

The interiors of the bunkhouses added to the illusion of arrested animation. On a deacon seat was a newspaper, the Aberdeen *Daily World*, of February 4, 1920. On a shelf above a broken-down cot was a Prince Albert tin, with a few flakes of tobacco in it, and a steel tool called a set, with which to drive calks into boots. Even the big barrel stove had been left in the center of the room, some few sticks of kindling resting between its forelegs.

A strange feeling came over me that must also have come over the first excavators at Pompeii, a feeling that I had somehow stepped into a hiatus in the life of this particular place; that the citizens were still somewhere about, watching, waiting to see what the intruder was up to. I felt like an uninvited guest.

The big range was gone from the cookhouse, but the mixing board, the shelves, and the sinks were as they had been left when some chef had taken off his apron, put on his coat, and walked out the door. A faucet at the sink still dripped slowly, as I suppose it had dripped since the last flunky washed the last dish, and called it a day.

The long tables of the dining room were still in place, nailed to the floor, apparently until Gabriel should blow. On the wall was a gaudy calendar for 1920. Some forgotten inhabitant of this deserted city had marked off the days of January, or nearly all of them, with a black pencil—no doubt a restless man trying to hurry Time till the day he should take the logging train down to the junction with the Northern Pacific, then in the cars to Aberdeen, where the lights were bright, and some of them red, even in the foggy murk of winter.

The silence, inside and out, was complete. I sat down on an empty box to muse on the scene, but not until I had read a legend on the box. "Atlas Stumping, 90 per cent," it said; and I knew it had held dynamite to aid the crew of gandy dancers who had cut and sawed and blasted a right of way for the logging railroad.

So, I sat safe enough on Atlas and looked at the scene. Where, now, were the lads who had lived here a week, or a month, or perhaps a year, and had cut the firs and left the stumps which had already started to disappear into the encroaching ground cover of new growth? Who was the filer who kept the teeth of their saws bright and sharp? Was he filing elsewhere now? Or not at all? What of the cook and his spanking-white apron? Had he fed these boys well, and on whose range and where was he cooking now? The feeling came over me that these loggers had left their city as it was, had walked out of it and out of the world, and were living on in some Valhalla beyond my knowing.

I took my leisure and looked at everything, for logging camps were slowly yet surely disappearing. I might—if my insurance man were not to lose on his gamble—I might well live to see the last logging camp in the Northwest go out of business. And I wanted to remember just how one looked, even if deserted like this one. What logger, I wondered, had thrown away a worn but perfectly good pair of boots in his haste to get out of there? Had a great thirst suddenly come upon him, or had the urge been biological? There lay the boots by a bunkhouse door, green with mold but patently serviceable. Where were the other boys—he who liked Prince Albert fine cut, and he who read the latest news in the Aberdeen *Daily World*? What of the flunky who scored Time on the cookhouse calendar? Had he caught Time, or had it caught him?

It was all futile, of course, this musing, but the scene held me. I reflected that if I had never known a logging camp, these ruins would have caused me no musing. I should have passed them without a glance or thought. What held me for an hour was the same circumstance that holds archeologists fast to their work: I could read the hieroglyphics, the characters of the inscriptions; I could recognize the significance of the relics and artifacts; and thus I could put together and comprehend the story of an abandoned and forgotten piece of civilization.

Although I have never returned there, I know well enough that the site of that particular camp could not now be found. Thirty years is long enough to have removed every trace. The place must now be again in the deep shadow of the forest, waiting for another generation of loggers. That is as it should be, for comparatively little of the land that grows Douglas fir is suitable for anything else. I've heard professional foresters say that four out of five acres of forest land in western Oregon and Washington are fit to grow trees and nothing else. This fact did not become known suddenly, as if by revelation. It was recognized slowly, and only after more than half a century of attempts to prove otherwise.

Beginning in the late eighties, logging outfits advertised cutover lands for sale to prospective farmers, or stump ranchers, as they came, with good reason, to be called. These lands could be had cheaply, and on the easiest of easy terms. Several of the larger companies had cutover-land departments. They engaged agricultural experts to experiment in order to find the crops most suitable, and to advise with settlers. Thousands of married couples bought these lands, build modest homes and barns, and partly cleared their forty or hundred acres of stumps and logging débris. As late as the middle 1920's, I recall, inventors were still getting patents on Improved Stump Burners. By then, too, thousands of stump ranchers had given up.

The unsuitability of the soil for crops was only one reason. What drove a majority of them from their hard-won acres was the appalling energy and power of the reviving forest, the second growth. You could hardly turn your back on a newly cleared field without the ferns and the fireweed marching across it. After them, and quickly, came the alders, the salal, and the huckleberries, and the firs, hemlocks, and cedars. The reviving forest overlooked no square foot of void. It began to fill the bare spots within a few weeks. By the end of a growing season, the field was sure to be covered deep. The forest's surge was so savage as to amaze a stump rancher over and over again, and so persistent as at last to discourage him. One day he reflected there *must* be an easier way to make a subsistence living, and he went away for good.

Here and there a few fortunates got land on which stood cedar stumps ten and more feet tall. These could be made into shingle bolts for sale to a mill, or split into shakes by hand at home. Then there were stump ranchers who ran bees in the fireweed and produced honey as fine as man has tasted. For a while there was a craze to raise goats on cut-over land. But both fireweed and fodder disappeared in the new forest. And not even goats could keep it out of a door-yard, much less out of a field.

The most fortunate of all stump ranchers were those who gave up quickly, yet retained ownership of their acres. By the time World War II came along, many of these former stump ranchers owned genuine forests fit to make lumber or, at the least pupwood. They were the ones who profited by their investment. As for the others, many a family made a living of a sort on a stump ranch, but few of them did more than that. Most gave up and moved away.

In the meantime, too, most of the larger logging outfits had ceased to advertise their cutover lands for sale. Nor did they let them revert to the counties in lieu of taxes, as many of them had been doing for fifty years and more. They kept their acres; they sought to protect them, and to grow new forests. I know of several operators who paid good money to buy back lands they had sold cheaply to stump ranchers.

As long ago as 1929, I noted this fact in print, and used the term "tree farmers" to describe these forward-looking logging operators. In more recent years the cutover lands of hundreds of concerns have been organized into individual company tree farms, registered as such with the American Forest Products Industries, Inc., and posted with signs asking the public to be careful of fire.

The conversion of stump ranches into tree farms is clearly the result of the knowledge that came slowly, both to logging companies and to stump ranchers, that all land is not suitable for agriculture. It is perhaps the greatest single piece of knowledge tending to permanence of an industry which for three hundred years was one of cut out and get out. It is knowledge which, at least to the Northwest, is of even greater importance than the fact that the Columbia River could be made to supply irrigation waters to the dry spots of the region, and electric power to all.

The implications of the shift from selling cutover lands to

making them into permanent forests are not yet fully understood or appreciated in the Northwest. Perhaps they never
will be understood by the public, nor does it matter much, so
long as Douglas-fir lands are recognized for what they are;
namely, a permanent source of the raw products for the
apparently illimitable number of things that can be made
from cellulose and lignin, either separately or in their natural
combination of what we call wood.

The timbered lands of the Northwest are really two forests. Douglas fir dominates the one that reaches from the
summit of the Cascade range westward to the sea. East of the
range is a pine forest.

Rain is the tree maker. Rain to a measure of 130 inches a
year falls in the coastal region. Between the coast and the
inland Cascades it averages some 40 inches, and rises to 80
inches in the higher elevations of the west slope of the
mountains. At the summit, however, the generous moisture
lessens markedly, and presently all but disappears. It is there
that the fir forest starts to peter out and the pine forest takes
over. That is the dividing line between two vastly different
climates. It often divides political thought in the states of
Oregon and Washington.

I can think of nowhere else in the United States where the
transition from one kind of climate to another is so sharp
and so sudden. It is best seen driving over any of the mountain passes, including the Columbia River Highway. Less
than half an hour takes you from one forest into the other.
Even those who do not know one species of tree from another are conscious of the change. It can be felt as well as
seen.

The west side, or fir forest, was both aged and immense
when the first white men saw it. Russians, Spaniards, English,
and Americans noted the great trees on their explorations,
but no heed was paid the forest until men of the Hudson's
Bay Company set up a little water-powered mill at their
post on the Columbia called Vancouver. They sawed boards
for export and for their own use. When the first genuine
settlers came, they found the fir forest to range unbroken,
except for a few natural clearings, from the Strait of Juan
de Fuca almost to San Francisco Bay, and from the ocean
east to the Cascades. The settlers thought of this forest, quite
naturally, only as a damnable nuisance, to be cut as quickly
as possible in order that crops could be planted. It had been

the same in the Pilgrims' day on the East coast. Throughout all history a clearing has been the first task of the settler in a wooded region. Most of the Northwest's fir trees had been ripe for cutting when the Declaration of Independence was signed, yet their existence was not known until twenty years later; and almost a century was to pass before logging in them was begun on a large scale. From that day to this, products of the fir forest have formed the major industry of the west side.

The dominant tree of the east side is ponderosa pine, a beautiful tree of great symmetry and of orange-and-brown colored bark. A stand of ponderosa is more like a park than like a jungle. It prefers relatively level ground. There is little underbrush; loggers do not, as in the fir region, have to clear a path to get close to a pine. In North Idaho is the superb western white pine, taller than ponderosa, yet hardly so large, and growing in much rougher country. It is peculiarly subject to blister rust, as are all other five-needled pines. White pine's bark is thin, and thus is poor protection against fire. Large stands of it have been killed by ground fires that would have damaged but not killed ponderosa.

Until recent years much of Idaho's white pine was logged in the classic manner of Maine and Michigan. Horses and sleighs (called sleds in Maine) took it in winter to the river. When the ice went out in the spring, loggers turned rivermen, grabbed their peaveys, and chased the sticks down to the mills. I was fortunate enough to see a number of these western-white-pine drives, in the Saint Joe, in the Priest and in the Clearwater rivers, all in Idaho. The last drive I saw was on the latter stream in 1943. It was almost a period piece. Driving logs on the Clearwater took place for another year or two, then ceased, as they have ceased on most, if not all, rivers in the Northwest. With the passing of the river drive disappeared the great drama of the logging woods.

In the summer of 1943, the cat-footed men of Potlatch Forests drove some eighty million feet of great and long white-pine logs a distance of 120 miles to the booms at Lewiston. Stan Profitt, a veteran of this and other streams, was boss of the Clearwater drive. With the waters running high and wild, and the logs ahead of them, Stan and forty drivers set out in late April with their two wanigans. These were noble craft, perfect for the likes of the Clearwater. Each was 24 by 84 feet. On one was a cookhouse and dining room, plus the cook's quarters. On the other were double-decked bunks. The wanigan rafts were of cedar logs, light as cork, bound crosswise with wild-cherry poles. The poles were kept in place with tough elastic saplings of cherry pegged into auger holes.

The shelters on the rafts were frame and canvas, with all furniture bolted into place to withstand the rocking and heaving that goes with shooting the white waters of the upper Clearwater. At each end of each raft was a big sweep, fifty feet long, with a sixteen-foot blade. These were manned by strong men under direction of Pilot Bill Atkins, a river mariner. Bill brought the lumberjack navy through the rough going near McKinnon's Cabin and Jump-off-Joe Riffles. Many times water surged up over the deck and into the cookhouse, but never high enough to douse the fire in Cook Bill Coon's stove, a stove, by the way, fed with small, round compact Presto logs, a product of the Potlatch mills, and made from what used to be sawmill waste.

There was one other craft in the navy during a part of the drive. This carried two caterpillar tractors for aid in breaking jams and for moving single logs off shoals and rocks and out of eddies. The cat raft transported the big machines through stretches where they could not travel along the riverbanks.

The spring of 1943 brought exceptionally high water on the Clearwater. Fewer logs than usual hung up, but the flood turned Little Canyon into a roaring chaos of rapids that no craft could navigate. So, for six days or so, the wanigans were tied up at the mouth of the Little Canyon, waiting till the high waters should abate somewhat. In the meantime, and for the first time in Clearwater driving history, the entire crew moved into the neat Helgeson Hotel at Orofino, taking it over lock, stock, and parlor, living like lords. On June 2 the river level dropped, and the wanigans cast off and went shooting down Little Canyon. It was an exciting run, and made safely, for Pilot Atkins and his crew manned the sweeps deftly, and kept the craft in the channel. Late on June 2 the whole shebang was in the broad stream of the main river.

From there on it was fine, compared to the upper stream. The logs jammed, of course, but men in bateaux, the classic boats of drivers East and West, were quick to break them up. Several times the cats were brought into use, and proved their worth. Resort to dynamite was made once to start a jam moving. Mostly, however, it was the skillful work with peavey and pikepole that jogged the sticks and sent them on their way.

The wanigans kept pace with the crew, tieing up at strategic places for the night. Evening found all hands at the wanigans. Eight hours on and in the water is likely to make a man ready for his bunk. But before retiring every man jack took care of his calked shoes. If the calks had blunted, they were removed with a chisel, the holes filled with little pegs of pine, then new calks driven into the wood. Each night the drivers rinsed their shoes and hung them on the handles of peaveys stuck into the raft. Before breakfast most of the old-timers filled their shoes with hot water and let them soak during the meal, just as I had seen old-timers do in Maine and New Hampshire.

Driving hours were from seven to four, seven days a week. Just sixty-two days were required to take the logs from the landings on the upper stream and put them into the booms at Lewiston. A week later most of the drivers were back in the Potlatch woods, turned loggers again.

Since then, as I remarked, the Clearwater drive has become a thing of the past. Trucks killed it and most other long-log drives, just as they have done away with all but a few logging railroads, both in the fir and in the pine regions of the Northwest.

In the past twenty-five years approximately three hundred logging railroads have disappeared in our region. Many of them were less than twenty miles long; but others, like Polson, Booth-Kelly, Weyerhaeuser, Shevlin-Hixon, Potlatch, and Joe Irving, operated over as much as one hundred and more miles of mainline and spurs. Their place has been taken by gasoline or Diesel trucks. Many of these monstrous vehicles, loaded high with great logs, use the highways, and they have come to present a problem which despite legislative efforts is still far from solved. The heavy loads quickly pound surfaces into crumbled concrete. Every little while a log or two rolls off a truck and crushes a passing automobile, including the occupants. Logging trucks are probably no harder on the highway surface than other heavy machines; but they seem to kill many more innocent bystanders than other trucks do.

Logging was almost the only industry in the Northwest that had its own special railroads. In 1923 there were 292 such rail lines in Oregon, Washington, and Idaho, many of which served more than one camp and had as many as twelve locomotives. I rode more than two hundred of them, on the log cars or in the cab or caboose, and never failed to be impressed with the ingenuity of the men who selected the devious ways by which the tracks wound up creeks and canyons, crossed them on staggeringly high trestles, clung to cliffs, went on piles over swamps, and climbed hills and mountains. Those unsung men were engineers of the first rank.

The logging railroad not only carried the product down to the waterway or sawmill; it was also the loggers' link with the rest of the world. It brought his supplies to camp, and his mail, his newspapers, and his mail-order goods. He himself entered and left camp by the railroad. It was the only way he could do so. The logging camp, as only those who have lived in one can know, was a separate and distinct unit of civilization, isolated from all else. I have been in some four hundred Northwest camps, and never found two of them any more alike than two different villages or cities. There were many similarities, but each had some individual flavor. It was there, at the very end of the track, and it quickly took on a character of its own.

Truck logging has changed all that. It has put the camp right on the road, the highway to town, any town, and now the loggers drive to and from camp in their own cars. I recall my astonishment when I first saw a camp in which the garage for loggers' automobiles was the largest structure. The barrier between the camp and the world had been demolished. The logger and the logging camp had become just another villager and village.

The next step will be abolishment of the logging camp. Many an outfit has already taken the step. The loggers live anywhere from one to thirty miles from the scene of activities, that is, the place where the camp would stand if there were any camp. This transition is happening rapidly.

Nearly all loggers, I think, and especially married loggers, welcome the change. Their lives are beginning to be more like the lives of other industrial workers. They live at home and drive to work in their own automobiles; drive, indeed, and on good hard roads, way back into the tall timber of the virgin forest.

The ramifications of this radical change in the lives of the Northwest's largest group of industrial workers are endless, and reach into every corner of the region. One wonders what the makers of Shay and Climax and Heisler and Willamette geared logging locomotives are up to nowadays; and where the 2,500 or 3,000 men who used to operate logging railroads are. The camp cook and his crew of flunkies are about to follow the railroaders into the shadows. The makers of bunks and cot beds will notice the change. So will the manufacturers of those barrel stoves that were typical of bunkhouses.

Another great change has been taking place along the Skidroads of Northwest towns and cities.* The Skidroad is that part of town where loggers and other footlose men were wont to relax periodically, usually in July and December. It presented, until quite recently, block upon block of rooming houses, houses of easy virtue, beer joints, pool halls, tattoo parlors, burlesque theaters, an I.W.W. or Wobbly hall, and the kind of store that has a pile of paper suitcases on open-handed display near the entrance, with every one chained down. This is the same store that stocks suits of a particularly hideous purple-blue favored by middle-aged loggers for at least half a century.

The Skidroads of the Northwest have centered around Yesler Way in Seattle (the original), Burnside Street in Portland, South F in Aberdeen, Pacific in Tacoma, and Trent in Spokane. All of them have felt the change that has been coming over the logging woods. Fewer loggers visit them. Bar lengths have shrunk. So have the size and number of employment offices. Pool halls, stores, all sorts of joints, are less in number. Many a mission has closed altogether. Business in all places that catered to itinerant loggers and other such workers is bad, and it is going to be progressively worse.

All this change is perhaps for the better, though I doubt if the Skidroad businessmen think so. My only complaint is that a logging operation without a camp is merely an open-air factory set in the woods, and that a logging camp without a railroad is only another small village. All of which reminds me that thirty years ago, I used to hear old-time loggers grumble that a camp without bull teams (oxen) was no

---

*Skidroad is the proper name. It originated in Seattle some seventy years ago, when logs were hauled through the town over an actual skidroad made of logs laid crosswise. Hotels, saloons, and other places seeking the logger trade grew up along the Skidroad, and the entire district was known as the Skidroad. From Seattle the term spread until cities all over the West had their Skidroad districts. Of recent years a corruption has appeared as "Skidrow," but its use is confined to those who wish to be known as men of the world, and who patently don't know what they are talking about.

camp at all, and they roughly damned the donkey engines and locomotives that had combined to drive the animals from the timber. Thus do things change, while grumbling meets every change and has no effect.

The time nears when almost all logging in the Northwest will be carried on without camps. It is none too early to act on the example set many years ago by the city of Rhinelander, Wisconsin, in its day one of the great lumber centers of the Lake States. Well before the last piece of equipment and camp furnishings had disappeared into the junk pile, Rhinelander established its Logging Museum. From rotting camps and from behind old stumps in Oneida County was mustered a fine collection of high wheels, steam haulers, geared locomotives, road-watering sleighs, snowplows and bateaux, and smaller items such as hanging lamps with reflectors, stoves, deacon seats, grindstones and much else. Then an authentic replica of an early-day camp was built. Into it and the camp yard went the equipment and furnishings. The whole business was accomplished at little expense. Rhinelander's Logging Museum is one of the town's show places, as well it should be. It is perhaps the most inclusive logging collection in the United States.

We ought to have something like it in the Northwest. Ten years ago Frank Lamb, the noted retired logging operator of Hoquiam, Washington, took the time and energy to draw up a plan for such a museum. His idea was that it should be established beside the main north-south highway, Route 99. I presented Mr. Lamb's plan to two different governors of the State of Washington, not with the idea of getting state money but in the hope that a good word from one or the other might result in a semiofficial committee and some sort of action. But each governor was being dreadfully badgered by pro- and anti-Christmas tree cutters (which was, and is, a minor war in itself), and harassed by hordes of what Washington officially and quaintly designates as its Senior Citizens. Added to these was the fact that, during a part of the period, the United States was at war. It was a poor time for talk of a museum. Nothing came of it, then or since.

When people in the Northwest get around to a logging museum, and are looking for a site, they might consider the Nisqually Flats, on Route 99 between Olympia, the state capital, and Tacoma. There, already established for more than a decade, is the great tree nursery of the fir region's lumber industry. It is a sight to cheer the bleakest soul. On forty acres of level ground, hedged by forest and the wild Pacific shore, are wide beds of young seedlings, trooping across the rich soil in bright green columns, some ten million of them in season.

A cooperative effort of lumbermen, and with no state or federal aid, the Nisqually Forest Industry Nursery supplies seedlings for transplanting on burned-over forest land. It is tended more carefully than most kitchen gardens are. The trees are grown from selected seeds. Harvest time comes in December and January. A bladed machine loosens the soil. The little trees, five inches tall and with a root system even longer, are picked by hand, then go into the nearby factory and are fed into a production line. One by one they travel on a belt at about fifteen miles an hour. Women trained for the job remove the sickly or imperfect trees as they are passing. The good ones go on to be automatically gathered into bundles of one hundred trees each. Wrapped in damp sphagnum moss and parchment-like paper, the trees are then packed into crates of six thousand trees each. They will keep thus for months without injury.

The crates of seedlings are taken from the nursery warehouse by the cooperating lumber companies, and go into the hills for planting by company crews. The planting goes on from December through April, five hundred seedlings to the acre, eight feet apart. Of five hundred planted, a few will be eaten by mountain beaver, a small rodent about the size of a rat but even lustier appetite. A few more will wilt and die in the summer sun; but this loss is negligible because the seedlings have been toughened, while in the nursery, by alternate wetting and drying, and the poorer specimens have been culled while packing. As for the rest, they will grow tall, mostly to more than two hundred feet.

Seeds are the Nisqually Nursery, as indicated, are selected with considerable care. They are gathered at elevations comparable to the areas where their seedlings will eventually be planted. And lest you think that the lumbermen may proceed with their admirable planting projects and reap nothing but cheers from the public, let me tell you about Mrs. Rice and the squirrels.

For several years Mrs. Cliff Rice, resident of Satsop, Washington, had made a business of gathering cones of fir, cedar, spruce, and hemlock, and extracting the seeds, which she sold to nurseries and tree-planting outfits. Mrs. Rice did her useful work ably and honestly, and the Nisqually people were happy to take as many of her seeds as she could supply.

It is safe to say that few persons other than her customers ever heard of Mrs. Rice and her occupation until, one day in 1947, a newspaperman who believed that all good stories are not founded solely either on sex or on violence, went to Satsop, a hamlet of 285 population, and there wrote a nice little story about Mrs. Rice, an unusual woman, surely, who with her crews ranged the woods collecting cones for their seeds.

Being gifted at his calling, and possessing no little imagination, the newspaperman inferred in his story that a portion of Mrs. Rice's harvest doubtless came from the hidden stores of squirrels. The story went out over the wires, and was printed in all parts of the United States. Then, the deluge. First-class mail by the hundred-weight began flowing into tiny Satsop. Both the postmaster and Mrs. Rice were astonished, and not a little dismayed, at the letters.

Nor are you to think that the letters favored Mrs. Rice and her occupation. Hardly. Much of her astounding correspondence was signed "Friend of Our Little Forest Creatures," or with titles of similar archness; and they denounced the whole business from beginning to end. One letter was addressed to the Mayor of Satsop, a nonexistent character, and demanded that he arrest Mrs. Rice forthwith, and incarcerate her in the city jail, a nonexistent structure. The charge in this and all of the thousands of other letters was of course that poor Mrs. Rice was committing burglary and theft in the storehouses of the lovely little squirrels.

Startled Mrs. Rice blinked in the dazzling light of sudden notoriety; while the postmaster of quiet little Satsop, his minute post office crowded to suffocation with what he had come to describe as "that goddam squirrel mail," looked around for an empty barn.

In her understandable desperation, Mrs. Rice called upon the Nisqually forester to do something. He did. He got a story on the wire citing eminent naturalists, from Louis Agassiz to Dr. Arthur Svihla of the University of Washington, to show that squirrels *(Familias sciuridae)* hoard so much food in summer and fall that they are not able, their memories being what they are, to find more than a small portion of what they have hidden. What was more, said the Nisqually man coldly, all of Mrs. Rice's cones were plucked from limbs by her tree-climbing employees; and our little furred friends of the forest had nothing to do with her harvest; a harvest, continued the Nisqually man, his pressure rising, of the greatest importance of the Northwest, where the public, including lovers of squirrels, carelessly set the forests on fire on an average of two thousand times every season, and thus made it necessary for lumbermen to restock their burned-over land at staggering expense.

The furor gradually subsided, though not before several lumbermen of the old school had time to remark on the futility, to say nothing of the dangers, inherent in trying to do *anything* in the way of forestry—a new-fangled idea, anyway, a path that could lead nowhere but to confusion.

The growing and replanting of nursery stock is the most expensive kind of forestry. It is also a necessity if burned-over land is to be reclaimed. It is the only way to reclaim it. From the Nisqually Nursery 34,000,000 seedlings have been transplanted, up to 1951, on 61,350 acres of fire-killed land in Oregon and Washington. The nursery would thus do as a suitable symbol of the forests of the future. The handsome Flats adjacent to the nursery ought to be a good place to establish a Northwest logging museum that would represent the past.

Years ago, and when it was almost, but not quite, too late, the sons and daughters of pioneers in the Northwest managed to round up a few authentic covered wagons and Concord coaches, and a considerable amount of early-day equipment and furnishings. You can see some or all of these things in our larger cities, and in a few of the smaller towns. They are highly prized, and properly so. No picture, no reproduction is quite like the object itself.

There is still time, though none too much, to collect and assemble an imposing exhibit of a typical Northwest camp of, say, the 1920's. It would show, as nothing else could, our basic industry as it was during the first quarter of the century, as it was before the last bearded logger had gone over to the other side of Round River, and as it was before the last logging locomotive powered by steam had blown its last whistle against a canyon of the Rock Candy mountains, a sound, I am sure, that will be as melancholy as that of an owl, and as despairing as the cry of a loon lost in a fog.

Thirty years ago the end product of Northwest forests was lumber, plus a comparatively small amount of pulp and paper. In mid-century, Northwest lumber is still made by billions of feet annually. Northwest paper output has increased a hundredfold. To these products has been added many another, including plywood. Though it has been made since ancient times, plywood came into its own only recently, with the discovery of waterproof phenolic resins that bond the three or five plies of veneer into a product of a strength almost beyond belief. Within the past twenty years, seventy-odd big plants have been erected in the Northwest to manufacture plywood.

Most people know that as a tree grows it puts on rings of bark and new wood. A growth ring represents a year in the life of a tree. To watch a lathe making veneer for plywood is to see the centuries peel away from a huge fir block, then flow in a continuous strip which spans Time from last Thursday to that dim past when America lay beyond the range of civilized man's imagination, and hence beyond the edge of a flat world.

The lathe operator must be alert. His keen eye must never leave the unwinding sheet of wood, for periodically some piece of history will appear in the block, and call for instant attention. It may be a length of barbed wire, grown over and imbedded deep since the day some forgotten homesteader sought to make a farm in the timber. Again, the object may be one of those old square handcut nails, dating from pioneer times. Or now and then a rifle bullet comes to light, telling of a shot that missed its mark, possibly a wild animal; though I like to think that here and there, at least in western Washington, the bullet might well be a relic of the greatest manhunt we ever had in these parts, that for John Turnow, called the Wild Man of the Olympics, for whom two thousand armed men beat the woods before the outlaw was taken, shooting till he fell.

In any case the man at the lathe must be alert when the past is unfolding at the rate of approximately twenty-five years a minute. He must stop his machine before the edge of its keen blade has been dulled on History.

A strictly native by-product of the Northwest lumber industry are the Presto logs already mentioned as being used on the Clearwater drive. These were developed at the plant of Potlatch Forests in Idaho. They are made by pressing finely ground bits of wood leftovers into short rock-hard sticks of equal size, ready for fireplace or stove. Their combustion is almost complete. Their cleanliness is most acceptable in city homes and apartments. They are much used in Eastern urban centers and elsewhere.

Other new by-products include several plastic and fiber items, put out by a number of the larger lumber companies, along with hard- and soft-faced boards, largely used as insulation. One outfit successfully processes Douglas-fir bark into packaged products under the registered name of Silvacon and Silvacel. Molasses and industrial alcohol are being made from wood in at least two plants affiliated with sawmills.

This and much more would seem to indicate that the well damned lumber industry is keeping step with the general technological advance in American industry. It was not always so, and I readily recall the protests that came to my editorial desk in 1927 when I instigated and published an article of a mildly prophetic nature. The piece suggested that every large sawmill in the Northwest should have an affiliated "factory" to produce chemical or mechanical by-products from the sawmill waste that was going into the burner stacks. The author of the article, a chemist-engineer friend, and the editor, who was me, were denounced as visionary. And one big lumberman, since dead, wrote in to say that the whole business was subversive. It appeared to him to be against God, and hence anti-American. When some years later I wrote his obituary, I had mellowed sufficiently to ignore this aspect of a type of mentality which had kept the lumber industry in thrall to traditional methods, and can report that I gave the old Nestor a right good send-off.

Actually I liked most of the old-timers, even when I had come to realize that their medieval thinking had resulted in a halting technology, and in very bad labor and public relations. They were bold fellows. For the most part they were kind and ruthless by turns. They were generous, and they were tightfisted. Some were crooked one day, and honest the next. They cherished old customs and old ways. They resented new things. It finally penetrated my understanding that they were much as other men of their generation; namely, the products of their era, as I am of mine.

The advance in applied forestry, in connection with lumber manufacture, has astonished both lumbermen and foresters. In the past decade forestry has made more progress than in the previous forty years, or since the first American forester was graduated from the first American forestry school. Federal foresters came first, and under Gifford Pinchot they put on a crusade of almost religious intensity. Meanwhile, the American Forestry Association took a hand in educating lumbermen and the public. A bit later the various states began to organize forestry departments. Then came private or company foresters. Ten years ago a handful of lumber concerns each had a single forester on their pay rolls. Now company foresters number several hundred in the Northwest alone. Great stimulus to company forestry was given when the West Coast Lumbermen's Association and Western Pine Association set up forestry departments under trained and competent professionals.

Private foresters have arrived along with tree farms, sustained yield, and reforestation practices generally. They are the result less of ideals than of economic conditions. Few lumbermen were interested in *growing* timber themselves, as a crop, until it was seen to be profitable. It is now profitable. Virgin timber on the stump is no longer to be had, as it was early this century, at $2.50 an acre. Moreover, to relocate a sawmill after holdings have been cut is both difficult and expensive. Lumbermen who mean to stay in business must grow their raw products as farmers grow wheat. To do so, they hire foresters to advise as to cutting practices, and as to getting the most from the forest yet leaving it in condition for quick and certain reproduction. They must also protect the woods from fire, disease, and parasites.

Along with economics, the influence of a number of men has been considerable. George S. Long, resident manager of the Weyerhaeuser interests for many years, took a lead in organizing the Western Forestry & Conservation Association and the first of the forest-fire protective groups. The brilliant E. T. Allen, born on the slopes of Mount Rainier, devoted much of his life to pleading, warning, and urging forestry practices in a day when most lumbermen thought them either foolish or dangerous. William (Bush) Osborne, working in a Portland cellar, devised and developed the forest-fire finder that bears his name, and has had an incalculable influence in forest protection work. When I first saw Leo Isaacs, thirty years ago, he was down on hands and knees, crawling over a huge canvas, counting the number of tree seeds dropped from a captive kite. For three decades, along with others, he has studied the reproductive habits of Douglas fir in the belief that if better wheat and better corn could be developed from selected seed, then so could better trees for timber.

Of great influence on forestry in our region has been that of Colonel William B. Greeley, former chief of the United States Forest Service, who left government employ to head the West Coast Lumbermen's Association. Greeley is a pragmatic forester; if some theory or other doesn't work, it isn't forestry. To him conservation means the wise use of timber, the harvesting of it in a volume and manner that will permit new growth to equal the amount cut. Both Northwest lumbermen and foresters have been given immeasurable encouragement by Greeley, a world-wide figure in the field. There are many others, too, who have contributed much to putting forestry into the lumber industry, but even to list those of my personal acquaintance would make this book over-long.

Here and there, the Federal forest service is able to give direct aid to local manufacture. In eastern Oregon, for instance, sawmills in the two communities of Paisley and Silver Lake are getting a regulated supply of logs from timber on the Fremont National Forest; and there are other similar arrangements in the Northwest.

An unusual and particularly happy cooperative sustained-yield agreement was made not long since between the forest service and a lumber company operating plants at Shelton and McCleary, Washington. The company, unlike most, had never sold any of its cut-over lands, nor permitted them to revert for taxes to country ownership. It was able to muster 170,000 acres on which new timber had been growing over a period spanning fifty years. In the cooperative agreement, the company merged its lands with 111,000 acres of Federal old-growth timber, to be logged and protected under unified management, and supply the company's plants for the next century, and beyond. New growth on this forest will equal the volume cut in any year.

In human terms this working circle, as it is called, means the security of two communities, on the edge of the combined forests, that otherwise might have faded. The entire log harvest will flow down from the green hills to the saw-mill, door, plywood, and fiberboard factories at Shelton and McCleary, and insure the livelihood of some ten thousand persons. It was the foresight of company officials that made this arrangement possible—foresight, dating from the nineties, plus the mere chance of location of company timber next to that of the Olympic National Forest. It couldn't happen everywhere, though it seems likely that one or more similar agreements may soon be made elsewhere in the Northwest.

High in the wild foothills of the Olympic Mountains, fifty miles from Puget Sound, is Camp Grisdale, woods headquarters for the company of the cooperative working circle. It is technically a logging camp, yet few loggers have seen its like. It has beauty and an air of permanence that set it apart. It is now, in 1951, four years old. The men who built it obviously had an eye for comfort, and another eye for what no lumberjack of my acquaintance ever called aesthetics. Camp Grisdale is handsome, both of itself and in its setting.

Seen from the air or a mountain peak, Grisdale sparkles in the dark green immensity of 280,000 acres like a toy village of Christmas candy. At close range it looks less like a conventional logging camp than it does a civilized town which takes no little pride in its appearance. Its population is about five hundred, man, woman, and child.

Camp Grisdale possibly contains more families than any other logging camp of comparable size in the country. The residential district has fifty-two houses—not shacks or bunkhouses—no two alike, set along streets bordered with lawns and flower gardens. Every house is heated with oil. Every house has a garage, for though Grisdale is set deep in a primeval forest, there is an excellent gravel road to the highway, and to Shelton and McCleary, where the company's plants are situated. There is also the company railroad, one of the few, as I have indicated, still operating in the timber of the Northwest.

Across town from the residential district are the bunkhouses for single men. But what bunkhouses! They are not great rambling barracks lined with bunks and heated by the classic barrel stoves. There are steam-heated rooms, equipped with running water, electric lights, and spring beds garnished with white sheets and slips. The beds are made daily and changed weekly—and may P. Bunyan roll in his grave— by a he-chambermaid. And the sons of lumberjacks who removed *their* whiskers with a finely whetted ax merely plug in their electric shavers.

These so-called bunkhouses also have something else: at the head of each bed is a reading lamp, the light from which may be trained fair on a book in the hand of one of the company's literate choker setters, rigging slingers, bull buckers, or high climbers. It is, as more than one startled newcomer to Grisdale has remarked, nigh incredible.

In the middle of town are the big dining room and the cookhouse, or kitchen. The latter is served by an overhead monorail from warehouse and the refrigerated meat house, and is slicked up with electrically driven mixers, slicers, dishwashers, and a band saw to fashion steaks and chops with speed and accuracy. The dining room gleams with spotless enamel and nickel and stainless steel.

Presiding over this imposing establishment is Head Cook Jim Devine, an artist who got his early training on ocean liners and in big-city hotels. I can easily recall the days when the camp cook was known to loggers as the Boiler, the Sizzler, or the Stew Builder. In those times it was quantity that counted in all logging camps; but no longer.

Today there is no better fed industrial worker on earth than the West Coast logger. Breakfast at Grisdale on any morning comprises fresh oranges, oatmeal, cornflakes, cream and milk, bacon and eggs, griddle cakes and honey, jam and marmalade, potatoes, toast, muffins, doughnuts, tea, and coffee. Dinner and supper always offer two kinds of meat, fresh vegetables, fruits, camp-made bread, biscuits, pies, cakes, and puddings beyond knowing. This generous fare is prepared by Head Cook Devine with the help of a meat cook and a baker, and is set forth by a squad of waitresses.

Near the residential district is the camp store, stocked with about everything a single man could want; and there housewives may select their wants from long open shelves, or dip into the deep-freeze bins for packaged meats, fruits, and vegetables. Next to the store is Grisdale Community Hall, neat as a pin inside and out. This is given over to bowling, volley ball, dancing, movies, and home-talent entertainments. Near the hall if Camp Grisdale School, modern in every respect, and taught by first-class professionals.

In the center of town is the village green, as handsome a little park as you'd care to see. High over its velvet lawn, bordered by azaleas, rhododendrons, and seasonal flowers, flies Old Glory, from sunrise to sunset. In the middle of the green, instead of a cast-iron general or a marble statesman, stands an honored piece of history, a relic of the company's beginnings. It is old Number 1, a proud little saddleback locomotive, painted and polished as if for a perennial party, which fifty-odd years ago wheeled the first logs out of the woods. This was the motive power that drove the company's bull teams from the Skidroad, never to return.

Camp Grisdale may well see the end of another era. The company's efficient logging railroad will probably go the way so many of its kind have gone in recent years. As cutting mounts higher in the mountains, making track difficult and expensive to lay and maintain, the company will doubtless change wholly to trucking. Even today trucks bring logs from the cutting areas to the railhead, where they are transferred to railroad flatcars. I am happy, though, that one of the great sights daily at Camp Grisdale is still the moment when the long train of great logs rolls past the town, pulled by a heavy mainline locomotive, bright with orange and green trimmings, her bell ringing, heading for the millpond in a bay of Puget Sound.

After sundown the camp is for many miles in every quarter a lone and bright beacon in the double-thick night of the woods. By day it shines with civilization amid the uncounted firs that reach two hundred and more feet toward the sky. It is a logger's dream camp come true.

I have mentioned a number of things tending to give permanence to our largest industry. Still another is utilization. For almost three hundred years the close utilization of logs was given no attention. How fast and how cheaply lumber could be made were what occupied the minds of lumbermen. But economic conditions have changed that. For the same reason that forestry has made progress in recent years, so has the advance toward complete utilization of the log. Twenty-five years ago every sawmill in the Northwest had beside it one of those great refuse burners that smoldered and flamed while consuming billions of feet of wood that was termed waste. It *was* waste, too, until economics and technology caught up with it. All of the newer big mills have been built without burners; and the burners at many, if not most, of the larger old mills now stand idle, relics of an era gone.

I like to think that these and other signs point to the time when standing timber will be measured not as at present by the number of board feet it contains, but by cubic feet. The perfect condition will have arrived if and when a piece of timberland is thought of as a *cubic acre*. There isn't such a thing, but there ought to be. It would be a square parcel of standing timber 208.7 feet on a side, *and* 208.7 tall. That's pretty tall timber, to be sure, and the unit of measure might better be by the half and by the quarter of a cubic acre. The idea, of course, would be the utilization of every part of the tree—bark, limbs, needles; everything.

Measurement by the cubic acre at present is pure idealism. As recently as ten years ago, a burnerless sawmill was idealism. As recently as thirty years ago not only was company forestry idealism, but the forester himself was classed with other odd if harmless people, such as butterfly collectors.

Today the bull of the woods, the boss logger of an operation, is as likely as not to be a graduate of a school of forestry. This of itself would be quite incredible to old-time loggers and lumbermen of, say, 1920. It is a wonderful thing for the forest, which I have seen in three decades change from a mine of timber that in time, like other kinds of mines, would play out and be abandoned, to be a farm of trees, cropped in cycles like any conventional farm.

No matter our new industries, it is still the forest on which the economic and the aesthetic health of the Northwest largely rests. I think it will remain so for another century, perhaps much longer.

Acknowledgments

A PROPER LIST OF INDIVIDUALS WHO HAVE CONTRIBUTED SOME-
thing or other to this book would run to several thousand
names. It would include many people whose names I never
knew or have long since forgotten, but whose trails and my own
have crossed during the past thirty years. It would include retired half-pay colonels, and remittance men; bearded Dukhobors; many loggers; moguls of business; professional men
and women; men of the cloth; men in jail; a few persons best described as barroom characters; and, perhaps most important of
all, a large number of newspapermen both active and retired.

Neither I nor any of these people knew why they were contributing to this book. I had no thought of writing it. The con-
tributors were persons casually met during my rather extensive
travel in all parts of the Northwest since 1920. From them I
learned much about the region. It is possible that no little I
learned will be termed erroneous. This does not worry me
overmuch because I long ago came to see that what is and
what isn't erroneous depend somewhat on where one is standing.

I shall not attempt to saddle my authorities, either named or
unnamed, with responsibility for the opinions, prejudices, and
other fallacies that may be found in this book. They are my
own opinions, prejudices, and fallacies. All I shall say in their
support is that they were not hastily arrived at. They have been
either mellowing or case-hardening for thirty years.

I trust, however, that I have been clear in stating what I
consider to be approximately true; what I believe are conscious falsehoods; and what I think are the myths, those
whopping great lies that Time has congealed and dignified
into the romantic fictions held to be truths and beloved by a
majority of my fellow citizens.

There are also a score or more individuals and institutions
whom I asked for help in varying degrees. In every case it was
given wholeheartedly, and to them I tender my wholehearted
thanks:

Leith Abbott, Harry Ault, Edith Bristol, Marshall Dana,
George L. Drake, M. T. Dunten, Dorothy Gilman, Emmett
Gulley, Glenn Hawkins, Herbert H. Hewitt, Fern Hobbs, Dave
James, Dorothy Johansen, Roderick Lull, Mr. and Mrs. Tress
McClintock, A. E. MacKinnon, Amanda Otto Marion, Walter
Mattila, Phil Metchan, Edward M. Miller, Roi Morin, Francis
Murphy, Philip H. Parrish, John Richards, Leslie M. Scott,
Edward P. Stamm, James Stevens, Minette Twist, Oswald
West, Edward C. Whitley, E. N. Wightman, and Jessie Booth
Williams; and the Oregon Historical Society, Portland Public
Library, and the Seattle Public Library.

The books, pamphlets, periodicals, and newspapers listed below either helped to confirm my opinions or to demolish or at
least soften them:

Bagley, Clarence B., *History of Seattle*. 3 vols., Chicago, 1916.
Baker, W. W., *Forty Years a Pioneer*. Seattle, 1934.
Crane (Ore.) *American,* a letter about Peter French, May 3,
1935.
De Voto, Bernard, *The Year of Decision: 1846*. Boston, 1943.
Estes, George, *The Rawhide Railroad*. Troutdale, Ore., 1924.
———, *The Stagecoach*. Troutdale, Ore., 1925.
Federal Writers' Project, *Idaho: A Guide in Word and Picture*.
1950.
Fuller, George W., *A History of the Pacific Northwest*. New
York, 1931.
Gaston, Joseph, *Portland, Oregon, Its History, etc.* Chicago,
1911.
Holbrook, Stewart H., editorials and signed articles in *The
Oregonian,* 1928–1951.
———, *Green Commonwealth*. Privately printed, 1945.
McClelland, John M., *Longview*. Portland, 1949.
McArthur, Lewis A., *Oregon Geographic Names*. Portland,
1944.
McDevitt, William, "Looking Backward After 50 Years," in
The Searchlight, San Francisco, 1949–1951.
Marshall, William I., *Acquisition of Oregon*. 2 vols., Seattle,
1905.
———, *History vs The Whitman Story*. Chicago, 1904.
Meany, Edmond S., *History of the State of Washington*. New
York, 1910.
Monroe, Ann Shannon, on Peter French, in *The Oregonian,*
April 14, 21, 1935.
Morrison, Wilma, article on French-glen, in *The Oregonian,*
Sept. 5, 1948.
Northwest Books. Portland, 1942.
Northwest Books, Supplement One. Lincoln, Neb., 1949.
Parrish, Philip H., *Before the Covered Wagon*. Portland, 1934.
———, *Wagons West*. Portland, 1943.

Pomeroy, Earl, articles on Peter French, in *The Oregonian,* Sept. 1–18, 1946.

Powers, Alfred, *History of Oregon Literature.* Portland, 1936.

Sanford, Marvin, "Freeland," in *The Searchlight,* San Francisco, 1949–1950.

Seattle Post-Intelligencer, March 14, 1892.

Seattle Press-Times, March 14, 1892.

Scott, Harvey W., *History of the Oregon Country.* 6 vols., Boston, 1924.

Scott, Leslie M., on The Whitman Story, *Oregon Historical Quarterly,* Vol. XII.

Smith, Charles W., *Pacific Northwest Americana,* revised and extended by Isabel Mayhew. Portland, 1950.

The Story of Port Angeles. Seattle, 1937.

Tacoma, Then and Now; 1883–1903. Tacoma, 1903.

Welsh, William D., *A Brief History of Port Angeles.* 1941.

———, *A Brief History of Port Townsend.* 1941.

Whiteley, Opal, *The Story of Opal.* Boston, 1920.

Whitley, Edward C., "Bridgeport Bar," in *Pacific Northwest Quarterly,* Jan., 1951.

[illegible] 1944.
[illegible]
[illegible] March [illegible]
[illegible] March [illegible]
[illegible]
[illegible] Vol. XII.
[illegible] and annotated by Isabel [illegible]
[illegible]
[illegible]
[illegible]
[illegible]
[illegible]

Index

243